Home Ownership: The American Myth

Home Ownership: The American Myth

By Mitchell A. Levy, MBA

Published by
Myth Breakers
19672 Stevens Creek Blvd.
Suite 200
Cupertino, CA 95014
408-257-7257

Myth Breakers®

Both the book and the spreadsheet do not make a recommendation to buy or sell a home. They are solely a set of tools that can help the reader determine if buying or selling is the correct option for them. Myth Breakers does not give professional legal or financial advice. Please talk to a professional before making any decision to buy or sell a home. Myth Breakers and all of its officers shall not be held responsible for any gain or loss either real or implied from reading this book or using the "Home Ownership: The American Myth" spreadsheets.

ISBN 0-9633302-1-7
Library of Congress Catalog Card Number: 92-62361

Dedication

This book is dedicated to my wife, Debra, whose patience and support helped carry me through this project. I'd also like to dedicate this book to all those who read it and are better off by the knowledge acquired.

yth Breakers®

Acknowledgments

Many people have helped in the creation of both the book and the accompanying spreadsheet. Let me first thank all of my friends who have had to listen to me talk about the benefits and disadvantages of home ownership for the last 10 years.

Specifically, I'd like to thank the reviewers of the book in alphabetical order: Terry Burns, Joyce Evan, Bill Fisher, Fred Heiman, Peggy Heiman, Royce Johnston, Debra Levy, Stuart Levy, and Bill Simpkins.

Additionally, I'd like to thank the following folks for helpful hints and bits of information along the way: Mike Davis, Dave Ferris, Grady Lawyer, William Mowsen, Broderick Perkins, Richard Seifert, Renn Vera, the folks at Advantage Graphix in Cupertino, the Publishers Marketing Association for the information and services it provides, and Dan Poynter for his book on self-publishing.

I'd also like to thank the following groups for information contained within this book: The District of Columbia Department of Finance and Revenue, The National Apartment Association, the National Association of Realtors and the newspapers, Chamber of Commerces and respective Apartment Associations in the cities where the information requested was not available at the national level.

Preface

The intent of this multimedia package (the book and the spreadsheet) is to dispel the common myths of home ownership. Please note that you do not need a computer to benefit from it. Just reading this book will enlighten you on the concepts of home ownership, renting and saving money. If you have a computer and decide to use the spreadsheet, you can input information relevant to your personal situation to help you make your own rent vs buy decision.

The purpose of this book is not to dissuade you from purchasing a home. The purpose is to give you the information necessary to either 1) Purchase a home for the "right" reasons or to 2) Rent a place and save a significant amount of money. Purchasing a home for purely investment purposes is not always prudent (this point is explored in detail in this book). However, even if you are in a situation where your home purchase will not pay off without significant housing price appreciation, you may still decide to purchase for emotional reasons (sometimes more important than the financial ones). This book should help you separate the financial and emotional reasons for purchasing a home.

Present value and inflation rates are not explored in this book. These concepts are predicated on predicting interest rates, and realistically no one knows what will happen with interest rates. The point of this book is wealth accumulation in nominal dollars. So I will ignore these concepts and focus primarily on nominal dollars.

Section 4, "Dynamics of the Spreadsheet" and section 5, "How to use the Spreadsheet to Evaluate Your Situation" are for those with a technical or financial orientation. For those that find these sections tough to read, the examples that follow in Section 5.1, "Silicon Valley," Section 5.2, "Detroit, Michigan" and Section 6, "When the Financial Numbers Scream Buy" apply the concepts in sections 4 and 5 and are easier to follow. In your reading, you may want to read sections 4 and 5 lightly, then come back to those sections after reading section's 5.1, 5.2 and 6.

In the Introduction and section 2, "The American Dream is no Free Lunch," the three common myths of home ownership are illustrated and discussed. In section 3, "Housing Prices are not Always Rising," the concept of housing price depreciation is explored. Both Houston, Texas and Boston,

Preface

Massachusetts are discussed in more detail in Appendixes A.1 and A.2. As you are aware, there are many other areas of the country that have experienced housing price depreciation.

Section 7, "What is Wrong with Renting" and the Conclusion, look at why renting could be a good alternative. This is especially true, if the renter wanted to save towards their retirement instead of betting on home-price appreciation.

A concern that is addressed in a couple of places within the book and specifically in Appendix B is equivalence. The point made in this Appendix, is that you should be comparing renting vs owning with the options you personally feel are relevant (e.g. your current/proposed rental and your proposed/current home). Only when you use your personal information can you make an analysis that is important to you.

Although it is easy to say that renting and saving can sometimes be a better alternative than owning, this statement is only true if the savings occur. Appendix C, "How to Plan & Save Money" can help you develop a methodology for savings. This Appendix can help you save regardless of your motivation. It applies years of practical experience that helped me save a significant amount of money.

Appendix D explores the rent vs buy analysis for over 25 metropolitan cities. The median cost of a single-family home and the average rent are used in this analysis. Please note that some of these numbers are "best guesses" at what the actual numbers would be. The use of this analysis is for illustrative purposes. If this type of analysis is important for you, you can either buy the spreadsheets and run the numbers yourself or have Myth Breakers run the numbers for your specific situation (order form at the back of this book). The point of the analysis is to get you thinking about what the numbers may mean for your situation, which of course differs across the country. After understanding the financial aspect of this decision, you are then free to contemplate the emotional one.

Congratulations on the first step in a better understanding of this extremely important decision; the purchase of this book. I hope you enjoy reading it.

Mitchell A. Levy

Table of Contents:

Table of Contents

Section 1

Introduction

---

1. INTRODUCTION

Why own a home when you can save money renting, have a lot less personal and financial responsibility and help reduce the federal budget deficit? Good reasons include:

- ❑ having security or piece of mind
- ❑ having control over what color you paint or how you remodel
- ❑ having the emotional satisfaction of owning your own "home"
- ❑ having a sound place for the kids to grow up
- ❑ having a financial situation where the numbers make sense

Poor reasons include:

- ❑ the desire to make money because housing prices have always gone up
- ❑ that it is "the thing to do" because your parents and friends have purchased homes

Myth #1: It is a myth in society that by owning a home you are better off because you will pay less tax. The taxes you pay will be less; however, the amount of interest you pay to the mortgage lender will be two to three times the taxes saved. The after-tax interest paid could be "a lot" more that you currently pay in rent. This myth will be explored in more detail in this book.

Myth #2: It is also a myth in society that it "absolutely pays" to own a home because the money you pay is an investment rather than money squandered away. While it is true that one will save money owning a home (principal), this book and associated spreadsheet will illustrate that with a rigid savings plan, one "could" save more money renting than would otherwise be earned by owning. Money saved by renting and saving is guaranteed equity (depending on your investment vehicle). With a home, over the short term, most of the money paid toward the mortgage goes towards interest. With an 8.5% fixed-rate 30-year loan, only one of your payments in the first year goes towards principal and it takes 23 years to pay down 50% of your mortgage.

Why own a home when you can save money renting, have a lot less personal and financial responsibility and help reduce the federal budget deficit?

Myth #3: The third housing myth is that housing prices always appreciate. With reasonable housing price appreciation, an investment in a home will pay more dividends than renting. It can be illustrated with the use of the spreadsheet, that housing price appreciation is necessary in most areas of the country in order for the home owner to make more money owning a home than renting (and saving). Unfortunately, over the last decade, there have been many areas of the country that have

Introduction

experienced significant decreases in housing prices. Two case studies (Houston, TX and Boston/Natick, MA) illustrating significant decreases in housing prices are explored in Appendix A.

This book will explore these myths of home ownership and help you determine what makes sense for you. There are certain areas of the country where buying a home makes good financial sense. There are also many areas of the country where you can save a large amount of money renting versus owning. Also available with this book, is a spreadsheet that can be used to input your personal numbers. The numbers discussed in this text are for illustration purposes. The spreadsheet's intent, is to allow you to input your numbers to help determine what makes sense for you. This book and spreadsheet will illustrate the following points:

- ❏ calculate the money that can be saved renting versus owning
- ❏ enable one to determine if they can afford a home
- ❏ quantify the annual appreciation necessary for the purchase of a home to pay off
- ❏ illustrate how to evaluate a potential home purchase from a financial viewpoint
- ❏ enable one to reduce the decision of renting versus owning from a financial oriented one to the sometimes more important emotional perspective
- ❏ illustrate when buying a home makes good financial sense

Section 2

The American Dream is no Free Lunch

THE AMERICAN DREAM IS NO FREE LUNCH

From childhood, we are conditioned to believe that the American dream consists of having a credit card, owning a car and of course, owning a home. How often have you heard someone say "Do not let your dream of owning a home pass you by"? The Government even creates incentive to own a home by allowing the home owner to deduct mortgage interest and property taxes from their income taxes.

By creating this incentive, the Government encourages folks to have their piece of the American dream. From its role of stimulating the economy, the Government does not lose out altogether. In this case, the Government stimulates a part of the financial sector of the economy, mortgage lenders (e.g., Banks, Savings & Loans, etc.). What the home owner does not pay to the Government in taxes, is paid approximately twofold to the lender in interest.

The interest, represents income to the lender, who then has to pay taxes on any profits (income less expenses) it makes. The Government will recoup some of the personal taxes lost, from the interest deduction of the home owner, in the form of commercial taxes from the lenders.

By creating this incentive, the Government encourages folks to have their piece of the American dream.

For some people, owning a home is a great feeling. It does, however, have a price. Besides the maintenance headache, the amount of after-tax money paid to the lender is usually greater than the amount of money otherwise paid in rent (this statement is not true around the entire country, please see Appendix D). To illustrate, let us buy a $250,000 house with a $25,000 down payment and $5,000 in closing costs. Although the specifics will be explored later, the reader can refer to figures 1 & 2 for more details. Looking at a 30 year fixed-rate loan with a 8.25% interest rate, the monthly mortgage payment would be $1,728. Since most of the initial mortgage payment goes towards interest, the after-tax layout (for someone in the 28% tax bracket) comes to approximately $1,244 (1,728 * (1 - 0.28)) per month. In most areas of the country, the equivalent rental property will run much less than $1,244.

As long as this relationship between housing prices and rental costs exists, the only time that owning a home will pay off is when housing prices appreciate by a reasonable amount.

An assumption made in this book is that a renter usually "steps up" when purchasing a home (i.e., they buy a home with larger square footage). "Equivalent rental property" will mean renting a home, town home, or apartment with the same (or one less) number of rooms. Please see Appendix B for a more detailed explanation of equivalence.

The American Dream is no Free Lunch

Any difference between the after-tax payment for the home versus rent could be put aside into a separate account and saved (see Appendix C on How to Plan and Save Money). Over an annual period, this amount will add up. Over a 30 year period, accruing interest, this amount will add up exponentially.

Besides the money saved each month in rent vs the after-tax mortgage, there will be additional taxes, insurance, repairs and utility expenses of owning a home. These expenses will increase the amount of money saved renting versus owning. In cases where the after-tax mortgage is not greater than rent, these additional expenses tend to push the total expenditure for owning to be more than that for renting. In cases where the after-tax mortgage plus the additional expenses is less than renting, it makes good sense to purchase (see Section 6 on When the Numbers Scream Buy).

In this example, assuming the equivalent rental property costs $910 per month (please note: when evaluating your personal situation, you can input a value into the spreadsheet that represents the proper rental price for your area) and increases 2.5% each year, **the savings over a 30 year time-frame would be over $400,000!** As long as this relationship between housing prices and rental costs exists, the only time that owning a home will pay off is when housing prices appreciate by a reasonable amount. Unfortunately, "reasonable" appreciation cannot be assumed to occur. This point is illustrated in the next section.

Section 3

Housing Prices are not Always Rising

3. HOUSING PRICES ARE NOT ALWAYS RISING

There are many examples of regions of the US, during certain periods of time, where housing prices have not appreciated. The pattern is typically one where there is a long period of prosperity. The economy is doing well; there is a large amount of expansion coupled with very low unemployment. The economic environment is so good, that euphoria is felt all around. Over a transitional period, however, the economy starts to slow down, expansion either slows down or stops and unemployment increases.

At this point, it becomes hard for some folks to pay their mortgages (which were acquired when times were good and housing prices were high) and they default on their loans. Now the lenders need to sell these homes along with other homes that may be on the market from home owners who want to cash in their profits before housing prices fall. Supply of homes for sale increases, while the demand for those homes decreases. Basic economics dictate that this situation will cause housing prices to fall. If a home was purchased at or near the peak of a market and had to be sold during a market depression, a significant loss could be in store. **A huge problem with a loss on a home, unlike a capital loss in the stock market, is that it is not tax deductible!**

Appendix's A.1 and A.2 focus on both Houston, Texas and Boston, Massachusetts where life was booming in the 70's and 80's respectively. Many millionaires were made in both states and it looked as if things could only get better. The question most people were asking when

Buying a home can always be a gamble!

Housing Prices are not Always Rising

evaluating the purchase of a home was not "can I afford it," but rather "could I afford to let these profits (from home-price appreciation) pass me by." Unfortunately, the economic situation did get worse and many folks lost a large amount of money when housing prices decreased significantly. Appendix's A.1 and A.2 illustrate situations with not just zero housing price appreciation, but situations with significant housing price depreciation.

The examples discussed in Appendix A.1 and A.2 point out situations where housing prices decreased significantly over a finite period of time. It must be noted that the risk of taking a loss in a home decreases as your time horizon increases.

Unfortunately, the economic situation did get worse and many folks lost a large amount of money when housing prices decreased significantly.

Section 4

Dynamics of the Spreadsheet

---

4. DYNAMICS OF THE SPREADSHEET

The approach taken with the spreadsheet and this analysis is to avoid the pitfalls usually taken when evaluating the rent vs buy question.

The spreadsheet has two sections. The first section allows the user to input their personal situational characteristics (figure 1). Once input, this section will also display high-level results of the comparison between renting and owning. The second section shows the detailed results of this comparison (figure 2).

The approach taken with the spreadsheet and this analysis is to avoid the pitfalls usually taken when evaluating the rent vs buy question. The major pitfall is to assume a certain amount of home price appreciation. The problem with making this assumption is that the home purchase is a very leveraged investment. This means that a very small amount of money is used to purchase an asset which is worth a lot more than what was initially spent.

If a 10% down payment is made on a $100,000 home, then only $10,000 was spent (ignoring closing costs) to own something worth $100,000. If real estate prices rise by approximately 5% per year for 2 years (i.e., the house is worth $110,000) the home owner has, on paper, doubled their money in a 2 year period (a return on investment that should make anyone happy). Likewise, if real estate prices drop by 10% (i.e., the house is worth $90,000) the home owner has had their initial investment (the down payment) completely wiped out. They would also need to spend an additional amount of money to pay for the closing cost of selling the home. If real estate prices happened to drop by 20%, the home owner would lose twice their initial investment plus the closing costs.

Likewise, if real estate prices drop by 10% (i.e., the house is worth $90,000) the home owner has had their initial investment completely wiped out.

Assuming a certain amount of appreciation on a leveraged investment has a large effect. The point of this book is that real estate prices do not have to go up. By making the assumption that real estate prices will appreciate, the cash flow generated from the analysis can look very good. It is very hard to argue with an analysis that shows a doubling of money in a 1 to 3 year period.

Instead of making the assumption about real estate appreciation and burying it in with the other numbers needed for the analysis, the spreadsheet requires assumptions about the other numbers and focuses on real estate appreciation as the end product. This is to allow the person performing the analysis to make "reasonable" assumptions about "relatively known" variables (e.g., what interest rate could they get on their loan, what tax bracket are they in, etc.) to allow them to focus on the

Dynamics of the Spreadsheet

final number; what real estate appreciation is needed over a certain time-frame to make renting and owning equivalent.

The person making the analysis can then focus on this appreciation percentage and look at the factors that may cause this number to be reached. More attention is given to this approach in the examples in Section 5 that follow.

RENT VS BUY ANALYSIS
INPUT PERSONAL CHARACTERISTICS

HOME:		**GENERAL:**	
Purchase Price:	$250,000	Tax Bracket:	28.0%
Closing Cost:	$5,000	Savings Rate:	5.0%
+Total Home Cost:	$255,000		
		RENT:	
+After-tax Cost:	$253,600	Starting Rental Amount:	$910
Down Payment:	$25,000	Monthly Rental Incr./Yr (in %):	2.5%
+Initial Principal:	$20,000	+Initial Monthly Savings Amt:	$796
+Starting Loan:	$230,000		
		COMPARISON (30 YRS):	
		Holding Period:	30
Mortgage Rate:	8.250%	+Principal Paid:	$230,000
Loan Length (in Yrs):	30	+Interest Paid:	$392,049
+Monthly Payment:	$1,728	+Amount Renter Can Save:	$420,261
		+Amount Difference Rent/Own:	$190,261
Real Estate Tax:	1.125%	+Appr. Required to Break Even:	$222,193
Add Repair/Utility Cost:	0.10%	+Required Home Sales Price:	$472,193
Closing Commission Rate:	6.0%	+Yearly % Appr. to Break Even:	2.1%
		+Total % Appr. to Break Even:	88.9%

Figure 1

Dynamics of the Spreadsheet

Dictionary applies to the values displayed on figure 1

HOME:

Purchase Price:	• Purchase price of the home
Closing Cost:	• Closing costs associated with the purchase of the home
+Total Home Cost	• Purchase price plus closing cost
+After-Tax Cost:	• Purchase price plus the after-tax closing cost
Down Payment	• Amount of personal money put toward the home purchase (outlay of cash)
+Initial Principal:	• Initial principal amount home owner owns
+Starting Loan:	• Initial loan value taken by the home owner
Mortgage Rate:	• Mortgage rate on the loan (in percent)
Loan Length (in Yrs):	• Number of years to pay off the loan
+Monthly Payment:	• Monthly payment of principal & interest to the lender
Real Estate Tax:	• Annual real estate tax (in percent)
Add Repair/Utility Cost:	• Represents the additional monthly cost of insurance, repairs and utilities of owning vs renting (in percent)
Closing Commission Rate:	• Closing commission rate charged by the broker to the home owner

GENERAL:

Tax Bracket:	• Evaluators personal tax bracket
Savings Rate:	• Rate which evaluator could invest money

RENT:

Starting Rental Amount:	• Current monthly rental amount
Monthly Rental Increase/Year:	• Amount that the monthly rental expense will increase by each year
+Initial Monthly Savings Amount:	• Represents the "Average Monthly Savings Amount" for year 1

Dictionary applies to the values displayed on figure 1

COMPARISON (IN YRS):

Holding Period:	• Expected length of time to hold the home **
+Principal Paid:	• Amount of principal paid over THP
+Interest Paid:	• Amount of interest paid over THP
+Amount Renter Can Save:	• After-tax amount renter can save over THP
+Amount Difference Rent/Own:	• After-tax amount saved renting less the amount saved owning (principal) over THP
+Appreciation Required to Break Even:	• Total dollar appreciation required for the home to break even over THP
+Required Home Sales Price:	• Required sales price of the home after THP in order to break even
+Yearly % Appreciation to Break Even:	• Annual percentage appreciation over THP for the home to break even
+Total % Appreciation to Break Even:	• Total percentage appreciation over THP for the home to break even

+ Denotes that the value is computed. All other values are manually input.

** Holding period is used in all the formulas below it. The holding period will be abbreviated with the acronym (THP).

Myth Breakers®

Figure 2 - Page 30

Yr	Summary Information							Home Ownership						Rental Difference			
	Current Loan	Mortgage Payment	After Tax Layout	Cumulative Principal Paid	Cumulative Interest Paid	Amount Renter Can Save	Amount Diff Rent/Own	Annual Principal Paid	Annual Interest Paid	Real Estate Tax	Income Tax Break	Repairs + Add Utils	Mthly Rent	Ave Mthly Savings Amount *	Before Int Diff Rent/Own	Int on Diff & **ATDP	
0	$230,000																
1	$228,172	$20,735	$20,466	$1,828	$18,907	$10,582	$8,754	$1,828	$18,907	$2,813	$6,081	$3,000	$910	$796	$9,546	$1,036	$1,036
2	$226,187	$20,735	$20,636	$3,813	$37,657	$21,401	$17,589	$1,985	$18,750	$2,883	$6,057	$3,075	$933	$787	$18,989	$1,377	$2,413
3	$224,032	$20,735	$20,812	$5,968	$56,237	$32,456	$26,488	$2,155	$18,580	$2,955	$6,030	$3,152	$956	$778	$28,328	$1,715	$4,128
4	$221,693	$20,735	$20,996	$8,307	$74,633	$43,741	$35,434	$2,339	$18,396	$3,029	$5,999	$3,231	$980	$770	$37,564	$2,049	$6,177
5	$219,153	$20,735	$21,187	$10,847	$92,828	$55,254	$44,407	$2,540	$18,195	$3,104	$5,964	$3,311	$1,004	$761	$46,697	$2,380	$8,557
6	$216,396	$20,735	$21,387	$13,604	$110,805	$66,992	$53,388	$2,758	$17,977	$3,182	$5,925	$3,394	$1,030	$753	$55,729	$2,707	$11,264
7	$213,402	$20,735	$21,595	$16,598	$128,546	$78,953	$62,355	$2,994	$17,741	$3,262	$5,881	$3,479	$1,055	$744	$64,660	$3,030	$14,294
8	$210,151	$20,735	$21,812	$19,849	$146,031	$91,134	$71,286	$3,250	$17,485	$3,343	$5,832	$3,566	$1,082	$736	$73,492	$3,349	$17,643
9	$206,622	$20,735	$22,040	$23,378	$163,237	$103,535	$80,157	$3,529	$17,206	$3,427	$5,777	$3,655	$1,109	$728	$82,226	$3,665	$21,308
10	$202,791	$20,735	$22,277	$27,209	$180,141	$116,153	$88,944	$3,831	$16,904	$3,512	$5,716	$3,747	$1,136	$720	$90,866	$3,978	$25,286
11	$198,631	$20,735	$22,526	$31,369	$196,716	$128,987	$97,619	$4,160	$16,575	$3,600	$5,649	$3,840	$1,165	$712	$99,414	$4,287	$29,573
12	$194,115	$20,735	$22,787	$35,885	$212,935	$142,040	$106,155	$4,516	$16,219	$3,690	$5,575	$3,936	$1,194	$705	$107,873	$4,593	$34,167
13	$189,212	$20,735	$23,060	$40,788	$228,767	$155,309	$114,522	$4,903	$15,832	$3,782	$5,492	$4,035	$1,224	$698	$116,247	$4,896	$39,063
14	$183,889	$20,735	$23,347	$46,111	$244,178	$168,799	$122,688	$5,323	$15,412	$3,877	$5,401	$4,136	$1,254	$691	$124,540	$5,196	$44,258
15	$178,110	$20,735	$23,648	$51,890	$259,134	$182,509	$130,619	$5,779	$14,956	$3,974	$5,300	$4,239	$1,286	$685	$132,758	$5,493	$49,751
16	$171,835	$20,735	$23,964	$58,165	$273,594	$196,445	$138,280	$6,275	$14,460	$4,073	$5,189	$4,345	$1,318	$679	$140,907	$5,787	$55,539
17	$165,023	$20,735	$24,296	$64,977	$287,517	$210,610	$145,633	$6,812	$13,923	$4,175	$5,067	$4,454	$1,351	$674	$148,992	$6,079	$61,618
18	$157,627	$20,735	$24,646	$72,373	$300,856	$225,010	$152,636	$7,396	$13,339	$4,280	$4,933	$4,565	$1,385	$669	$157,022	$6,369	$67,987
19	$149,597	$20,735	$25,015	$80,403	$313,561	$239,650	$159,247	$8,030	$12,705	$4,387	$4,786	$4,679	$1,419	$665	$165,005	$6,658	$74,645
20	$140,879	$20,735	$25,403	$89,121	$325,578	$254,541	$165,419	$8,718	$12,017	$4,496	$4,624	$4,796	$1,455	$662	$172,952	$6,944	$81,589
21	$131,414	$20,735	$25,813	$98,586	$336,848	$269,690	$171,104	$9,465	$11,270	$4,609	$4,446	$4,916	$1,491	$660	$180,871	$7,230	$88,819
22	$121,137	$20,735	$26,246	$108,863	$347,307	$285,110	$176,247	$10,276	$10,459	$4,724	$4,251	$5,039	$1,528	$659	$188,777	$7,514	$96,333
23	$109,981	$20,735	$26,704	$120,019	$356,885	$300,813	$180,794	$11,157	$9,578	$4,842	$4,038	$5,165	$1,567	$659	$196,681	$7,799	$104,132
24	$97,868	$20,735	$27,188	$132,132	$365,507	$316,815	$184,683	$12,113	$8,622	$4,963	$3,804	$5,294	$1,606	$660	$204,599	$8,084	$112,216
25	$84,717	$20,735	$27,700	$145,283	$373,091	$333,134	$187,851	$13,151	$7,584	$5,087	$3,548	$5,426	$1,646	$662	$212,548	$8,369	$120,585
26	$70,440	$20,735	$28,243	$159,560	$379,548	$349,788	$190,227	$14,278	$6,457	$5,214	$3,268	$5,562	$1,687	$666	$220,546	$8,656	$129,241
27	$54,938	$20,735	$28,818	$175,062	$384,782	$366,801	$191,739	$15,501	$5,234	$5,345	$2,962	$5,701	$1,729	$672	$228,614	$8,946	$138,187
28	$38,109	$20,735	$29,429	$191,891	$388,688	$384,197	$192,306	$16,829	$3,906	$5,478	$2,627	$5,843	$1,772	$680	$236,773	$9,238	$147,425
29	$19,837	$20,735	$30,078	$210,163	$391,151	$402,007	$191,844	$18,272	$2,463	$5,615	$2,262	$5,989	$1,817	$690	$245,049	$9,534	$156,958
30	$0	$20,735	$30,767	$230,000	$392,049	$420,261	$190,261	$19,837	$898	$5,756	$1,863	$6,139	$1,862	$702	$253,469	$9,834	$166,792

* Represents the approximate amount of money which should be saved monthly
** After Tax Down Payment is the initial principal plus the after-tax value of the closing cost

Dictionary applies to the columns displayed on figure 2

SUMMARY INFORMATION:

Current Loan:
- Current end-of-year loan amount (year 0 represents the starting loan amount)

Mortgage Payment:
- Annual payment of principal and interest to the lender

After Tax Layout:
- Annual mortgage payment minus the income tax break plus the after-tax real estate tax and the additional amount paid for insurance, repairs and utilities owning vs renting

Cumulative Principal Paid:
- Cumulative principal amount paid; represents your ownership of the home

Cumulative Interest Paid:
- Cumulative interest amount paid

Amount Renter Can Save:
- After-tax amount of money renter can save by saving the "Average Monthly Savings Amount" (includes the after-tax interest on the down payment)

Amount Diff Rent/Own:
- After-tax amount saved renting vs owning minus the amount saved owning (Cumulative Principal Paid)

HOME OWNERSHIP:

Annual Principal Paid:
- Annual principal amount paid; represents evaluators ownership of the home

Annual Interest Paid:
- Annual interest amount paid; value calculated by summing the results of monthly data (stored below the annual data in the spreadsheet)

Real Estate Tax:
- Annual amount of real estate tax **

Income Tax Break:
- Annual income tax break on both the interest of the mortgage payment and the real estate tax paid

Repairs + Add Utils:
- Annual additional cost of insurance, repairs and utility expenses of owning vs renting **

Dynamics of the Spreadsheet

Dictionary applies to the columns displayed on figure 2

RENTAL DIFFERENCE:

Mthly Rent:
- Monthly rental amount, increased annually by amount input in figure 1

Ave Mthly Savings Amount:
- Average monthly amount which should be saved by the renter to achieve the "Amount Renter Can Save"; value calculated by dividing the "Before Int Diff Rent/Own" by 12

Before Int Diff Rent/Own:
- Before interest difference of renting vs owning (can be calculated by taking the "Average Mthly Savings Amt" and multiplying by 12)

Int on Diff & ATDP:
- After-tax interest on both the "Before Int Diff Rent/Own" and the After-Tax Down Payment

Cumulative Interest Earned:
- Interest in above line cumulated over the holding period

** These values are calculated from the percentages input in figure 1 and are assumed to be constant over the life of the loan

Section 5

How to use the Spreadsheet to Evaluate

Your Own Situation

---

5. HOW TO USE THE SPREADSHEET TO EVALUATE YOUR SITUATION

Although this section has a "How to use the spreadsheet" title, it contains information on the logic and assumptions used in the spreadsheet and the book. For the non-technical reader, you may want to gloss over the "How to use" instructions and focus on how the calculations and values in the spreadsheet were arrived at. The logic and assumptions used in this analysis may contain information that the reader will find interesting.

User interaction with the spreadsheet should be with the section displayed in figure 1. The screen is titled "Rent vs Buy Analysis - Input Personal Characteristics." If you are not at that location, you need to do the following for either Lotus or Excel. Press the F5 key (go to), then input the word "info" and press return. You should now be at that screen. Please note that you can only input values in the highlighted spreadsheet cells. The rest of the cells, signified by the "+" sign, are calculated based on the values you fill in.

There are a number of different types of loans that can be obtained when purchasing a home. The differences stem from the lending institutions desire to tailor a loan to your financial situation.

To start, type in your tax bracket on the right-hand side of the spreadsheet. This is the tax rate you feel you would be in as a renter. This tax-rate is used in a number of calculations throughout the spreadsheet. It is used to calculate the following:

- ❏ the after-tax closing cost on the home purchase
- ❏ the tax benefit of the mortgage payments
- ❏ the after-tax cost of the real estate (property) tax
- ❏ the after-tax interest earned on the down payment
- ❏ the after-tax interest earned on the difference between renting and owning

Next, input data about the home. Move the cursor to the purchase price field and input the purchase price, the closing cost, and the down payment being considered. There are closing costs associated with both buying and selling a home. If you are not sure what the closing costs would be for the purchase price being considered, ask a banker, a mortgage broker, or a Realtor for suggestions. Once inputting the items above, the total home cost, the after-tax home cost, the initial principal amount and the starting loan amount should reflect your personal situation. As mentioned above, the after-tax home cost is calculated by using your personal tax rate. This number is calculated by adding the after-tax value of the closing cost to the purchase price.

To determine your monthly mortgage payment, input the mortgage rate, in percent (e.g., 0.10 for 10%), and the loan length (typically 30 years).

How to use the Spreadsheet to Evaluate Your Own Situation

If you input 15 (for a 15-year mortgage) please ignore the numbers displayed in figure 2 after the 15-year time-period.

In order to evaluate the effects of an adjustable rate loan, one needs to make assumptions about the direction of interest rates. It is the author's view that no one can accurately predict interest rates and that this type of assumption can only skew the results of your analysis.

There are a number of different types of loans that can be obtained when purchasing a home. The differences stem from the lending institutions desire to tailor a loan to your financial situation. From a simplistic viewpoint, there are essentially two types of loans; fixed and variable. The fixed-rate loan is a loan that has a constant interest rate for the entire life of the loan. The monthly mortgage payment made during the first year of the loan will be the same as those made during the final year of the loan.

The variable-rate (adjustable) loan is one where the interest rate is changed at set intervals of time over the life of the loan. The initial rate that the lender charges is usually less than the current "going" rate, since the rate will be adjusted over time (initially, the adjustment will be upward). The benefit to the borrower is that it is easier to qualify for an adjustable rate loan since the initial mortgage payments are less than with a fixed-rate loan.

In order to evaluate the effects of an adjustable rate loan, one needs to make assumptions about the direction of interest rates. It is the author's view that no one can accurately predict interest rates and that this type of assumption can only skew the results of your analysis. As a result, only fixed-rate loans are used in the book and the spreadsheet. Please talk to a mortgage broker, an accountant, a tax advisor, or a Realtor for a discussion of what type of loan might be best for your personal situation.

This is the average monthly amount that should be saved during the first year in order to make this comparison valid. This amount represents the difference between your proposed rent and the after-tax layout for the home.

After examining the monthly mortgage payment, input the yearly real estate (property) tax, in percent, and the commission rate paid to the broker to sell the home (typically 6 %, input as 0.06). This percentage varies throughout the country and you should input a value that is relevant for your situation.

The next value that needs to be input is the additional cost of owning versus renting. The areas that should be taken into consideration are the additional cost of insurance, utilities, repairs, and upkeep. Typically home owner's insurance is 3 to 4 times the cost of renter's insurance. In a number of situations, the rent paid by the renter includes some of the utilities (e.g., electricity, gas, water, etc.). Additionally, it is customary that the renter does not pay for large maintenance bills or the cost of keeping the place in a reasonable condition (e.g., painting the exterior, replacing the roof, outdoor gardening expenses, etc.)

All these costs can add up to a lot of money. The spreadsheet requires that this value be input as a monthly percentage of the home cost. A good rule of thumb is 1/10 of 1 percent of the initial home price per month. This rule implies that a little more than 1 percent (1.2 percent) of the home cost is applied to additional utilities, upkeep and maintenance. In the example shown in figure 2, this rule means that the cost of additional insurance, utilities, repairs and upkeep comes to $3,000 per year. If you are a home owner or have friends who are, ask them if they feel that this is a reasonable rule for the type of home and area of the country they live in. Real estate taxes and the additional cost of repairs and utilities are increased by the same percentage rate specified below for the rental increase.

Now that the home data is loaded, input data regarding your general financial and rental situation. Since you have already entered your personal tax bracket, you can now enter your savings rate. If you are not sure of your savings rate, use 3 or 4% representing the amount of money that might be earned by placing your money in a savings account. Next, input the monthly rental amount followed by the percentage you expect the rent to be increased by each year. It is quite common for your rent not to be increased each year. Try to come up with a percentage value you feel comfortable with. This percentage will also be applied against the real estate tax and the additional cost of repairs.

The interest paid over the majority of the loan (22 years for a 30-year loan at 8.5%) will be a much larger percent of the monthly mortgage payment than the principal paid.

The next field, the initial monthly savings amount, will be populated automatically. This is the average monthly amount that should be saved during the first year to make this comparison valid (see figure 2 to determine the "average monthly savings amount" for all other years). This amount represents the difference between your proposed rent and the after-tax layout for the home. **If this amount seems high, you may want to reconsider this purchase since this amount will be the after-tax amount of money, above the current rent, that must be laid out monthly to own this home.**

Finally input the number of years you expect to hold the home for before selling. It is a good exercise to input a number of different time periods to see how this effects the end result. Once you have input this number, please execute the update macro. For Lotus, you can do this by holding down the "Alt" key (for versions 1.x and 2.x) or the "Ctrl" key (for version 3.x) and pressing the letter "u". For Excel, please click the mouse

How to use the Spreadsheet to Evaluate Your Own Situation

on the "Update" button. For both Lotus and Excel, the next eight fields will be calculated automatically. These fields should help you evaluate your situation.

The principal and interest paid fields are interesting numbers to evaluate. These fields show where the monthly mortgage payment, over the holding period number of years, has been applied. The interest paid over the majority of the loan (22 years for a 30-year loan at 8.5%) will be a much larger percent of the monthly mortgage payment than the principal paid. Nevertheless, owning a home is a forced savings account as represented by the principal paid. The problem with this savings account, as seen in Appendix A, is that it does not necessarily pay interest.

Knowing the appreciation required to break even leads to the required sales price that the home must sell for, after the holding period number of years, to break even.

The amount the renter can save is the total after-tax amount of money that could be saved (including interest calculated at the after-tax interest rate) by the renter, if the money that would otherwise be applied to a home was saved. The number represents the operating cash flow difference between renting and owning. In a large number of cases, this could be a very large number. In the example illustrated in figure 1, this amount is $420,269! As long the renter is willing to save the amount of money they would otherwise pay for the home, they would be able to accumulate this amount of savings.

In evaluating your personal situation, you need to determine if real estate prices are likely to rise by the required amount.

The amount difference between renting and owning represents the amount of money a renter can save less the amount of money a home owner can save (Cumulative Principal Paid). In our example, this amount is $237,793. Still a big difference. However, this number ignores the amount of money paid in closing cost to both purchase and sell the home.

The appreciation required to break even is the total appreciation amount by which the house must increase by in order to break even. **This is the real amount to use to compare renting vs owning.** To calculate this amount, (the difference between renting and owning) is added to (the after-tax closing cost from the purchase of the home plus the commission dollars paid on the sale of the home). The after-tax closing cost of buying a home can be obtained by subtracting the after-tax cost from the purchase price on Figure 1. The closing cost of selling a home is determined by taking the closing commission rate paid to the Realtor. This is a very simplistic view of the sellers closing cost, the actual cost will vary across the country and you can take this into consideration by modifying the closing commission rate entered into Figure 1.

How to use the Spreadsheet to Evaluate Your Own Situation

The appreciation required to break even represents the net difference between the money the renter would save and the money the home owner would have after paying the closing costs for both the purchase and the sale of the home. Please note that the amount of tax the home owner would pay on the appreciation of the home is not included in this evaluation. Tax on appreciation is ignored because the home owner who has made a profit on the sale of their home can roll those profits to their next home as long as that next home is purchased within a 2-year period. Please consult a professional money manager if you find yourself in this situation and are wondering what to do.

A library, the local chamber of commerce, a Realtor, or a financial advisor can be good sources for this type of information.

The next two numbers show the appreciation required to break even in percentage terms. The yearly percentage and the total percentage appreciation to break even is the appreciation amount to break even expressed in both annual and total percentage terms. In this example, the home would need to appreciate by 2.1% a year or by 88.9% over the 30-year period to break even.

In the example above, if you felt that real estate prices were going to increase by at least 2.1% per year for thirty years, then it makes financial sense to purchase.

Please note that there is a difference in risk between the savings rate used in this example and the appreciation percentage required to break even from the home purchase. When making a comparison of the risks and rewards of an investment, it makes sense to either compare investments of equal risk or to analyze and understand the differences in risk. The savings account return has a much smaller risk of loss and is much more liquid (e.g. you can get your money when you want to). Based on this understanding, it makes sense for you to require a higher rate of return than the appreciation percent required to break even shown above.

Knowing the appreciation required to break even leads to the required sales price that the home must sell for, after the holding period number of years, to break even. This number may seem high by today's standards. **In our example, after 30 years, the $250,000 home would need to be sold for $472,193**.

In evaluating your personal situation, you need to determine if real estate prices are likely to rise by the required amount. To determine what the appreciation in your area may be, you should take historical, regional,

How to use the Spreadsheet to Evaluate Your Own Situation

state, and local trends into consideration. A library, the local chamber of commerce, a Realtor, or a financial advisor can be good sources for this type of information. After performing your evaluation, you need to come up with an appreciation percentage you have confidence in.

In the example above, if you felt that real estate prices were going to increase by at least 2.1% per year for thirty years, then it makes financial sense to purchase. You will make money if real estate prices appreciate by any percentage above that amount. If, over the thirty-year period you did not expect real estate prices to increase by 88.9%, then from a purely investment perspective, it makes sense to rent and save the difference.

Section 5.1

Silicon Valley

5.1. SILICON VALLEY

Homes in Silicon Valley (between San Francisco and San Jose, California) represent some of the most expensive homes in the country. As in most areas, there is a large variance in price and size depending on the city and the neighborhood. Focusing on a 3 bedroom, 2 bathroom home with between 1,200 and 1,500 square feet, the home price could be as low as $200,000 in San Jose or as high as $500,000 in Palo Alto.

Let us examine one couple's exploration of the real estate market. Both the husband and wife work for high-flying Silicon Valley companies and are making good money. They are currently paying rent of $960 per month for a nice 2 bedroom, 2 bathroom apartment and have money left over to save. After exploring the housing market, they contemplate buying a 3 bedroom, 2 bathroom home in a nice neighborhood with a good school district. After negotiation, they feel they could get the home for $327,500. **They have a desire to sell the home after three years in order to move up to a four-bedroom place.**

The couple inputs their parameters into the spreadsheet (see figure 3). They expect to make a 20% down payment and get a 30-year fixed-rate jumbo loan at a 8.25% rate. The real estate tax is 1.125% and real estate brokers typically earn a 6% fee from the seller.

After talking with friends, they feel that in Silicon Valley it would cost 1/10 of 1 percent of the purchase price per month in additional insurance, utilities, upkeep and maintenance to own a home versus continuing to rent. They expect their rent to be raised by 3.0% each year.

RENT VS BUY ANALYSIS

INPUT PERSONAL CHARACTERISTICS

HOME:

Purchase Price:	$327,500
Closing Cost:	$8,000
+Total Home Cost:	$335,500
+After-tax Cost:	$333,020
Down Payment:	$66,500
+Initial Principal:	$58,500
+Starting Loan:	$269,000
Mortgage Rate:	8.250%
Loan Length (in Yrs):	30
+Monthly Payment:	$2,021
Real Estate Tax:	1.125%
Add Repair/Utility Cost:	0.10%
Closing Commission Rate:	6.0%

GENERAL:

Tax Bracket:	31.0%
Savings Rate:	5.0%

RENT:

Starting Rental Amount:	$960
Monthly Rental Increase/Yr:	3.0%
+Initial Monthly Savings Amt:	$1,029

COMPARISON (3 YRS):

Holding Period:	3
+Principal Paid:	$6,979
+Interest Paid:	$65,773
+Amount Renter Can Save:	$45,348
+Amount Difference Rent/Own:	$38,369
+Appr. Required to Break Even:	$67,594
+Required Home Sales Price:	$395,094
+Yearly % Appr. to Break Even:	6.5%
+Total % Appr. to Break Even:	20.6%

Figure 3

Myth Breakers

	Summary Information							Home Ownership					Rental Difference				
	Current Loan	Mortgage Payment	After Tax Layout	Cumulative Principal Paid	Cumulative Interest Paid	Amount Renter Can Save	Amount Diff Rent/Own	Annual Principal Paid	Annual Interest Paid	Real Estate Tax	Income Tax Break	Repairs + Add Utils	Mthly Rent *	Ave Mthly Savings Amount	Before Int Diff Rent/Own	Int on Diff & **ATDP	Int on Diff & **ATDP
Yr 0	$269,000																
Yr 1	$266,862	$24,251	$23,868	$2,138	$22,113	$14,787	$12,649	$2,138	$22,113	$3,684	$7,997	$3,930	$960	$1,029	$12,348	$2,439	$2,439
Yr 2	$264,541	$24,251	$24,119	$4,459	$44,042	$29,904	$25,445	$2,321	$21,930	$3,795	$7,975	$4,048	$989	$1,021	$24,602	$2,864	$5,303
Yr 3	$262,021	$24,251	$24,381	$6,979	$65,773	$45,348	$38,369	$2,520	$21,731	$3,909	$7,948	$4,169	$1,018	$1,013	$36,761	$3,284	$8,587
Yr 4	$259,284	$24,251	$24,654	$9,716	$87,288	$61,116	$51,400	$2,736	$21,515	$4,026	$7,918	$4,294	$1,049	$1,005	$48,826	$3,702	$12,290
Yr 5	$256,314	$24,251	$24,939	$12,686	$108,568	$77,205	$64,519	$2,971	$21,280	$4,147	$7,882	$4,423	$1,080	$998	$60,799	$4,117	$16,406
Yr 6	$253,089	$24,251	$25,236	$15,911	$129,594	$93,614	$77,703	$3,225	$21,026	$4,271	$7,842	$4,556	$1,113	$990	$72,680	$4,528	$20,934
Yr 7	$249,587	$24,251	$25,547	$19,413	$150,343	$110,342	$90,929	$3,501	$20,749	$4,399	$7,796	$4,693	$1,146	$983	$84,471	$4,936	$25,871
Yr 8	$245,786	$24,251	$25,872	$23,214	$170,793	$127,387	$104,172	$3,802	$20,449	$4,531	$7,744	$4,833	$1,181	$975	$96,175	$5,341	$31,212
Yr 9	$241,658	$24,251	$26,211	$27,342	$190,916	$144,748	$117,407	$4,127	$20,124	$4,667	$7,685	$4,978	$1,216	$968	$107,793	$5,744	$36,955
Yr 10	$237,177	$24,251	$26,567	$31,823	$210,686	$162,427	$130,605	$4,481	$19,770	$4,807	$7,619	$5,128	$1,253	$961	$119,329	$6,143	$43,098
Yr 11	$232,312	$24,251	$26,939	$36,688	$230,072	$180,424	$143,736	$4,865	$19,386	$4,951	$7,545	$5,282	$1,290	$955	$130,786	$6,539	$49,638
Yr 12	$227,031	$24,251	$27,330	$41,969	$249,041	$198,740	$156,771	$5,282	$18,969	$5,100	$7,461	$5,440	$1,329	$949	$142,170	$6,933	$56,571
Yr 13	$221,296	$24,251	$27,739	$47,704	$267,558	$217,379	$169,675	$5,734	$18,516	$5,253	$7,369	$5,603	$1,369	$943	$153,483	$7,325	$63,895
Yr 14	$215,070	$24,251	$28,168	$53,930	$285,583	$236,343	$182,413	$6,226	$18,025	$5,411	$7,265	$5,771	$1,410	$938	$164,734	$7,714	$71,609
Yr 15	$208,311	$24,251	$28,618	$60,689	$303,074	$255,637	$194,947	$6,759	$17,491	$5,573	$7,150	$5,944	$1,452	$933	$175,927	$8,101	$79,710
Yr 16	$200,972	$24,251	$29,092	$68,028	$319,986	$275,266	$207,239	$7,339	$16,912	$5,740	$7,022	$6,123	$1,496	$929	$187,071	$8,486	$88,195
Yr 17	$193,005	$24,251	$29,589	$75,995	$336,270	$295,239	$219,243	$7,967	$16,283	$5,912	$6,881	$6,306	$1,541	$925	$198,174	$8,870	$97,065
Yr 18	$184,354	$24,251	$30,112	$84,646	$351,870	$315,562	$230,917	$8,650	$15,601	$6,090	$6,724	$6,496	$1,587	$923	$209,245	$9,252	$106,317
Yr 19	$174,963	$24,251	$30,663	$94,037	$366,730	$336,247	$242,210	$9,391	$14,859	$6,272	$6,551	$6,691	$1,634	$921	$220,296	$9,633	$115,950
Yr 20	$164,767	$24,251	$31,243	$104,233	$380,784	$357,304	$253,070	$10,196	$14,055	$6,461	$6,360	$6,891	$1,683	$920	$231,339	$10,015	$125,965
Yr 21	$153,697	$24,251	$31,854	$115,303	$393,965	$378,747	$263,444	$11,070	$13,181	$6,654	$6,149	$7,098	$1,734	$921	$242,387	$10,396	$136,360
Yr 22	$141,678	$24,251	$32,499	$127,322	$406,198	$400,593	$273,271	$12,019	$12,232	$6,854	$5,917	$7,311	$1,786	$922	$253,455	$10,777	$147,138
Yr 23	$128,630	$24,251	$33,180	$140,370	$417,400	$422,858	$282,488	$13,049	$11,202	$7,060	$5,661	$7,530	$1,839	$926	$264,561	$11,159	$158,297
Yr 24	$114,463	$24,251	$33,898	$154,537	$427,484	$445,564	$291,027	$14,167	$10,084	$7,271	$5,380	$7,756	$1,895	$930	$275,724	$11,544	$169,841
Yr 25	$99,082	$24,251	$34,658	$169,918	$436,354	$468,735	$298,817	$15,381	$8,870	$7,490	$5,072	$7,989	$1,951	$937	$286,964	$11,930	$181,771
Yr 26	$82,384	$24,251	$35,461	$186,616	$443,907	$492,395	$305,779	$16,699	$7,552	$7,714	$4,733	$8,229	$2,010	$945	$298,305	$12,320	$194,090
Yr 27	$64,254	$24,251	$36,311	$204,746	$450,028	$516,575	$311,830	$18,130	$6,121	$7,946	$4,361	$8,475	$2,070	$956	$309,772	$12,713	$206,804
Yr 28	$44,571	$24,251	$37,212	$224,429	$454,429	$541,309	$316,880	$19,683	$4,568	$8,184	$3,953	$8,730	$2,132	$969	$321,394	$13,112	$219,915
Yr 29	$23,201	$24,251	$38,166	$245,799	$457,477	$566,634	$320,835	$21,370	$2,881	$8,430	$3,506	$8,992	$2,196	$984	$333,203	$13,516	$233,431
Yr 30	$0	$24,251	$39,178	$269,000	$458,527	$592,591	$323,591	$23,201	$1,050	$8,682	$3,017	$9,261	$2,262	$1,003	$345,233	$13,927	$247,358

* Represents the approximate amount of money which should be saved monthly
** After Tax Down Payment is the initial principal plus the after-tax value of the closing cost

Figure 4 - Page 48

Tax-wise, they are in the 31% tax bracket. Their money is currently in a money market account earning 5 percent.

After buying the home for $327,500, do they expect to sell it for more than $395,094 after 3 years?

After typing in the parameters above, the holding period of 3 years and executing the update macro, some interesting numbers are displayed. After three years, only $6,979 of the $72,752 paid to the lender would go towards principal. More importantly, if they continue to rent instead of own, they could save $45,348!

To save this amount, they would need to put aside an average of $1,029 a month during the first year and $1,021, $1,013 a month (see figure 4) during years' two and three respectively. The monthly savings amount represents the difference between (their current rental amount, which increases by 3.0% each year, plus the interest they would earn on their after-tax down payment and their after-tax closing cost) and (the after-tax layout of their mortgage payment plus the additional cost of insurance, utilities, repairs, and upkeep).

If the couple did not expect the home to appreciate by this amount, then buying this home for purely financial reasons would not make sense.

From the perspective of renters, this couple could save $45,348 (in cash) by saving the amount of money that would otherwise be put towards a home. **This number is the operating cash flow difference between renting and owning.** To reach this amount, they need to set aside the monthly amount, mentioned above, for three years and continue to allow the amount of money used for the down payment and the after-tax closing cost to earn interest.

Since it is important for folks to see the equity they have built up in their house, the "Amount Difference Rent/Own" field is shown. Ignoring closing cost, this field shows the amount of money the renter can save less the amount of money the home owner can save. In this example, this number comes to $38,369, the $45,348 saved as a renter less the $6,979 saved as an owner (Principal Paid).

An option available to this couple if they did not expect the home to appreciate by the required amount, would be to rent for three years and save the money that would otherwise be spent on the home.

The number to use for comparison between renting and owning from a "total cost" perspective is the appreciation required to break even. This number takes the "operating cash-flow" difference between renting and owning and includes the closing costs of both buying and selling the home. The number comes to $67,594 and it represents the total difference between renting and owning. In percentage terms, the home would need to appreciate by 20.6% over this three year period, or by 6.5% per year for the ownership of the home to be the equivalent of their current rental situation.

From a purely investment perspective, the couple must answer the following questions to make a decision of whether it makes sense to buy or continue to rent. After buying the home for $327,500, do they expect to sell it for more than $395,094 after 3 years? Would they expect to see appreciation greater than 6.5% per year for three years? If the answers to these questions are yes, then buying this home would produce a financial return that is greater than continuing to rent.

If the couple did not expect the home to appreciate by this amount, then buying this home for purely financial reasons would not make sense. There may be non-investment reasons to purchase this home, but the desire to make more money than they would otherwise make renting would not be one of them.

An option available to this couple, if they did not expect the home to appreciate by the required amount, would be to rent for three years and save the money that would otherwise be spent on the home. The additional $45,348 may be the boost they need to purchase the 4 bedroom, 2 bathroom house three years down the road.

Section 5.2

Detroit, Michigan

5.2. DETROIT, MICHIGAN

Homes in Detroit, Michigan are "reasonably" priced compared to homes in Silicon Valley. As in the previous example, there is a large variance in price and size depending on city and neighborhood. Focusing on a 3 or 4 bedroom, 2 to 2.5 bathroom home with between 1,800 and 2,000 square feet, the home price could be as low as $70,000 in Rosedale Park or as high as $300,000 in Birmingham.

Let us examine another couple's exploration of the real estate market. Both the husband and wife work for a large car company and together make a good living. They have two children that are 8 and 10 years old. They pay rent of $600 per month for a 3 bedroom, 2 bathroom town home and have some money left over to save. After exploring the housing market, they contemplate buying a 4 bedroom, 2 bathroom home in a nice neighborhood with a good school district. After negotiation, they feel they could get the home for $120,000. They also have a desire to sell the home after ten years, when the kids grow up, and move to sunny California.

The couple inputs their parameters into the spreadsheet (see figure 5). They expect to make a 10% down payment and get a 30-year fixed-rate loan at a 7.75% rate. The real estate tax of 4.4% is the highest effective rate in the nation and Realtors earn a 6% fee from the seller.

Just like their Silicon Valley counterparts, they feel it would cost 1/10 of 1 percent per month in additional insurance, utilities, upkeep and maintenance to own a home versus continuing to rent. They expect their

RENT VS BUY ANALYSIS
INPUT PERSONAL CHARACTERISTICS

HOME:		**GENERAL:**	
Purchase Price:	$120,000	Tax Bracket:	28.0%
Closing Cost:	$4,000	Savings Rate:	4.0%
+Total Home Cost:	$124,000		
		RENT:	
+After-tax Cost:	$122,880	Starting Rental Amount:	$600
Down Payment:	$12,000	Monthly Rental Increase/Yr:	2.5%
+Initial Principal:	$8,000	+Initial Monthly Savings Amt:	$437
+Starting Loan:	$112,000		
		COMPARISON (10 YRS):	
		Holding Period:	10
Mortgage Rate:	7.750%	+Principal Paid:	$14,262
Loan Length (in Yrs):	30	+Interest Paid:	$82,024
+Monthly Payment:	$802	+Amount Renter Can Save:	$62,027
		+Amount Difference Rent/Own:	$47,766
Real Estate Tax:	4.400%	+Appr. Required to Break Even:	$61,538
Add Repair/Utility Cost:	0.10%	+Required Home Sales Price:	$181,538
Closing Commission Rate:	6.0%	+Yearly % Appr. to Break Even:	4.2%
		+Total % Appr. to Break Even:	51.3%

Figure 5

Myth Breakers®

			Summary Information					Home Ownership						Rental Difference			
Yr	Current Loan	Mortgage Payment	After Tax Layout	Cumulative Principal Paid	Cumulative Interest Paid	Amount Renter Can Save	Amount Diff Rent/Own	Annual Principal Paid	Annual Interest Paid	Real Estate Tax	Income Tax Break	Repairs + Add Utils	Mthly Rent	Ave Mthly Savings Amount	Before Int Diff Rent/Own	Int on Diff	**ATDP
0	$112,000																
1	$111,017	$9,629	$12,449	$983	$8,646	$5,645	$4,662	$983	$8,646	$5,280	$3,899	$1,440	$600	$437	$5,249	$395	$395
2	$109,955	$9,629	$12,603	$2,045	$17,212	$11,413	$9,368	$1,062	$8,567	$5,412	$3,914	$1,476	$615	$435	$10,472	$546	$941
3	$108,808	$9,629	$12,761	$3,192	$25,694	$17,305	$14,113	$1,147	$8,481	$5,547	$3,928	$1,513	$630	$433	$15,668	$696	$1,637
4	$107,568	$9,629	$12,924	$4,432	$34,083	$23,321	$18,890	$1,239	$8,389	$5,686	$3,941	$1,551	$646	$431	$20,839	$845	$2,482
5	$106,229	$9,629	$13,093	$5,771	$42,372	$29,461	$23,690	$1,339	$8,290	$5,828	$3,953	$1,589	$662	$429	$25,985	$994	$3,476
6	$104,783	$9,629	$13,268	$7,217	$50,554	$35,724	$28,507	$1,446	$8,182	$5,974	$3,964	$1,629	$679	$427	$31,106	$1,142	$4,617
7	$103,220	$9,629	$13,449	$8,780	$58,620	$42,112	$33,332	$1,563	$8,066	$6,123	$3,973	$1,670	$696	$425	$36,205	$1,289	$5,906
8	$101,532	$9,629	$13,636	$10,468	$66,561	$48,624	$38,156	$1,688	$7,940	$6,276	$3,981	$1,712	$713	$423	$41,283	$1,435	$7,341
9	$99,709	$9,629	$13,830	$12,291	$74,366	$55,262	$42,971	$1,824	$7,805	$6,433	$3,987	$1,755	$731	$421	$46,340	$1,581	$8,922
10	$97,738	$9,629	$14,030	$14,262	$82,024	$62,027	$47,766	$1,970	$7,658	$6,594	$3,991	$1,798	$749	$420	$51,378	$1,726	$10,649
11	$95,610	$9,629	$14,238	$16,390	$89,524	$68,920	$52,530	$2,128	$7,500	$6,759	$3,993	$1,843	$768	$418	$56,400	$1,871	$12,520
12	$93,311	$9,629	$14,454	$18,689	$96,854	$75,943	$57,253	$2,299	$7,329	$6,928	$3,992	$1,889	$787	$417	$61,407	$2,016	$14,536
13	$90,827	$9,629	$14,677	$21,173	$103,998	$83,096	$61,923	$2,484	$7,145	$7,101	$3,989	$1,937	$807	$416	$66,401	$2,160	$16,695
14	$88,143	$9,629	$14,910	$23,857	$110,943	$90,384	$66,527	$2,684	$6,945	$7,279	$3,983	$1,985	$827	$415	$71,385	$2,303	$18,999
15	$85,244	$9,629	$15,151	$26,756	$117,673	$97,808	$71,052	$2,899	$6,730	$7,461	$3,973	$2,035	$848	$415	$76,362	$2,447	$21,445
16	$82,112	$9,629	$15,401	$29,888	$124,169	$105,371	$75,483	$3,132	$6,497	$7,647	$3,960	$2,086	$869	$414	$81,336	$2,590	$24,035
17	$78,729	$9,629	$15,661	$33,271	$130,415	$113,077	$79,806	$3,383	$6,245	$7,838	$3,943	$2,138	$891	$414	$86,308	$2,733	$26,769
18	$75,074	$9,629	$15,932	$36,926	$136,388	$120,929	$84,003	$3,655	$5,973	$8,034	$3,922	$2,191	$913	$415	$91,284	$2,876	$29,645
19	$71,125	$9,629	$16,213	$40,875	$142,068	$128,933	$88,058	$3,949	$5,680	$8,235	$3,896	$2,246	$936	$415	$96,268	$3,020	$32,665
20	$66,859	$9,629	$16,506	$45,141	$147,431	$137,093	$91,952	$4,266	$5,363	$8,441	$3,865	$2,302	$959	$416	$101,264	$3,164	$35,829
21	$62,251	$9,629	$16,812	$49,749	$152,451	$145,415	$95,665	$4,608	$5,020	$8,652	$3,828	$2,360	$983	$418	$106,278	$3,308	$39,136
22	$57,272	$9,629	$17,130	$54,728	$157,101	$153,904	$99,177	$4,979	$4,650	$8,868	$3,785	$2,419	$1,008	$420	$111,315	$3,452	$42,589
23	$51,894	$9,629	$17,462	$60,106	$161,351	$162,569	$102,463	$5,378	$4,250	$9,090	$3,735	$2,479	$1,033	$422	$116,382	$3,598	$46,187
24	$46,084	$9,629	$17,809	$65,916	$165,170	$171,417	$105,501	$5,810	$3,818	$9,317	$3,678	$2,541	$1,059	$425	$121,486	$3,744	$49,931
25	$39,807	$9,629	$18,171	$72,193	$168,521	$180,457	$108,264	$6,277	$3,352	$9,550	$3,612	$2,605	$1,085	$429	$126,634	$3,892	$53,823
26	$33,026	$9,629	$18,549	$78,974	$171,369	$189,699	$110,725	$6,781	$2,848	$9,789	$3,538	$2,670	$1,112	$433	$131,835	$4,041	$57,865
27	$25,700	$9,629	$18,944	$86,300	$173,672	$199,153	$112,853	$7,326	$2,303	$10,034	$3,454	$2,736	$1,140	$439	$137,097	$4,192	$62,056
28	$17,786	$9,629	$19,358	$94,214	$175,386	$208,832	$114,618	$7,914	$1,715	$10,284	$3,360	$2,805	$1,169	$444	$142,431	$4,345	$66,401
29	$9,236	$9,629	$19,791	$102,764	$176,465	$218,748	$115,984	$8,550	$1,079	$10,541	$3,254	$2,875	$1,198	$451	$147,847	$4,499	$70,900
30	$0	$9,629	$20,245	$112,000	$176,857	$228,764	$116,916	$9,236	$392	$10,805	$3,135	$2,947	$1,228	$459	$153,358	$4,657	$75,557

* Represents the approximate amount of money which should be saved monthly
** After Tax Down Payment is the initial principal plus the after-tax value of the closing cost

Figure 6 - Page 56

Copyright © Myth Breakers - 1993

rent to be raised by 2.5% each year. Tax-wise, they are in the 28% tax bracket. They currently have their money in a credit union savings account earning 4 percent interest.

After ten years, only $14,262 of the $96,286 paid to the lender would go towards principal.

After typing in the parameters above, the holding period of 10 years and executing the update macro, some interesting numbers are displayed. After ten years, only $14,262 of the $96,286 paid to the lender would go towards principal. What is more important, if they continue to rent instead of own, they could save $62,027!

To save this amount, they would need to put aside an average of $437 a month during the first year and $435, $433, $431, $429, $427, $425, $423, $421, $420 a month (see figure 6) during years' two through ten respectively. Notice that this amount goes down each year. This is because less of the money paid to the lender goes towards interest, hence less of a tax deduction.

More than the $62,027 can be saved if the couple was more aggressive about savings, maybe continuing to save the $437 per month that is recommended in year one (figure 6) of the spreadsheet. The monthly savings amount represents the difference between (their current rental amount, which increases by $2.5% each year, plus the interest that could

Detroit, Michigan

have been earned on their down payment and their after-tax closing cost) and (the after-tax cost of their mortgage payment plus the additional cost of insurance, utilities, repairs, and upkeep.

As in the Silicon Valley example, from the perspective of renters, the couple could save $62,027 by saving the amount of money that would otherwise be put towards a home. To reach this amount, they would need to set aside the monthly amount, mentioned above, for ten years and continue to allow the amount of money used for the down payment and the after-tax closing cost to earn interest.

The real number to use for comparison is $61,538, which is the appreciation required to break even. Starting with the amount required to break even, the difference between the $62,027 (amount renter can save) and the $61,538 (appreciation required to break even) is as follows:

❑ Subtract the principal earned as a home owner ($14,262)
❑ Add the after-tax closing cost on the purchase of the home ($2,880)
❑ Add the commission paid to the Realtor to sell the home ($10,892 = $181,538 * 0.06)

As you can see, the appreciation required to break even takes the operating cash flow difference between renting and owning and subtracts the amount of principal saved as a home owner and adds the closing cost of getting into and out of the home. In percentage terms, the home would need to appreciate by 51.3% over this ten year period, or by 4.2% per year for the ownership of the home to be the equivalent of their current rental situation.

They may decide to make this purchase because they want more control over the environment their kids grow up in, but the decision to purchase would not be made because they feel they would make more money owning a home than they would otherwise make renting.

From a purely investment perspective, the couple must answer the following questions in order to make this decision. After buying the home for $120,000, do they expect to sell it for more than $181,538 after 10 years? Would they expect to see appreciation of 4.2% or greater per year for ten years? If the answers to these questions are yes, then buying this home would produce a financial return that is greater than continuing to rent.

If the couple did not expect the home to appreciate by this amount, then buying this home as an investment would not make sense. There may be emotional reasons to purchase. For instance, they may decide to make this purchase because they want more control over the environment their kids grow up in, but the decision to purchase would not be made

Detroit, Michigan

because they feel they would make more money owning a home than they would otherwise make renting.

The situation where it is better to purchase a home versus rent is explored in more detail in the next section.

Section 6

When the Financial Numbers Scream Buy

---

6. WHEN THE FINANCIAL NUMBERS SCREAM "BUY"

Looking at the rent versus buy decision throughout the country, there are a large number of situations where renting will allow one to save a lot a money compared to owning. However, there are also situations where the rent is so high, that the amount of money paid to rent is much more than the amount of money paid to own. An example of such a situation is displayed in figures 7 and 8.

The town is in New England, the situation is one where from almost day one, owning a home would be financially more sound than renting. Only a "large" decrease in housing prices, while owning the home, would change this situation.

The basic parameters used in the previous examples apply here. Those that change include the purchase price, which is $130,000, and the monthly rent, which is $1,300 per month. This rent is very high compared to the monthly mortgage paid to own the home. Please look at figure 7 to examine all the figures input into the spreadsheet.

During the first year, the difference between renting and owning would be ($5,139). This means that the renter would pay out $5,139 more than the home owner. Unfortunately, there would still be a cost to buy and sell the home. Taking this additional amount into consideration, the home would need to appreciate by $5,067, or by 3.9% to break even.

After just 2 years, the closing costs associated with buying and selling the home are covered. The home could decrease in price by $2,121 before renting and owning would be equivalent. After 5 years, the amount the home owner would save over the renter would be $27,443. The home could depreciate all the way down to $102,552, over the five year period, before renting and owning would be equivalent. As you can imagine, any appreciation in the home, would really make the ownership of this home pay off.

Please look at figure 8 to view the 30 year relationship. The "Amount Diff Rent/Own" is a very interesting column to look at. The negative difference increases tremendously fast because the renter is not only paying more for rent than they would pay by owning, they are also not saving any money as a home owner (principal).

After 13 years, the additional amount of money that the renter has paid plus the principal that the renter has not saved would completely pay for the home. This does not include any appreciation on the home. After 30 years, the difference would be $545,035, the $423,635 that the renter paid over owning plus the $121,400 in principal (starting loan amount) that could have been paid "saved" over this period.

This is clearly a situation where owning outweighs renting. Not only that, this is a situation where (if your financial situation permitted) it would make sense to purchase the home as an investment. Then, rent out the home, since the rent would more than offset the mortgage payment.

If you find yourself in a situation like this, please print off a copy of this spreadsheet and consult a tax accountant on your options. Generally, unless circumstances do not permit buying, when the financial numbers appear as they do in this example, purchasing a home makes good financial sense.

RENT VS BUY ANALYSIS
INPUT PERSONAL CHARACTERISTICS

HOME:

Purchase Price:	$130,000
Closing Cost:	$4,400
+Total Home Cost:	$134,400

+After-tax Cost:	$133,168
Down Payment:	$13,000
+Initial Principal:	$8,600
+Starting Loan:	$121,400

Mortgage Rate:	7.750%
Loan Length (in Yrs):	30
+Monthly Payment:	$870

Real Estate Tax:	0.890%
Add Repair/Utility Cost:	0.10%
Closing Commission Rate:	6.0%

GENERAL:

Tax Bracket:	28.0%
Savings Rate:	4.0%

RENT:

Starting Rental Amount:	$1,300
Monthly Rental Increase/Yr:	2.5%
+Initial Monthly Savings Amt:	($450)

COMPARISON (1 YR):

+Principal Paid:	$1,066
+Interest Paid:	$9,371
+Amount Renter Can Save:	($5,139)
+Amount Difference Rent/Own:	($6,205)
+Appr. Required to Break Even:	$5,067
+Required Home Sales Price:	$135,067
+Yearly % Appr. to Break Even:	3.9%
+Total % Appr. to Break Even:	3.9%

COMPARISON (2 YRS):

+Principal Paid:	$2,217
+Interest Paid:	$18,657
+Amount Renter Can Save:	($10,745)
+Amount Difference Rent/Own:	($12,962)
+Appr. Required to Break Even:	($2,121)
+Required Home Sales Price:	$127,879
+Yearly % Appr. to Break Even:	-0.8%
+Total % Appr. to Break Even:	-1.6%

COMPARISON (5 YRS):

+Principal Paid:	$6,255
+Interest Paid:	$45,929
+Amount Renter Can Save:	($30,515)
+Amount Difference Rent/Own:	($36,769)
+Appr. Required to Break Even:	($27,448)
+Required Home Sales Price:	$102,552
+Yearly % Appr. to Break Even:	-4.6%
+Total % Appr. to Break Even:	-21.1%

Figure 7

Myth Breakers®

Summary Information | Home Ownership | Rental Difference

Yr	Current Loan	Mortgage Payment	After Tax Layout	Cumulative Principal Paid	Cumulative Interest Paid	Amount Renter Can Save	Amount Diff Rent/Own	Annual Principal Paid	Annual Interest Paid	Real Estate Tax	Income Tax Break	Repairs + Add Utils	Mthly Rent	Ave Mthly Savings Amount *	Before Int Diff Rent/Own	Int on Diff &	**ATDP
0	$121,400																
1	$120,334	$10,437	$10,206	$1,066	$9,371	($5,139)	($6,205)	$1,066	$9,371	$1,157	$2,948	$1,560	$1,300	($450)	($5,394)	$255	$255
2	$119,183	$10,437	$10,290	$2,217	$18,657	($10,745)	($12,962)	$1,151	$9,286	$1,186	$2,932	$1,599	$1,333	($475)	($11,095)	$95	$349
3	$117,940	$10,437	$10,377	$3,460	$27,850	($16,833)	($20,293)	$1,244	$9,193	$1,216	$2,914	$1,639	$1,366	($501)	($17,108)	($74)	$275
4	$116,596	$10,437	$10,468	$4,804	$36,943	($23,417)	($28,221)	$1,343	$9,093	$1,246	$2,895	$1,680	$1,400	($528)	($23,439)	($253)	$22
5	$115,145	$10,437	$10,562	$6,255	$45,929	($30,515)	($36,769)	$1,451	$8,985	$1,277	$2,874	$1,722	$1,435	($555)	($30,097)	($440)	($418)
6	$113,577	$10,437	$10,661	$7,823	$54,797	($38,141)	($45,963)	$1,568	$8,869	$1,309	$2,850	$1,765	$1,471	($582)	($37,086)	($637)	($1,055)
7	$111,884	$10,437	$10,764	$9,516	$63,540	($46,311)	($55,828)	$1,694	$8,743	$1,342	$2,824	$1,809	$1,508	($611)	($44,413)	($844)	($1,898)
8	$110,054	$10,437	$10,871	$11,346	$72,147	($55,044)	($66,390)	$1,830	$8,607	$1,375	$2,795	$1,854	$1,545	($639)	($52,085)	($1,060)	($2,958)
9	$108,077	$10,437	$10,984	$13,323	$80,607	($64,353)	($77,677)	$1,977	$8,460	$1,410	$2,763	$1,901	$1,584	($669)	($60,109)	($1,286)	($4,245)
10	$105,941	$10,437	$11,101	$15,459	$88,908	($74,258)	($89,716)	$2,136	$8,301	$1,445	$2,729	$1,948	$1,624	($698)	($68,490)	($1,523)	($5,768)
11	$103,634	$10,437	$11,224	$17,766	$97,038	($84,774)	($102,539)	$2,307	$8,130	$1,481	$2,691	$1,997	$1,664	($729)	($77,236)	($1,770)	($7,538)
12	$101,142	$10,437	$11,352	$20,258	$104,982	($95,918)	($116,176)	$2,492	$7,944	$1,518	$2,649	$2,047	$1,706	($760)	($86,352)	($2,028)	($9,566)
13	$98,450	$10,437	$11,487	$22,950	$112,727	($107,708)	($130,658)	$2,692	$7,744	$1,556	$2,604	$2,098	$1,748	($791)	($95,846)	($2,296)	($11,862)
14	$95,541	$10,437	$11,628	$25,859	$120,255	($120,160)	($146,020)	$2,909	$7,528	$1,595	$2,554	$2,150	$1,792	($823)	($105,723)	($2,576)	($14,438)
15	$92,398	$10,437	$11,776	$29,002	$127,549	($133,293)	($162,295)	$3,142	$7,294	$1,635	$2,500	$2,204	$1,837	($856)	($115,990)	($2,866)	($17,304)
16	$89,004	$10,437	$11,931	$32,396	$134,591	($147,124)	($179,520)	$3,395	$7,042	$1,676	$2,441	$2,259	$1,883	($889)	($126,652)	($3,168)	($20,472)
17	$85,336	$10,437	$12,094	$36,064	$141,360	($161,670)	($197,734)	$3,667	$6,769	$1,718	$2,376	$2,316	$1,930	($922)	($137,717)	($3,481)	($23,953)
18	$81,375	$10,437	$12,265	$40,025	$147,835	($176,949)	($216,974)	$3,962	$6,475	$1,761	$2,306	$2,374	$1,978	($956)	($149,189)	($3,806)	($27,760)
19	$77,094	$10,437	$12,445	$44,306	$153,992	($192,978)	($237,283)	$4,280	$6,157	$1,805	$2,229	$2,433	$2,028	($990)	($161,074)	($4,143)	($31,903)
20	$72,471	$10,437	$12,635	$48,929	$159,804	($209,774)	($258,704)	$4,624	$5,813	$1,850	$2,146	$2,494	$2,078	($1,025)	($173,379)	($4,492)	($36,396)
21	$67,475	$10,437	$12,834	$53,925	$165,246	($227,355)	($281,280)	$4,995	$5,442	$1,896	$2,054	$2,556	$2,130	($1,061)	($186,107)	($4,853)	($41,249)
22	$62,079	$10,437	$13,045	$59,321	$170,286	($245,739)	($305,060)	$5,396	$5,040	$1,943	$1,955	$2,620	$2,183	($1,096)	($199,264)	($5,226)	($46,475)
23	$56,249	$10,437	$13,267	$65,151	$174,893	($264,941)	($330,092)	$5,830	$4,607	$1,992	$1,848	$2,686	$2,238	($1,132)	($212,853)	($5,612)	($52,087)
24	$49,951	$10,437	$13,501	$71,449	$179,032	($284,979)	($356,427)	$6,298	$4,139	$2,042	$1,731	$2,753	$2,294	($1,169)	($226,881)	($6,010)	($58,098)
25	$43,148	$10,437	$13,748	$78,252	$182,665	($305,868)	($384,121)	$6,804	$3,633	$2,093	$1,603	$2,822	$2,351	($1,206)	($241,349)	($6,421)	($64,519)
26	$35,797	$10,437	$14,009	$85,603	$185,751	($327,626)	($413,228)	$7,350	$3,086	$2,145	$1,465	$2,892	$2,410	($1,243)	($256,262)	($6,845)	($71,364)
27	$27,857	$10,437	$14,285	$93,543	$188,248	($350,266)	($443,809)	$7,941	$2,496	$2,199	$1,315	$2,964	$2,470	($1,280)	($271,621)	($7,281)	($78,645)
28	$19,279	$10,437	$14,577	$102,121	$190,106	($373,805)	($475,927)	$8,578	$1,858	$2,254	$1,151	$3,039	$2,532	($1,317)	($287,429)	($7,731)	($86,376)
29	$10,011	$10,437	$14,887	$111,389	$191,276	($398,257)	($509,645)	$9,267	$1,170	$2,310	$974	$3,115	$2,595	($1,355)	($303,687)	($8,193)	($94,569)
30	$0	$10,437	$15,215	$121,400	$191,701	($423,635)	($545,035)	$10,011	$425	$2,368	$782	$3,192	$2,660	($1,392)	($320,397)	($8,668)	($103,238)

* Represents the approximate amount of money which should be saved monthly
** After Tax Down Payment is the initial principal plus the after-tax value of the closing cost

Copyright © Myth Breakers - 1993

Figure 8 - Page 65

When the Financial Numbers Scream Buy

Section 7

What is Wrong with Renting

---

7. WHAT IS WRONG WITH RENTING

Nothing, absolutely nothing is wrong with renting. The problem is, it is hard to feel good about renting because the American dream is to own a home. With reasonable real estate appreciation, this dream not only provides the home owner with a place they can call their own, but also a part (or all) of their retirement fund. **Without reasonable real estate appreciation, this retirement fund will not pay off.**

As illustrated in figures 1 and 2, if the renter saved as much as they would otherwise pay to own a home, they could save a large amount of money; $420,261 after-tax over a 30-year period. Depending on their economic circumstances, this amount can be a significant chunk (or even more than expected) of their retirement fund.

With an emphasis on retirement planning, home ownership should not be so important. An individual or family should not feel bad about renting an apartment, town home or home. What is important, if renting is the chosen alternative, is that they save for their retirement or some other worthy cause. The additional cash that is not spent on home ownership should be <u>saved</u> instead of consumed.

As a single person, renting options should include a hotel or motel. With a number of establishments offering rates of $32 per night, there might be a bargain that could be struck on a month-to-month lease. Instead of paying $960 a month ($32 per night), the hotel/motel owner might accept $500 for a steady rental of one of their units. Instead of getting maid service nightly, a semiweekly schedule might be worked out.

A $500 apartment with semiweekly maid service is a pretty good deal in much of the country.

As long as you are not spending all the additional cash, but apply it towards your retirement fund...you should feel good about renting.

For a family, renting a home may be the desired alternative. There are many home owners that would prefer to rent their property to a nice family who will take pride in their rented home. In this situation, the home owner would probably be willing to accept a discount to the market rate knowing that their investment would be taken care of.

The key point is that renting is not bad. Do not feel left out if you do not own a home. As long as you are not spending all the additional cash, but apply it towards your retirement fund or some other worthy cause, you should feel good about renting.

What is Wrong with Renting

Section 8

Conclusion

---

8. CONCLUSION

Home ownership is not for everyone. The decision too own should be viewed from both a financial and emotional perspective. From the financial perspective, as illustrated in this book, there are no guarantees that this purchase will pay off. As with any investment, there are good times and bad times to purchase a home. Since an investment in a home is usually a highly leveraged one, the potential gain or loss could be very large. Losing money on a home purchase can and does happen. Unfortunately, the economic circumstances that can cause housing prices to decrease can also result in a loss of employment.

If a lifetime goal is raising your children in a home, then the financial implications may take on less importance. What is important, is that you take the time to evaluate your own circumstances from both a financial and emotional perspective.

It is important to recognize the amount of money that could be saved by renting instead of owning. If the individual or family can save the amount of money that would otherwise be put into a home, there can be significant savings. Additionally, without the occasionally large expenditure for major repair work on the home, there may be some extra money that could lead to a slightly higher standard of living.

From an emotional perspective, it is important to separate out the old financial myths of home ownership. As illustrated in this book, 1) you are not necessarily better off by paying less taxes, 2) it does not necessarily pay to own a home and 3) housing prices do not always appreciate. In weighing home ownership from this perspective, it is important to look at your other "lifetime" goals; including retirement. Depending on the circumstances, a guaranteed amount of money saved (by renting and saving) could be a much safer alternative than hoping that housing prices will appreciate. If a lifetime goal is raising your children in a home, then the financial implications may take on less importance.

What is important, is that you take the time to evaluate your own circumstances from both a financial and emotional perspective. With the help of this spreadsheet, you can view the financial implications of renting vs owning. With these numbers at hand, you can then weigh your financial and emotional goals and come to a decision that you can feel good about.

Good luck!

Conclusion

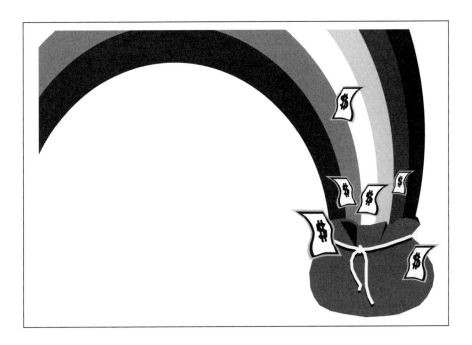

YOU TOO, CAN SAVE A LOT OF

MONEY - TRY IT!

Conclusion

Appendix A

Examples Where Housing Prices

Did Not Rise

APPENDIX A: EXAMPLES WHERE HOUSING PRICES DID NOT RISE

APPENDIX A.1: HOUSTON, TEXAS

Life was good in this oil-rich state during the 70's and early 80's. Real estate prices reflected this prosperity. During the four year period from 1979 to 1983, real estate prices increased 36 percent. The median price of a home increased from $59,000 to $80,000. Until 1983, it looked like real estate prices were going up and would continue to do so for quite a while.

Trouble in this region came when the OPEC oil cartel started to unravel and oil prices started to plummet. Oil prices fell far enough to make it unprofitable to drill for oil domestically. Many local oil concerns (and supporting businesses) went bankrupt. Unemployment went up and real estate prices went down.

This scenario not only demonstrates a situation with zero housing-price appreciation, it demonstrates one that would generate a significant loss.

From a high of $80,000 in 1983 for a single-family dwelling, median housing prices decreased to a low of $62,000 in 1988 (a 23 percent decrease). From 1988 to 1991, housing prices crept back up to a price of $71,000. This means that a home purchased in 1983, at the peak of the market, and held for eight years would still have depreciated 11 percent!

Please see Table 1 for an analysis of this situation in financial terms. If a home was purchased in 1983 with a 10% down payment, the initial outlay of cash would be approximately $8,000 (the down payment). The $8,000 cash outlay in 1983, would have produced a loss of ($23,670) in 1988 (yes, the home owner would have lost the initial $8,000 down payment and would still owe the lender another $15,670 [$23,670-$8,000] to payoff the mortgage). This amount does not include the amount of interest that would have otherwise been earned had the $8,000 been put into a bank account (plus the difference between owning and renting) instead of purchasing the home.

In 1991, this 8,000 cash outlay would have generated a loss of $15,210. It would cost the initial outlay of cash plus an additional $7,210 to live in this home for eight years. This scenario not only demonstrates a situation with zero housing-price appreciation, it demonstrates one that would generate a significant loss.

Analysis of Home Ownership

in Houston, Texas

PURCHASED					SOLD			
Year	Price	Down Payment	After-tax Closing Cost	Total Home Price	Year	Price	Comm- ission	Gain or Loss
1983	$80,000	$8,000	$1,950	$81,950	1988	$62,000	$3,720	($23,670)
1983	$80,000	$8,000	$1,950	$81,950	1991	$71,000	$4,260	($15,210)

Table 1

APPENDIX A.2: BOSTON, MASSACHUSETTS

Boston was in its heyday during the 70's and much of the 80's. There were many computer companies along Route 128, right outside of Boston, that were doing extremely well. These companies attracted many talented individuals and the stock options given by these companies created many millionaires. Because of this environment, this area was dubbed the Silicon Valley of the East.

This means that the cost of living in a home for one year would be over forty-one thousand dollars!

Housing prices started to reflect this prosperity in the 80's. The median price of a single family dwelling increased from $83,000 in 1983 to a high of $182,000 in 1989 (a 119 percent increase). Folks that invested in a home in 1983 were looking at some healthy profits in 1989. With a 10 percent down payment, the initial cash investment in a home would be $8,300. This investment in 1983 would have generated a gain of $86,080 in 1989, an outstanding return for six years. Please see Table 2 for an analysis of this situation.

In 1989, the economic situation on the east coast started to change. The computer companies along Route 128 weren't doing as well. Announcements of layoffs were seen in the papers every other week.

Examples Where Housing Prices did not Rise

Housing prices started to tumble. From 1989 to the beginning of 1991, housing prices decreased to $160,000 (a 12% decrease). Folks that purchased in 1983, watched their profits decrease by $20,680. Instead of turning their initial $8,300 investment into $86,080, it was now only worth $65,400. Still not a bad return for an 8-year investment.

The point is, do not buy a home just because housing prices "always" go up; they do not.

However, folks that purchased at the peak, in 1989, did not fare very well. The initial outlay of cash to get into a home in 1989 with a 10% down payment would have been $18,200. In 1991, this cash outlay would have generated a loss of $34,850. If the home owner had to sell in 1991, they would have to pay an additional $16,650 to pay off the mortgage. In this situation, it would cost approximately **thirty-five thousand dollars** to live in a home for two years.

In a town outside of Boston (Natick, Massachusetts), very close to Route 128, the situation was even worse. From January to August 1990, the median price of a home was $170,000. During the same time-frame in 1991, the median price of a home decreased to $140,000, a 17.6 percent decrease. The $17,000 it would take to purchase a home in 1990 would be worth ($41,325) the next year. This means that the cost of living in a home for one year would be over **forty-one thousand dollars**!

Analysis of Home Ownership

in Boston/Natick, Massachusetts

		PURCHASED					SOLD		
Year	Price	Down Payment	After-tax Closing Cost	Total Home Price	Year	Price	Comm-ission	Gain or Loss
Boston								
1983	$83,000	$8,300	$2,000	$85,000	1989	$182,000	$10,920	$86,080
1983	$83,000	$8,300	$2,000	$85,000	1991	$160,000	$9,600	$65,400
1989	$182,000	$18,200	$3,250	$185,250	1991	$160,000	$9,600	($34,850)
Natick								
Jan.-Aug. 1990	$170,000	$17,000	$2,925	$172,925	Jan.-Aug. 1991	$140,000	$8,400	($41,325)

Table 2

Examples Where Housing Prices did not Rise

Hindsight has 20/20 vision. Folks that purchased in 1983 or before would still be sitting on some very healthy profits. Folks that purchased in 1989 or 1990 may see housing prices come back and their losses covered.

As with any investment, there are good times and bad times to purchase a home. There are many examples of people who purchased at a good time and they will be more than happy to share their story with you. Unfortunately, there are a large number of folks who purchased at a bad time and they may not be so happy to share their story with you. The point is, do not buy a home just because housing prices "always" go up; they do not.

Appendix B

Equivalence

Appendix B: Equivalence

When evaluating renting vs owning, the question of equivalence comes into play. Depending on whom you ask, the answer to this question will take on a different meaning The theoretical and practical answers are different. The theoretical answer is as follows:

❑ Equivalence means looking at exactly the same piece of property for both renting and owning

Those that want to argue with the outcome of some of the examples shown in this book will take this definition to heart. However, the practical answer to this question can and often is a lot different from the theoretical one. The practical view of equivalence is as follows:

❑ Equivalence means looking at what type of apartment, town home or home the renter "will be happy with" because they are renting compared to what they would "have to" have in order to be happy as a home owner

Please notice that this latter definition takes an emotional element into account. As a renter, one is often happy living in an accommodation that is not 100% of what they would want if they were owning. This does not mean that there is anything wrong with the rental situation. Nor does it mean that the renter is unhappy renting. It only means that if the renter were going too own, they would "need" to own a place that had "more" of what they wanted. One possible reason for this is flexibility. If the rental situation got bad, the renter could just pick up and move. Another reason is that one takes more pride in something owned than something rented. Please take the time to come up with your own reasons.

The exact definition of equivalence is personal...it is important to look at the particular rental property and the particular home that each person making the rent vs buy decision would look at.

The point is, that the exact definition of equivalence is personal. As a renter, one needs to look at what type of accommodation is necessary to satisfy the basic needs of renting. These accommodations can range from practically nothing to renting a mansion. As a home owner, one needs to look at what type of accommodation is necessary to satisfy the basic needs of owning. As mentioned before, the requirements placed here are often more stringent than those placed when renting.

The practical definition of equivalence is the one used in this book. The author feels that the entire rent vs buy question is a personal one and must be evaluated on a case by case basis. It is important to look at the particular rental property and the particular home that each person making the rent vs buy decision would look at. Research conducted by this author shows that the typical renter wants to "step up" when evaluating the purchase of a home. This means that if the renter is

Equivalence

currently renting a 2 bedroom by 2 bathroom (2x2) place, they would want to own a 3x2 place. Similarly, if the renter were renting a 3x2 place, they would want to own a 4x2 place.

Of course, this is an assumption and no assumption is an absolute truth. That is why the spreadsheet is sold separately*. The reader is invited to purchase the spreadsheet and plug in whatever numbers are relevant for their particular situation.

* For those without a computer, Myth Breakers will run the numbers for you (order form enclosed at the back of the book)

Appendix C

How to Plan & Save Money

APPENDIX C: HOW TO PLAN AND SAVE MONEY

OVERVIEW:

Saving money is easy if you take the following five steps and then believe in step four:

1 - Draft a plan detailing your monthly income and expenditures

2 - Set a goal of how much money you want to save in a certain time-frame

3 - Based on your plan, and your goal of how much money you want to save, determine a "realistic" Amount of Money per PAy Check (AMPAC) you can save

4 - <u>Treat your AMPAC as an expense</u> (i.e., a forced savings account)

5 - Set up a separate bank account which you will put your AMPAC into

Believing in step four is vital to saving money. If a sudden opportunity to travel arises, take out a loan or use your credit card before you would think about tapping into your AMPAC. Obviously, you need to be careful about taking out loans to pay for vacations. The point is, treat the AMPAC as an expense; an item that must be paid for with every pay check. If you do this, you would be surprised at your ability to save money.

ADDITIONAL DETAIL:

In order to save money, you first need to get an understanding of your personal financial situation. Most people know how much money they make each month, not as many know how they are spending it. Creating a plan is not difficult. The next three paragraphs will walk you through the steps necessary to create a plan. Feel free to do it on a medium you feel comfortable with. Find a pencil, piece of paper and a calculator.

First right down your monthly net income, the amount of money you take home each month after taxes. Underneath that, write down your fixed expenses. Fixed expenses are those that must be paid for each month. Items in this category include rent, car loan, insurance, telephone expense, electric, gas, and so on. Please calculate a total of your fixed expenses.

The money you should save annually should feel comfortable to you.

Underneath your fixed expenses, write down your variable expenses. Variable expenses are those that could vary based on either your desire to consume them or their propensity to crop up. Items in this category include food, clothes, entertainment, gifts, vacation, car repair, and so on. Please calculate the total of your variable expenses.

How to Plan & Save Money

Add together the total of your fixed and variable expenses. This is your current total expenses for the month. If you subtract your total expenses from your monthly net income you should come up with a positive dollar amount. If not, or if this difference is not as large as you would like, you should take a look at your variable expenses to see if there is anything that you could decrease or eliminate. This difference is your personal operating income and a portion (or all) of it should be used as your AMPAC.

Step two is to quantify your financial goals. You could have as many goals as you would like. Typically having as many goals as you can count on one hand makes sense. For illustration purposes, we will set two goals (a vacation fund and a child's college fund). For the first goal, we will say that we want to save $4,000 by next year to take a trip to Europe. For the second goal, we will save everything else we can for the college fund (essentially the personal operating income less the vacation fund savings).

With every paycheck you receive, you should write a check (or transfer the money) for your AMPAC. This is your "forced savings account."

Step three is to determine your AMPAC. First take your personal operating income and annualize it (multiply this number by 12). This should be the total amount of money you could save in a year. Now determine if this amount is either okay, too much, or too little to save. If it is not enough, please look over your variable expenses and determine what can be decreased or eliminated. If this is too much, do not save it all. Include some of this money in a variable expense called "rainy day fund."

The money you should save annually should feel comfortable to you. In our example, it must be at least $4,000 and hopefully some value large enough to make a dent in a college fund. Once you determine the amount you want to save in a year, divide that value by the number of paychecks you receive in a year. This is your AMPAC.

Step four is to write down your AMPAC as a fixed expense in your budget. With every paycheck you receive, you should write a check (or transfer the money) for your AMPAC. This is your "forced savings account."

Step five is to set up a bank account for each goal. You could group all your goals into one account, as long as you keep separate track of how much money has been contributed for each goal. What is important, is that you keep one account for your regular use and a separate account for your AMPAC.

How to Plan & Save Money

Appendix D

Rent vs Buy Analysis for Various

Metropolitan Cities

APPENDIX D: RENT VS BUY ANALYSIS FOR VARIOUS METROPOLITAN CITIES

This appendix includes a rent versus buy analysis for 29 cities. The comparitive results are seen on the next page. The same methodology used in the book is applied here. For more information, please read Section 5. The following assumptions were made in this analaysis:

❏ Median home price taken from National Association of Realtors' "Home Sales" monthly publication, where available

❏ Average rent taken from the National Apartment Association "1992 Survey of Income & Operation Expenses", where available

❏ Effective property tax taken from the Department of Finance & Revenue "Tax Rates & Tax Burdens in the District of Columbia", where available

❏ A 30-year fixed-rate loan is used with a rate of 7.75% for loans under $202,300 and 8.25% for loans over that amount

❏ Additional assumptions: down payment of 10%, additional cost of repairs & utilities of 1.2% (per year) of the home price, tax bracket of 31.0%, savings rate of 4.0%, and a rental increase of 2.5% per year

These numbers are "best guesses" at what the actual numbers would be for each city. The use of this appendix is to give the reader a general feeling for the rent vs buy analysis for a city they can relate to. As seen on the next page, the results differ across the country. San Francisco is the city where the average renter can save the most amount of money compared to owning while New Orleans is the city where the renter can save the least; even losing money over 10 years. What does this mean for your situation? Is it better to own, or is it better to rent and save?

Comparison of Rent vs Buy Analysis for 3, 5 & 10 Year Periods for Various Metropolitan Cities

#	City	Med Home Price	Average Rent	Effective Property Tax	Amount Rentor Can Save 3 yrs	Yrly % Appr. to Break Even 3 yrs	Tot % Appr. to Break Even 3 yrs	Amount Rentor Can Save 5 yrs	Yrly % Appr. to Break Even 5 yrs	Tot % Appr. to Break Even 5 yrs	Amount Rentor Can Save 10 yrs	Yrly % Appr. to Break Even 10 yrs	Tot % Appr. to Break Even 10 yrs
1	San Francisco (Bay Area), CA	$262,000	$785	1.25%	$38,565	6.8%	21.7%	$65,655	5.5%	30.6%	$138,319	4.3%	53.1%
2	Honolulu, HI	$339,500	$1,200	0.37%	$36,264	5.5%	17.3%	$61,049	4.2%	23.0%	$124,931	3.1%	36.0%
3	Newark, NJ*	$188,900	$525	3.14%	$35,924	8.1%	26.2%	$61,632	6.7%	38.4%	$129,115	5.5%	70.7%
4	Los Angeles, CA	$216,600	$685	0.63%	$25,969	5.9%	18.7%	$43,986	4.6%	25.3%	$91,462	3.5%	41.1%
5	NYC, NY*	$174,800	$542	0.87%	$22,300	6.1%	19.6%	$37,851	4.9%	26.7%	$79,134	3.7%	44.3%
6	Chicago, IL	$138,100	$540	2.05%	$16,928	6.0%	19.0%	$28,695	4.7%	25.8%	$59,784	3.6%	42.2%
7	Seattle, WA	$145,900	$517	1.05%	$16,720	5.7%	18.2%	$28,274	4.5%	24.3%	$58,546	3.3%	38.9%
8	Boston, MA	$173,300	$739	0.89%	$14,427	4.7%	14.8%	$24,062	3.4%	18.5%	$48,018	2.3%	25.6%
9	Washington, DC	$159,900	$707	0.91%	$12,418	4.5%	14.2%	$20,635	3.3%	17.4%	$40,763	2.1%	23.3%
10	Albany, NY	$110,200	$483	2.15%	$11,755	5.5%	17.4%	$19,824	4.2%	22.9%	$40,757	3.1%	35.5%
11	Denver, CO	$95,500	$404	0.97%	$8,246	4.8%	15.2%	$13,778	3.6%	19.1%	$27,632	2.4%	27.0%
12	Baltimore, MD	$113,300	$629	2.46%	$7,753	4.2%	13.2%	$12,788	3.0%	15.7%	$24,741	1.8%	19.4%
13	Houston, TX	$79,700	$372	2.00%	$7,364	5.0%	15.9%	$12,343	3.8%	20.2%	$24,968	2.6%	29.6%
14	Portland, OR	$97,400	$538	2.64%	$7,162	4.4%	13.8%	$11,865	3.1%	16.6%	$23,239	2.0%	21.5%
15	Philadelphia, PA	$120,700	$716	2.64%	$6,976	3.9%	12.1%	$11,375	2.6%	13.7%	$21,272	1.4%	14.9%
16	Phoenix, AZ	$87,200	$414	1.47%	$6,762	4.5%	14.2%	$11,236	3.3%	17.4%	$22,192	2.1%	23.3%
17	Charlotte, NC	$99,700	$484	1.20%	$6,718	4.2%	13.2%	$11,070	2.9%	15.5%	$21,357	1.8%	19.0%
18	Albuquerque, NM	$90,700	$417	1.04%	$6,687	4.4%	13.8%	$11,079	3.1%	16.7%	$21,707	2.0%	21.6%
19	Milwaukee, WI	$95,700	$625	3.75%	$5,681	3.9%	12.3%	$9,280	2.7%	14.0%	$17,457	1.5%	15.6%
20	Las Vegas, NV	$105,600	$541	1.02%	$5,604	3.7%	11.6%	$9,077	2.4%	12.8%	$16,633	1.2%	12.9%
21	Indianapolis, IN	$84,100	$461	1.75%	$4,668	3.8%	11.9%	$7,588	2.5%	13.3%	$14,059	1.3%	14.0%
22	Detroit, MI	$79,400	$552	4.40%	$4,566	3.9%	12.1%	$7,442	2.6%	13.6%	$13,902	1.4%	14.8%
23	Atlanta, GA	$87,500	$512	1.74%	$3,584	3.3%	10.3%	$5,663	2.0%	10.6%	$9,583	0.8%	7.8%
24	Memphis, TN	$85,500	$447	0.54%	$3,277	3.2%	10.0%	$5,140	1.9%	10.1%	$8,474	0.7%	6.7%
25	Cleveland, OH	$92,300	$586	2.00%	$2,545	2.9%	8.9%	$3,808	1.6%	8.0%	$5,214	0.2%	2.1%
26	Jacksonville, FL	$74,700	$471	2.15%	$2,388	3.0%	9.1%	$3,659	1.7%	8.7%	$5,530	0.4%	3.8%
27	St. Louis, MO	$81,700	$529	1.15%	$322	2.1%	6.4%	($14)	0.7%	3.7%	($3,036)	-0.8%	-7.8%
28	Minneapolis, MN	$95,100	$632	1.39%	$270	2.1%	6.3%	($200)	0.7%	3.5%	($3,952)	-0.9%	-8.2%
29	New Orleans, LA	$73,700	$500	1.61%	$174	2.1%	6.3%	($217)	0.7%	3.4%	($3,203)	-0.9%	-8.4%

Newark & NYC Rents are low because of rent control

Table 3

Rent vs Buy Analysis for Various Metropolitan Cities

Albany, NY

Using the Median Home Price and the Average Monthly Rent

HOME:

Purchase Price:	$110,200
Closing Cost:	$3,700
+Total Home Cost:	$113,900
+After-tax Cost:	$112,753
Down Payment:	$11,000
+Initial Principal:	$7,300
+Starting Loan:	$102,900
Mortgage Rate:	7.750%
Loan Length (in Yrs):	30
+Monthly Payment:	$737
Real Estate Tax:	2.150%
Add Repair/Utility Cost:	0.10%
Closing Commission Rate:	6.0%

GENERAL:

Tax Bracket:	31.0%
Savings Rate:	4.0%

RENT:

Starting Rental Amount:	$483
Monthly Rental Incr./Yr (in %):	2.5%
+Initial Monthly Savings Amt:	$295

COMPARISON (3 YRS):

+Principal Paid:	$2,933
+Interest Paid:	$23,606
+Amount Renter Can Save:	$11,755
+Amount Difference Rent/Own:	$8,822
+Appr. Required to Break Even:	$19,135
+Required Home Sales Price:	$129,335
+Yearly % Appr. to Break Even:	5.5%
+Total % Appr. to Break Even:	17.4%

COMPARISON (5 YRS):

+Principal Paid:	$5,302
+Interest Paid:	$38,930
+Amount Renter Can Save:	$19,824
+Amount Difference Rent/Own:	$14,522
+Appr. Required to Break Even:	$25,199
+Required Home Sales Price:	$135,399
+Yearly % Appr. to Break Even:	4.2%
+Total % Appr. to Break Even:	22.9%

COMPARISON (10 YRS):

+Principal Paid:	$13,103
+Interest Paid:	$75,360
+Amount Renter Can Save:	$40,757
+Amount Difference Rent/Own:	$27,654
+Appr. Required to Break Even:	$39,169
+Required Home Sales Price:	$149,369
+Yearly % Appr. to Break Even:	3.1%
+Total % Appr. to Break Even:	35.5%

Figure 9

Myth Breakers

		Summary Information						Home Ownership					Rental Difference				
Yr	Current Loan	Mortgage Payment	After Tax Layout	Cumulative Principal Paid	Interest Paid	Amount Renter Can Save	Amount Diff Rent/Own	Annual Principal Paid	Annual Interest Paid	Real Estate Tax	Income Tax Break	Repairs + Add Utils	Mthly Rent *	Ave Mthly Savings Amount	Before Int Diff Rent/Own	Int on Diff	Int on Diff & **ATDP
0	$102,900																
1	$101,997	$8,846	$9,341	$903	$7,943	$3,870	$2,967	$903	$7,943	$2,369	$3,197	$1,322	$483	$295	$3,545	$325	$325
2	$101,021	$8,846	$9,458	$1,879	$15,814	$7,789	$5,910	$976	$7,871	$2,429	$3,193	$1,355	$495	$291	$7,042	$422	$747
3	$99,967	$8,846	$9,558	$2,933	$23,606	$11,755	$8,822	$1,054	$7,792	$2,489	$3,187	$1,389	$507	$287	$10,490	$518	$1,265
4	$98,828	$8,846	$9,642	$4,072	$31,313	$15,767	$11,695	$1,139	$7,708	$2,551	$3,180	$1,424	$520	$283	$13,890	$612	$1,877
5	$97,598	$8,846	$9,749	$5,302	$38,930	$19,824	$14,522	$1,230	$7,616	$2,615	$3,172	$1,460	$533	$279	$17,242	$705	$2,582
6	$96,269	$8,846	$9,862	$6,631	$46,447	$23,925	$17,294	$1,329	$7,517	$2,681	$3,161	$1,496	$546	$275	$20,546	$797	$3,379
7	$94,834	$8,846	$9,978	$8,066	$53,858	$28,069	$20,003	$1,436	$7,411	$2,748	$3,149	$1,534	$560	$271	$23,802	$888	$4,267
8	$93,283	$8,846	$10,100	$9,617	$61,153	$32,257	$22,639	$1,551	$7,295	$2,816	$3,135	$1,572	$574	$268	$27,013	$977	$5,244
9	$91,607	$8,846	$10,226	$11,293	$68,324	$36,486	$25,193	$1,676	$7,171	$2,887	$3,118	$1,611	$588	$264	$30,177	$1,065	$6,309
10	$89,797	$8,846	$10,358	$13,103	$75,360	$40,757	$27,654	$1,810	$7,036	$2,959	$3,098	$1,651	$603	$260	$33,297	$1,151	$7,460
11	$87,842	$8,846	$10,496	$15,058	$82,250	$45,070	$30,012	$1,955	$6,891	$3,033	$3,076	$1,693	$618	$256	$36,373	$1,237	$8,697
12	$85,729	$8,846	$10,639	$17,171	$88,984	$49,425	$32,254	$2,113	$6,734	$3,109	$3,051	$1,735	$634	$253	$39,407	$1,321	$10,018
13	$83,447	$8,846	$10,789	$19,453	$95,548	$53,823	$34,370	$2,282	$6,564	$3,186	$3,023	$1,778	$650	$249	$42,401	$1,404	$11,422
14	$80,981	$8,846	$10,945	$21,919	$101,929	$58,264	$36,346	$2,465	$6,381	$3,266	$2,991	$1,823	$666	$246	$45,356	$1,486	$12,908
15	$78,318	$8,846	$11,108	$24,582	$108,112	$62,750	$38,168	$2,663	$6,183	$3,348	$2,954	$1,869	$682	$243	$48,274	$1,567	$14,476
16	$75,441	$8,846	$11,279	$27,459	$114,081	$67,282	$39,822	$2,877	$5,969	$3,431	$2,914	$1,915	$700	$240	$51,159	$1,647	$16,123
17	$72,332	$8,846	$11,458	$30,568	$119,818	$71,861	$41,294	$3,108	$5,738	$3,517	$2,869	$1,963	$717	$238	$54,012	$1,726	$17,849
18	$68,974	$8,846	$11,645	$33,926	$125,307	$76,492	$42,566	$3,358	$5,488	$3,605	$2,819	$2,012	$735	$235	$56,838	$1,805	$19,654
19	$65,346	$8,846	$11,841	$37,554	$130,525	$81,175	$43,621	$3,628	$5,218	$3,695	$2,763	$2,062	$753	$233	$59,639	$1,882	$21,536
20	$61,427	$8,846	$12,046	$41,473	$135,452	$85,915	$44,442	$3,919	$4,927	$3,788	$2,702	$2,114	$772	$232	$62,419	$1,959	$23,496
21	$57,193	$8,846	$12,262	$45,707	$140,064	$90,715	$45,008	$4,234	$4,612	$3,882	$2,633	$2,167	$791	$230	$65,184	$2,036	$25,531
22	$52,619	$8,846	$12,489	$50,281	$144,337	$95,581	$45,300	$4,574	$4,272	$3,979	$2,558	$2,221	$811	$229	$67,938	$2,112	$27,643
23	$47,678	$8,846	$12,727	$55,222	$148,242	$100,518	$45,295	$4,941	$3,905	$4,079	$2,475	$2,277	$832	$229	$70,687	$2,188	$29,831
24	$42,339	$8,846	$12,977	$60,561	$151,750	$105,531	$44,970	$5,338	$3,506	$4,181	$2,384	$2,334	$852	$229	$73,436	$2,264	$32,095
25	$36,572	$8,846	$13,240	$66,328	$154,829	$110,628	$44,300	$5,767	$3,079	$4,285	$2,283	$2,392	$874	$230	$76,193	$2,340	$34,435
26	$30,342	$8,846	$13,518	$72,558	$157,445	$115,816	$43,258	$6,230	$2,616	$4,393	$2,173	$2,452	$895	$231	$78,965	$2,416	$36,851
27	$23,612	$8,846	$13,810	$79,288	$159,561	$121,105	$41,816	$6,730	$2,116	$4,502	$2,052	$2,513	$918	$233	$81,761	$2,493	$39,343
28	$16,341	$8,846	$14,118	$86,559	$161,136	$126,504	$39,944	$7,271	$1,575	$4,615	$1,919	$2,576	$941	$236	$84,590	$2,570	$41,914
29	$8,486	$8,846	$14,443	$94,414	$162,127	$132,024	$37,610	$7,855	$991	$4,730	$1,774	$2,640	$964	$239	$87,461	$2,649	$44,563
30	$0	$8,846	$14,786	$102,900	$162,488	$137,678	$34,778	$8,486	$360	$4,849	$1,615	$2,706	$988	$244	$90,386	$2,729	$47,292

* Represents the approximate amount of money which should be saved monthly
** After Tax Down Payment is the initial principal plus the after-tax value of the closing cost

Copyright © Myth Breakers - 1993

Figure 10 - Page 99

Albuquerque, NM

Using the Median Home Price and the Average Monthly Rent

HOME:

Purchase Price:	$90,700
Closing Cost:	$3,000
+Total Home Cost:	$93,700
+After-tax Cost:	$92,770
Down Payment:	$9,100
+Initial Principal:	$6,100
+Starting Loan:	$84,600
Mortgage Rate:	7.750%
Loan Length (in Yrs):	30
+Monthly Payment:	$606
Real Estate Tax:	1.040%
Add Repair/Utility Cost:	0.10%
Closing Commission Rate:	6.0%

GENERAL:

Tax Bracket:	31.0%
Savings Rate:	4.0%

RENT:

Starting Rental Amount:	$417
Monthly Rental Incr./Yr (in %):	2.5%
+Initial Monthly Savings Amt:	$165

COMPARISON (3 YRS):

+Principal Paid:	$2,411
+Interest Paid:	$19,408
+Amount Renter Can Save:	$6,687
+Amount Difference Rent/Own:	$4,275
+Appr. Required to Break Even:	$12,540
+Required Home Sales Price:	$103,240
+Yearly % Appr. to Break Even:	4.4%
+Total % Appr. to Break Even:	13.8%

COMPARISON (5 YRS):

+Principal Paid:	$4,359
+Interest Paid:	$32,006
+Amount Renter Can Save:	$11,079
+Amount Difference Rent/Own:	$6,720
+Appr. Required to Break Even:	$15,140
+Required Home Sales Price:	$105,840
+Yearly % Appr. to Break Even:	3.1%
+Total % Appr. to Break Even:	16.7%

COMPARISON (10 YRS):

+Principal Paid:	$10,773
+Interest Paid:	$61,958
+Amount Renter Can Save:	$21,707
+Amount Difference Rent/Own:	$10,934
+Appr. Required to Break Even:	$19,624
+Required Home Sales Price:	$110,324
+Yearly % Appr. to Break Even:	2.0%
+Total % Appr. to Break Even:	21.6%

Figure 11

Myth Breakers®

Yr	Current Loan	Mortgage Payment	After Tax Layout	Cumulative Principal Paid	Cumulative Interest Paid	Amount Renter Can Save	Amount Diff Rent/Own	Annual Principal Paid	Annual Interest Paid	Real Estate Tax	Income Tax Break	Repairs + Add Utils	*Mthly Rent	Ave Mthly Savings Amount	Before Int Diff Rent/Own	Int on Diff & **ATDP (annual)	Int on Diff & **ATDP (cum)
0	$84,600																
1	$83,857	$7,273	$6,988	$743	$6,530	$2,239	$1,496	$743	$6,530	$943	$2,317	$1,088	$417	$165	$1,984	$255	$255
2	$83,055	$7,273	$7,050	$1,545	$13,001	$4,469	$2,924	$802	$6,471	$967	$2,306	$1,116	$427	$160	$3,905	$309	$564
3	$82,189	$7,273	$7,114	$2,411	$19,408	$6,687	$4,275	$867	$6,406	$991	$2,293	$1,144	$438	$155	$5,762	$361	$925
4	$81,253	$7,273	$7,182	$3,347	$25,745	$8,891	$5,543	$936	$6,337	$1,016	$2,279	$1,172	$449	$149	$7,554	$411	$1,336
5	$80,241	$7,273	$7,252	$4,359	$32,006	$11,079	$6,720	$1,011	$6,262	$1,041	$2,264	$1,201	$460	$144	$9,283	$460	$1,796
6	$79,149	$7,273	$7,325	$5,451	$38,187	$13,248	$7,797	$1,093	$6,180	$1,067	$2,247	$1,231	$472	$139	$10,946	$506	$2,303
7	$77,968	$7,273	$7,401	$6,632	$44,279	$15,398	$8,766	$1,180	$6,093	$1,094	$2,228	$1,262	$484	$133	$12,544	$551	$2,854
8	$76,693	$7,273	$7,481	$7,907	$50,277	$17,526	$9,619	$1,275	$5,998	$1,121	$2,207	$1,294	$496	$128	$14,077	$595	$3,449
9	$75,316	$7,273	$7,565	$9,284	$56,173	$19,629	$10,345	$1,378	$5,895	$1,149	$2,184	$1,326	$508	$122	$15,545	$636	$4,084
10	$73,827	$7,273	$7,652	$10,773	$61,958	$21,707	$10,934	$1,488	$5,785	$1,178	$2,158	$1,359	$521	$117	$16,947	$675	$4,760
11	$72,220	$7,273	$7,743	$12,380	$67,623	$23,758	$11,378	$1,608	$5,665	$1,207	$2,131	$1,393	$534	$111	$18,285	$713	$5,473
12	$70,483	$7,273	$7,839	$14,117	$73,159	$25,780	$11,663	$1,737	$5,536	$1,238	$2,100	$1,428	$547	$106	$19,558	$749	$6,222
13	$68,607	$7,273	$7,939	$15,993	$78,556	$27,773	$11,779	$1,876	$5,397	$1,269	$2,066	$1,464	$561	$101	$20,767	$783	$7,005
14	$66,580	$7,273	$8,044	$18,020	$83,802	$29,735	$11,714	$2,027	$5,246	$1,300	$2,029	$1,500	$575	$96	$21,914	$816	$7,821
15	$64,390	$7,273	$8,155	$20,210	$88,885	$31,665	$11,455	$2,190	$5,083	$1,333	$1,989	$1,538	$589	$90	$22,998	$846	$8,667
16	$62,024	$7,273	$8,271	$22,576	$93,792	$33,564	$10,988	$2,366	$4,907	$1,366	$1,945	$1,576	$604	$85	$24,021	$875	$9,543
17	$59,468	$7,273	$8,393	$25,132	$98,510	$35,431	$10,299	$2,556	$4,717	$1,400	$1,896	$1,616	$619	$80	$24,985	$903	$10,446
18	$56,707	$7,273	$8,521	$27,893	$103,022	$37,266	$9,374	$2,761	$4,512	$1,435	$1,844	$1,656	$635	$76	$25,892	$928	$11,374
19	$53,725	$7,273	$8,656	$30,875	$107,312	$39,070	$8,195	$2,983	$4,290	$1,471	$1,786	$1,698	$650	$71	$26,743	$953	$12,327
20	$50,503	$7,273	$8,798	$34,097	$111,363	$40,843	$6,746	$3,222	$4,051	$1,508	$1,723	$1,740	$667	$67	$27,541	$975	$13,302
21	$47,022	$7,273	$8,947	$37,578	$115,155	$42,588	$5,009	$3,481	$3,792	$1,546	$1,655	$1,783	$683	$62	$28,289	$997	$14,299
22	$43,261	$7,273	$9,105	$41,339	$118,667	$44,305	$2,966	$3,761	$3,512	$1,584	$1,580	$1,828	$700	$58	$28,990	$1,017	$15,315
23	$39,198	$7,273	$9,272	$45,402	$121,878	$45,998	$596	$4,063	$3,210	$1,624	$1,499	$1,874	$718	$55	$29,647	$1,035	$16,350
24	$34,810	$7,273	$9,448	$49,790	$124,762	$47,668	($2,122)	$4,389	$2,884	$1,665	$1,410	$1,921	$736	$51	$30,265	$1,053	$17,403
25	$30,068	$7,273	$9,634	$54,532	$127,294	$49,321	($5,211)	$4,741	$2,532	$1,706	$1,314	$1,969	$754	$49	$30,848	$1,069	$18,473
26	$24,946	$7,273	$9,831	$59,654	$129,445	$50,959	($8,695)	$5,122	$2,151	$1,749	$1,209	$2,018	$773	$46	$31,402	$1,085	$19,557
27	$19,413	$7,273	$10,039	$65,187	$131,184	$52,589	($12,598)	$5,534	$1,740	$1,793	$1,095	$2,068	$792	$44	$31,932	$1,100	$20,657
28	$13,435	$7,273	$10,259	$71,165	$132,479	$54,216	($16,950)	$5,978	$1,295	$1,837	$971	$2,120	$812	$43	$32,444	$1,114	$21,771
29	$6,977	$7,273	$10,493	$77,623	$133,294	$55,846	($21,777)	$6,458	$815	$1,883	$836	$2,173	$833	$42	$32,947	$1,128	$22,899
30	$0	$7,273	$10,740	$84,600	$133,591	$57,488	($27,112)	$6,977	$296	$1,930	$690	$2,227	$853	$42	$33,447	$1,142	$24,041

Summary Information · *Home Ownership* · *Rental Difference*

* Represents the approximate amount of money which should be saved monthly
** After Tax Down Payment is the initial principal plus the after-tax value of the closing cost

Figure 12 - Page 101

Atlanta, GA

Using the Median Home Price and the Average Monthly Rent

HOME:

Purchase Price:	$87,500
Closing Cost:	$2,900
+Total Home Cost:	$90,400
+After-tax Cost:	$89,501
Down Payment:	$8,800
+Initial Principal:	$5,900
+Starting Loan:	$81,600
Mortgage Rate:	7.750%
Loan Length (in Yrs):	30
+Monthly Payment:	$585
Real Estate Tax:	1.740%
Add Repair/Utility Cost:	0.10%
Closing Commission Rate:	6.0%

GENERAL:

Tax Bracket:	31.0%
Savings Rate:	4.0%

RENT:

Starting Rental Amount:	$512
Monthly Rental Incr./Yr (in %):	2.5%
+Initial Monthly Savings Amt:	$85

COMPARISON (3 YRS):

+Principal Paid:	$2,326
+Interest Paid:	$18,720
+Amount Renter Can Save:	$3,584
+Amount Difference Rent/Own:	$1,258
+Appr. Required to Break Even:	$9,053
+Required Home Sales Price:	$96,553
+Yearly % Appr. to Break Even:	3.3%
+Total % Appr. to Break Even:	10.3%

COMPARISON (5 YRS):

+Principal Paid:	$4,204
+Interest Paid:	$30,871
+Amount Renter Can Save:	$5,663
+Amount Difference Rent/Own:	$1,459
+Appr. Required to Break Even:	$9,266
+Required Home Sales Price:	$96,766
+Yearly % Appr. to Break Even:	2.0%
+Total % Appr. to Break Even:	10.6%

COMPARISON (10 YRS):

+Principal Paid:	$10,391
+Interest Paid:	$59,760
+Amount Renter Can Save:	$9,583
+Amount Difference Rent/Own:	($807)
+Appr. Required to Break Even:	$6,855
+Required Home Sales Price:	$94,355
+Yearly % Appr. to Break Even:	0.8%
+Total % Appr. to Break Even:	7.8%

Figure 13

Myth Breakers®

				Summary Information				Home Ownership						Rental Difference		
Yr	Current Loan	Mortgage Payment	After Tax Layout	Cumulative Principal Paid	Cumulative Interest Paid	Amount Renter Can Save	Amount Diff Rent/Own	Annual Principal Paid	Annual Interest Paid	Real Estate Tax	Income Tax Break	Repairs + Add Utils	Mthly Rent	Ave Mthly Savings Amount	Before Int Diff Rent/Own	Int on Diff & **ATDP
0	$81,600															
1	$80,884	$7,015	$7,163	$716	$6,299	$1,252	$536	$716	$6,299	$1,523	$2,425	$1,050	$512	$85	$1,019	$233
2	$80,110	$7,015	$7,233	$1,490	$12,540	$2,448	$958	$774	$6,241	$1,561	$2,419	$1,076	$525	$78	$1,955	$260
3	$79,274	$7,015	$7,306	$2,326	$18,720	$3,584	$1,258	$836	$6,179	$1,600	$2,411	$1,103	$538	$71	$2,806	$285
4	$78,371	$7,015	$7,382	$3,229	$24,832	$4,657	$1,428	$903	$6,112	$1,640	$2,403	$1,131	$551	$64	$3,572	$307
5	$77,396	$7,015	$7,461	$4,204	$30,871	$5,663	$1,459	$976	$6,040	$1,681	$2,393	$1,159	$565	$57	$4,252	$327
6	$76,342	$7,015	$7,544	$5,258	$36,833	$6,600	$1,342	$1,054	$5,961	$1,723	$2,382	$1,188	$579	$49	$4,844	$344
7	$75,203	$7,015	$7,629	$6,397	$42,709	$7,463	$1,067	$1,138	$5,877	$1,766	$2,369	$1,218	$594	$42	$5,348	$359
8	$73,973	$7,015	$7,719	$7,627	$48,494	$8,250	$624	$1,230	$5,785	$1,810	$2,354	$1,248	$609	$35	$5,763	$372
9	$72,645	$7,015	$7,812	$8,955	$54,181	$8,958	$3	$1,329	$5,686	$1,855	$2,338	$1,279	$624	$27	$6,089	$382
10	$71,209	$7,015	$7,909	$10,391	$59,760	$9,583	($807)	$1,435	$5,580	$1,901	$2,319	$1,311	$639	$20	$6,325	$390
11	$69,659	$7,015	$8,010	$11,941	$65,225	$10,123	($1,818)	$1,551	$5,464	$1,949	$2,298	$1,344	$655	$12	$6,470	$395
12	$67,983	$7,015	$8,116	$13,617	$70,565	$10,575	($3,042)	$1,675	$5,340	$1,998	$2,275	$1,378	$672	$5	$6,524	$397
13	$66,174	$7,015	$8,226	$15,426	$75,770	$10,936	($4,491)	$1,810	$5,205	$2,048	$2,248	$1,412	$689	($3)	$6,488	$397
14	$64,219	$7,015	$8,342	$17,381	$80,830	$11,203	($6,178)	$1,955	$5,060	$2,099	$2,219	$1,447	$706	($11)	$6,360	$395
15	$62,106	$7,015	$8,463	$19,494	$85,733	$11,376	($8,118)	$2,112	$4,903	$2,151	$2,187	$1,484	$723	($18)	$6,142	$390
16	$59,825	$7,015	$8,590	$21,775	$90,466	$11,450	($10,325)	$2,282	$4,733	$2,205	$2,151	$1,521	$742	($26)	$5,834	$383
17	$57,360	$7,015	$8,723	$24,240	$95,016	$11,425	($12,815)	$2,465	$4,550	$2,260	$2,111	$1,559	$760	($33)	$5,436	$373
18	$54,697	$7,015	$8,862	$26,903	$99,369	$11,299	($15,604)	$2,663	$4,352	$2,317	$2,067	$1,598	$779	($41)	$4,949	$361
19	$51,820	$7,015	$9,008	$29,780	$103,507	$11,071	($18,710)	$2,877	$4,138	$2,375	$2,019	$1,638	$799	($48)	$4,375	$346
20	$48,712	$7,015	$9,162	$32,888	$107,414	$10,739	($22,149)	$3,108	$3,907	$2,434	$1,966	$1,679	$819	($55)	$3,715	$329
21	$45,354	$7,015	$9,323	$36,246	$111,071	$10,304	($25,942)	$3,358	$3,658	$2,495	$1,907	$1,721	$839	($62)	$2,970	$309
22	$41,727	$7,015	$9,493	$39,873	$114,459	$9,765	($30,108)	$3,627	$3,388	$2,557	$1,843	$1,764	$860	($69)	$2,144	$287
23	$37,808	$7,015	$9,671	$43,792	$117,556	$9,123	($34,669)	$3,919	$3,097	$2,621	$1,772	$1,808	$881	($75)	$1,238	$263
24	$33,575	$7,015	$9,859	$48,025	$120,338	$8,378	($39,647)	$4,233	$2,782	$2,687	$1,695	$1,853	$903	($82)	$255	$237
25	$29,002	$7,015	$10,057	$52,598	$122,780	$7,531	($45,067)	$4,573	$2,442	$2,754	$1,611	$1,899	$926	($88)	($800)	$209
26	$24,062	$7,015	$10,266	$57,538	$124,854	$6,586	($50,953)	$4,940	$2,075	$2,823	$1,518	$1,947	$949	($94)	($1,924)	$179
27	$18,724	$7,015	$10,487	$62,876	$126,532	$5,544	($57,332)	$5,337	$1,678	$2,893	$1,417	$1,995	$973	($99)	($3,113)	$147
28	$12,958	$7,015	$10,719	$68,642	$127,781	$4,409	($64,233)	$5,766	$1,249	$2,966	$1,307	$2,045	$997	($104)	($4,361)	$113
29	$6,729	$7,015	$10,965	$74,871	$128,567	$3,186	($71,685)	$6,229	$786	$3,040	$1,186	$2,096	$1,022	($108)	($5,663)	$78
30	$0	$7,015	$11,225	$81,600	$128,853	$1,879	($79,721)	$6,729	$286	$3,116	$1,054	$2,149	$1,048	($112)	($7,011)	$41

* Represents the approximate amount of money which should be saved monthly
** After Tax Down Payment is the initial principal plus the after-tax value of the closing cost

Figure 14 - Page 103

Baltimore, MD

Using the Median Home Price and the Average Monthly Rent

HOME:

Purchase Price:	$113,300
Closing Cost:	$3,700
+Total Home Cost:	$117,000
+After-tax Cost:	$115,853
Down Payment:	$11,300
+Initial Principal:	$7,600
+Starting Loan:	$105,700
Mortgage Rate:	7.750%
Loan Length (in Yrs):	30
+Monthly Payment:	$757
Real Estate Tax:	2.460%
Add Repair/Utility Cost:	0.10%
Closing Commission Rate:	6.0%

GENERAL:

Tax Bracket:	31.0%
Savings Rate:	4.0%

RENT:

Starting Rental Amount:	$629
Monthly Rental Incr./Yr (in %):	2.5%
+Initial Monthly Savings Amt:	$191

COMPARISON (3 YRS):

+Principal Paid:	$3,013
+Interest Paid:	$24,248
+Amount Renter Can Save:	$7,753
+Amount Difference Rent/Own:	$4,740
+Appr. Required to Break Even:	$14,990
+Required Home Sales Price:	$128,290
+Yearly % Appr. to Break Even:	4.2%
+Total % Appr. to Break Even:	13.2%

COMPARISON (5 YRS):

+Principal Paid:	$5,446
+Interest Paid:	$39,989
+Amount Renter Can Save:	$12,788
+Amount Difference Rent/Own:	$7,342
+Appr. Required to Break Even:	$17,758
+Required Home Sales Price:	$131,058
+Yearly % Appr. to Break Even:	3.0%
+Total % Appr. to Break Even:	15.7%

COMPARISON (10 YRS):

+Principal Paid:	$13,459
+Interest Paid:	$77,410
+Amount Renter Can Save:	$24,741
+Amount Difference Rent/Own:	$11,281
+Appr. Required to Break Even:	$21,949
+Required Home Sales Price:	$135,249
+Yearly % Appr. to Break Even:	1.8%
+Total % Appr. to Break Even:	19.4%

Figure 15

Figure 16 - Page 105

Myth Breakers®

			Summary Information					Home Ownership					Rental Difference			
Yr	Current Loan	Mortgage Payment	After Tax Layout	Cumulative Principal Paid	Cumulative Interest Paid	Amount Renter Can Save	Amount Diff Rent/Own	Annual Principal Paid	Annual Interest Paid	Real Estate Tax	Income Tax Break	Repairs + Add Utils	* Mthly Rent	Ave Mthly Savings Amount	Before Int Diff Rent/Own	Int on Diff & **ATDP
0	$105,700															
1	$104,772	$9,087	$9,840	$928	$8,159	$2,607	$1,679	$928	$8,159	$2,787	$3,393	$1,360	$629	$191	$2,292	$314
2	$103,770	$9,087	$9,946	$1,930	$16,244	$5,192	$3,262	$1,002	$8,085	$2,857	$3,392	$1,394	$645	$184	$4,501	$376
3	$102,687	$9,087	$10,055	$3,013	$24,248	$7,753	$4,740	$1,083	$8,004	$2,928	$3,389	$1,428	$661	$177	$6,626	$436
4	$101,518	$9,087	$10,168	$4,182	$32,166	$10,286	$6,103	$1,170	$7,917	$3,001	$3,385	$1,464	$677	$170	$8,665	$494
5	$100,254	$9,087	$10,285	$5,446	$39,989	$12,788	$7,342	$1,264	$7,823	$3,077	$3,379	$1,501	$694	$163	$10,619	$549
6	$98,889	$9,087	$10,407	$6,811	$47,711	$15,256	$8,445	$1,365	$7,722	$3,153	$3,371	$1,538	$712	$156	$12,486	$601
7	$97,414	$9,087	$10,534	$8,286	$55,323	$17,689	$9,403	$1,475	$7,612	$3,232	$3,362	$1,577	$729	$148	$14,267	$651
8	$95,821	$9,087	$10,666	$9,879	$62,817	$20,082	$10,203	$1,593	$7,494	$3,313	$3,350	$1,616	$748	$141	$15,961	$699
9	$94,100	$9,087	$10,803	$11,600	$70,183	$22,433	$10,833	$1,721	$7,366	$3,396	$3,336	$1,657	$766	$134	$17,568	$745
10	$92,241	$9,087	$10,946	$13,459	$77,410	$24,741	$11,281	$1,859	$7,228	$3,481	$3,320	$1,698	$786	$127	$19,087	$788
11	$90,232	$9,087	$11,095	$15,468	$84,489	$27,002	$11,534	$2,009	$7,078	$3,568	$3,300	$1,740	$805	$119	$20,520	$828
12	$88,062	$9,087	$11,250	$17,638	$91,406	$29,215	$11,577	$2,170	$6,917	$3,657	$3,278	$1,784	$825	$112	$21,867	$867
13	$85,718	$9,087	$11,412	$19,982	$98,148	$31,378	$11,395	$2,344	$6,743	$3,748	$3,252	$1,829	$846	$105	$23,127	$902
14	$83,185	$9,087	$11,580	$22,515	$104,703	$33,489	$10,974	$2,533	$6,554	$3,842	$3,223	$1,874	$867	$98	$24,302	$936
15	$80,449	$9,087	$11,757	$25,251	$111,054	$35,548	$10,297	$2,736	$6,351	$3,938	$3,190	$1,921	$889	$91	$25,394	$967
16	$77,493	$9,087	$11,941	$28,207	$117,185	$37,553	$9,346	$2,956	$6,131	$4,037	$3,152	$1,969	$911	$84	$26,403	$996
17	$74,300	$9,087	$12,133	$31,400	$123,079	$39,503	$8,104	$3,193	$5,894	$4,138	$3,110	$2,018	$934	$77	$27,331	$1,023
18	$70,851	$9,087	$12,334	$34,849	$128,716	$41,400	$6,550	$3,450	$5,637	$4,241	$3,062	$2,069	$957	$71	$28,180	$1,047
19	$67,124	$9,087	$12,545	$38,576	$134,077	$43,242	$4,666	$3,727	$5,360	$4,347	$3,009	$2,121	$981	$64	$28,953	$1,069
20	$63,098	$9,087	$12,766	$42,602	$139,138	$45,031	$2,429	$4,026	$5,061	$4,456	$2,950	$2,174	$1,006	$58	$29,652	$1,090
21	$58,749	$9,087	$12,997	$46,951	$143,876	$46,768	($183)	$4,349	$4,738	$4,567	$2,885	$2,228	$1,031	$52	$30,282	$1,108
22	$54,051	$9,087	$13,240	$51,649	$148,264	$48,455	($3,195)	$4,698	$4,388	$4,681	$2,812	$2,284	$1,056	$47	$30,844	$1,124
23	$48,975	$9,087	$13,495	$56,725	$152,275	$50,094	($6,631)	$5,076	$4,011	$4,798	$2,731	$2,341	$1,083	$42	$31,345	$1,139
24	$43,491	$9,087	$13,763	$62,209	$155,879	$51,689	($10,520)	$5,483	$3,603	$4,918	$2,642	$2,399	$1,110	$37	$31,788	$1,152
25	$37,568	$9,087	$14,044	$68,132	$159,042	$53,244	($14,889)	$5,924	$3,163	$5,041	$2,543	$2,459	$1,138	$33	$32,180	$1,163
26	$31,168	$9,087	$14,340	$74,532	$161,729	$54,763	($19,769)	$6,400	$2,687	$5,167	$2,435	$2,521	$1,166	$29	$32,526	$1,173
27	$24,254	$9,087	$14,651	$81,446	$163,903	$56,254	($25,192)	$6,914	$2,173	$5,296	$2,316	$2,584	$1,195	$26	$32,834	$1,182
28	$16,785	$9,087	$14,980	$88,915	$165,521	$57,721	($31,193)	$7,469	$1,618	$5,429	$2,185	$2,648	$1,225	$23	$33,112	$1,190
29	$8,717	$9,087	$15,325	$96,983	$166,539	$59,175	($37,809)	$8,069	$1,018	$5,565	$2,041	$2,714	$1,256	$21	$33,368	$1,197
30	$0	$9,087	$15,690	$105,700	$166,909	$60,623	($45,077)	$8,717	$370	$5,704	$1,883	$2,782	$1,287	$20	$33,612	$1,204

* Represents the approximate amount of money which should be saved monthly
** After Tax Down Payment is the after-tax value of the closing cost

Copyright © Myth Breakers - 1993

Rent vs Buy Analysis for Various Metropolitan Cities

Boston, MA

Using the Median Home Price and the Average Monthly Rent

HOME:

Purchase Price:	$173,300
Closing Cost:	$5,700
+Total Home Cost:	$179,000
+After-tax Cost:	$177,233
Down Payment:	$17,300
+Initial Principal:	$11,600
+Starting Loan:	$161,700
Mortgage Rate:	7.750%
Loan Length (in Yrs):	30
+Monthly Payment:	$1,158
Real Estate Tax:	0.890%
Add Repair/Utility Cost:	0.10%
Closing Commission Rate:	6.0%

GENERAL:

Tax Bracket:	31.0%
Savings Rate:	4.0%

RENT:

Starting Rental Amount:	$739
Monthly Rental Incr./Yr (in %):	2.5%
+Initial Monthly Savings Amt:	$359

COMPARISON (3 YRS):

+Principal Paid:	$4,609
+Interest Paid:	$37,095
+Amount Renter Can Save:	$14,427
+Amount Difference Rent/Own:	$9,818
+Appr. Required to Break Even:	$25,691
+Required Home Sales Price:	$198,991
+Yearly % Appr. to Break Even:	4.7%
+Total % Appr. to Break Even:	14.8%

COMPARISON (5 YRS):

+Principal Paid:	$8,331
+Interest Paid:	$61,175
+Amount Renter Can Save:	$24,062
+Amount Difference Rent/Own:	$15,731
+Appr. Required to Break Even:	$31,981
+Required Home Sales Price:	$205,281
+Yearly % Appr. to Break Even:	3.4%
+Total % Appr. to Break Even:	18.5%

COMPARISON (10 YRS):

+Principal Paid:	$20,590
+Interest Paid:	$118,422
+Amount Renter Can Save:	$48,018
+Amount Difference Rent/Own:	$27,428
+Appr. Required to Break Even:	$44,425
+Required Home Sales Price:	$217,725
+Yearly % Appr. to Break Even:	2.3%
+Total % Appr. to Break Even:	25.6%

Figure 17

Myth Breakers

			Summary Information					Home Ownership						Rental Difference		
Yr	Current Loan	Mortgage Payment	After Tax Layout	Cumulative Principal Paid	Cumulative Interest Paid	Amount Renter Can Save	Amount Diff Rent/Own	Annual Principal Paid	Annual Interest Paid	Real Estate Tax	Income Tax Break	Repairs + Add Utils	* Mthly Rent	Ave Mthly Savings Amount	Before Int Diff Rent/Own	Int on Diff	Int on Diff & **ATDP
0	$161,700																
1	$160,281	$13,901	$13,176	$1,419	$12,482	$4,801	$3,381	$1,419	$12,482	$1,542	$4,348	$2,080	$739	$359	$4,308	$493	$493
2	$158,748	$13,901	$13,290	$2,952	$24,850	$9,611	$6,658	$1,533	$12,368	$1,581	$4,324	$2,132	$757	$350	$8,508	$610	$1,103
3	$157,091	$13,901	$13,408	$4,609	$37,095	$14,427	$9,818	$1,656	$12,245	$1,620	$4,298	$2,185	$776	$341	$12,599	$725	$1,828
4	$155,302	$13,901	$13,532	$6,398	$49,207	$19,245	$12,847	$1,789	$12,112	$1,661	$4,270	$2,240	$796	$332	$16,581	$836	$2,664
5	$153,369	$13,901	$13,661	$8,331	$61,175	$24,062	$15,731	$1,933	$11,968	$1,702	$4,238	$2,295	$816	$323	$20,454	$944	$3,608
6	$151,280	$13,901	$13,796	$10,420	$72,988	$28,874	$18,455	$2,088	$11,813	$1,745	$4,203	$2,353	$836	$314	$24,217	$1,049	$4,657
7	$149,024	$13,901	$13,937	$12,676	$84,633	$33,679	$21,003	$2,256	$11,645	$1,789	$4,165	$2,412	$857	$304	$27,870	$1,152	$5,809
8	$146,587	$13,901	$14,084	$15,113	$96,097	$38,473	$23,360	$2,437	$11,464	$1,833	$4,122	$2,472	$878	$295	$31,413	$1,251	$7,060
9	$143,954	$13,901	$14,239	$17,746	$107,366	$43,253	$25,508	$2,633	$11,268	$1,879	$4,076	$2,534	$900	$286	$34,847	$1,347	$8,407
10	$141,110	$13,901	$14,400	$20,590	$118,422	$48,018	$27,428	$2,844	$11,057	$1,926	$4,025	$2,597	$923	$277	$38,172	$1,440	$9,847
11	$138,037	$13,901	$14,569	$23,663	$129,251	$52,766	$29,102	$3,073	$10,828	$1,974	$3,969	$2,662	$946	$268	$41,389	$1,530	$11,377
12	$134,717	$13,901	$14,746	$26,983	$139,832	$57,493	$30,510	$3,320	$10,582	$2,024	$3,908	$2,729	$970	$259	$44,499	$1,617	$12,994
13	$131,131	$13,901	$14,932	$30,569	$150,147	$62,200	$31,631	$3,586	$10,315	$2,074	$3,841	$2,797	$994	$250	$47,504	$1,702	$14,696
14	$127,257	$13,901	$15,127	$34,443	$160,174	$66,885	$32,442	$3,874	$10,027	$2,126	$3,767	$2,867	$1,019	$242	$50,406	$1,783	$16,479
15	$123,071	$13,901	$15,332	$38,629	$169,890	$71,548	$32,919	$4,185	$9,716	$2,179	$3,687	$2,938	$1,044	$233	$53,208	$1,862	$18,340
16	$118,549	$13,901	$15,547	$43,151	$179,270	$76,189	$33,038	$4,522	$9,380	$2,234	$3,600	$3,012	$1,070	$225	$55,911	$1,937	$20,278
17	$113,665	$13,901	$15,773	$48,035	$188,286	$80,808	$32,773	$4,885	$9,016	$2,290	$3,505	$3,087	$1,097	$217	$58,520	$2,011	$22,288
18	$108,388	$13,901	$16,011	$53,312	$196,910	$85,407	$32,095	$5,277	$8,624	$2,347	$3,401	$3,164	$1,124	$210	$61,037	$2,081	$24,370
19	$102,687	$13,901	$16,262	$59,013	$205,111	$89,988	$30,974	$5,701	$8,200	$2,406	$3,288	$3,243	$1,153	$203	$63,469	$2,149	$26,519
20	$96,528	$13,901	$16,527	$65,172	$212,853	$94,553	$29,381	$6,159	$7,743	$2,466	$3,165	$3,325	$1,181	$196	$65,819	$2,215	$28,734
21	$89,875	$13,901	$16,806	$71,825	$220,101	$99,107	$27,281	$6,653	$7,248	$2,527	$3,030	$3,408	$1,211	$190	$68,094	$2,279	$31,013
22	$82,687	$13,901	$17,100	$79,013	$226,815	$103,653	$24,640	$7,188	$6,714	$2,591	$2,884	$3,493	$1,241	$184	$70,300	$2,341	$33,354
23	$74,922	$13,901	$17,411	$86,778	$232,951	$108,198	$21,420	$7,765	$6,136	$2,655	$2,725	$3,580	$1,272	$179	$72,444	$2,401	$35,754
24	$66,533	$13,901	$17,740	$95,167	$238,464	$112,749	$17,582	$8,389	$5,513	$2,722	$2,553	$3,670	$1,304	$174	$74,535	$2,459	$38,213
25	$57,471	$13,901	$18,088	$104,229	$243,302	$117,313	$13,083	$9,062	$4,839	$2,790	$2,365	$3,761	$1,337	$171	$76,583	$2,516	$40,729
26	$47,681	$13,901	$18,455	$114,019	$247,414	$121,899	$7,880	$9,790	$4,111	$2,859	$2,161	$3,855	$1,370	$168	$78,598	$2,572	$43,301
27	$37,104	$13,901	$18,845	$124,596	$250,738	$126,519	$1,924	$10,576	$3,325	$2,931	$1,939	$3,952	$1,404	$166	$80,591	$2,627	$45,929
28	$25,678	$13,901	$19,257	$136,022	$253,214	$131,186	($4,836)	$11,426	$2,475	$3,004	$1,699	$4,051	$1,439	$165	$82,575	$2,682	$48,611
29	$13,335	$13,901	$19,695	$148,365	$254,772	$135,913	($12,452)	$12,344	$1,558	$3,079	$1,437	$4,152	$1,475	$166	$84,565	$2,737	$51,348
30	$0	$13,901	$20,159	$161,700	$255,338	$140,716	($20,984)	$13,335	$566	$3,156	$1,154	$4,256	$1,512	$168	$86,577	$2,792	$54,140

* Represents the approximate amount of money which should be saved monthly

** After Tax Down Payment is the initial principal plus the after-tax value of the closing cost

Figure 18 - Page 107

Rent vs Buy Analysis for Various Metropolitan Cities

Charlotte, NC

Using the Median Home Price and the Average Monthly Rent

HOME:

Purchase Price:	$99,700
Closing Cost:	$3,300
+Total Home Cost:	$103,000
+After-tax Cost:	$101,977
Down Payment:	$10,000
+Initial Principal:	$6,700
+Starting Loan:	$93,000

Mortgage Rate:	7.750%
Loan Length (in Yrs):	30
+Monthly Payment:	$666
Real Estate Tax:	1.200%
Add Repair/Utility Cost:	0.10%
Closing Commission Rate:	6.0%

GENERAL:

Tax Bracket:	31.0%
Savings Rate:	4.0%

RENT:

Starting Rental Amount:	$484
Monthly Rental Incr./Yr (in %):	2.5%
+Initial Monthly Savings Amt:	$165

COMPARISON (3 YRS):

+Principal Paid:	$2,651
+Interest Paid:	$21,335
+Amount Renter Can Save:	$6,718
+Amount Difference Rent/Own:	$4,067
+Appr. Required to Break Even:	$13,113
+Required Home Sales Price:	$112,813
+Yearly % Appr. to Break Even:	4.2%
+Total % Appr. to Break Even:	13.2%

COMPARISON (5 YRS):

+Principal Paid:	$4,792
+Interest Paid:	$35,184
+Amount Renter Can Save:	$11,070
+Amount Difference Rent/Own:	$6,279
+Appr. Required to Break Even:	$15,466
+Required Home Sales Price:	$115,166
+Yearly % Appr. to Break Even:	2.9%
+Total % Appr. to Break Even:	15.5%

COMPARISON (10 YRS):

+Principal Paid:	$11,842
+Interest Paid:	$68,109
+Amount Renter Can Save:	$21,357
+Amount Difference Rent/Own:	$9,515
+Appr. Required to Break Even:	$18,908
+Required Home Sales Price:	$118,608
+Yearly % Appr. to Break Even:	1.8%
+Total % Appr. to Break Even:	19.0%

Figure 19

Myth Breakers®

			Summary Information					Home Ownership					Rental Difference				
Yr	Current Loan	Mortgage Payment	After Tax Layout	Cumulative Principal Paid	Interest Paid	Amount Renter Can Save	Amount Diff Rent/Own	Annual Principal Paid	Annual Interest Paid	Real Estate Tax	Income Tax Break	Repairs + Add Utils	Mthly Rent	* Ave Mthly Savings Amount	Before Int Diff Rent/Own	Int on Diff	Int on Diff & **ATDP
0	$93,000																
1	$92,184	$7,995	$7,792	$816	$7,179	$2,261	$1,445	$816	$7,179	$1,196	$2,596	$1,196	$484	$165	$1,984	$277	$277
2	$91,302	$7,995	$7,862	$1,698	$14,292	$4,501	$2,803	$882	$7,113	$1,226	$2,585	$1,226	$496	$159	$3,893	$331	$608
3	$90,349	$7,995	$7,936	$2,651	$21,335	$6,718	$4,067	$953	$7,043	$1,257	$2,573	$1,257	$509	$153	$5,727	$383	$991
4	$89,320	$7,995	$8,013	$3,680	$28,301	$8,909	$5,229	$1,029	$6,966	$1,288	$2,559	$1,288	$521	$147	$7,496	$432	$1,423
5	$88,208	$7,995	$8,093	$4,792	$35,184	$11,070	$6,279	$1,112	$6,883	$1,321	$2,543	$1,321	$534	$140	$9,168	$479	$1,902
6	$87,007	$7,995	$8,177	$5,993	$41,978	$13,200	$7,208	$1,201	$6,794	$1,354	$2,526	$1,354	$548	$134	$10,773	$525	$2,427
7	$85,710	$7,995	$8,264	$7,290	$48,676	$15,296	$8,006	$1,298	$6,698	$1,387	$2,506	$1,387	$561	$127	$12,301	$568	$2,995
8	$84,308	$7,995	$8,355	$8,692	$55,269	$17,356	$8,664	$1,402	$6,593	$1,422	$2,485	$1,422	$575	$121	$13,752	$609	$3,604
9	$82,794	$7,995	$8,450	$10,206	$61,750	$19,377	$9,171	$1,514	$6,481	$1,458	$2,461	$1,458	$590	$114	$15,125	$648	$4,252
10	$81,158	$7,995	$8,549	$11,842	$68,109	$21,357	$9,515	$1,636	$6,359	$1,494	$2,435	$1,494	$604	$108	$16,421	$685	$4,936
11	$79,390	$7,995	$8,653	$13,610	$74,337	$23,294	$9,685	$1,767	$6,228	$1,531	$2,405	$1,531	$620	$102	$17,639	$719	$5,655
12	$77,481	$7,995	$8,761	$15,519	$80,423	$25,187	$9,668	$1,909	$6,086	$1,570	$2,373	$1,570	$635	$95	$18,780	$752	$6,407
13	$75,419	$7,995	$8,875	$17,581	$86,356	$27,033	$9,451	$2,063	$5,933	$1,609	$2,338	$1,609	$651	$89	$19,844	$782	$7,189
14	$73,190	$7,995	$8,995	$19,810	$92,122	$28,831	$9,021	$2,228	$5,767	$1,649	$2,299	$1,649	$667	$82	$20,832	$810	$7,999
15	$70,783	$7,995	$9,120	$22,217	$97,710	$30,581	$8,364	$2,407	$5,588	$1,690	$2,256	$1,690	$684	$76	$21,745	$836	$8,835
16	$68,182	$7,995	$9,251	$24,818	$103,105	$32,280	$7,463	$2,601	$5,395	$1,733	$2,209	$1,733	$701	$70	$22,585	$860	$9,695
17	$65,373	$7,995	$9,389	$27,627	$108,291	$33,930	$6,303	$2,809	$5,186	$1,776	$2,158	$1,776	$719	$64	$23,352	$882	$10,578
18	$62,338	$7,995	$9,534	$30,662	$113,251	$35,529	$4,867	$3,035	$4,960	$1,820	$2,102	$1,820	$736	$58	$24,049	$903	$11,480
19	$59,059	$7,995	$9,687	$33,941	$117,967	$37,078	$3,137	$3,279	$4,716	$1,866	$2,041	$1,866	$755	$52	$24,677	$921	$12,401
20	$55,517	$7,995	$9,847	$37,483	$122,420	$38,577	$1,094	$3,542	$4,453	$1,913	$1,973	$1,913	$774	$47	$25,239	$937	$13,338
21	$51,690	$7,995	$10,016	$41,310	$126,589	$40,028	($1,282)	$3,827	$4,169	$1,960	$1,900	$1,960	$793	$42	$25,738	$952	$14,290
22	$47,556	$7,995	$10,194	$45,444	$130,450	$41,431	($4,012)	$4,134	$3,861	$2,009	$1,820	$2,009	$813	$37	$26,177	$964	$15,254
23	$43,091	$7,995	$10,382	$49,909	$133,979	$42,790	($7,120)	$4,466	$3,529	$2,060	$1,733	$2,060	$833	$32	$26,560	$976	$16,230
24	$38,266	$7,995	$10,580	$54,734	$137,150	$44,107	($10,627)	$4,825	$3,171	$2,111	$1,637	$2,111	$854	$28	$26,891	$986	$17,216
25	$33,054	$7,995	$10,790	$59,946	$139,933	$45,385	($14,561)	$5,212	$2,783	$2,164	$1,534	$2,164	$875	$24	$27,176	$994	$18,209
26	$27,423	$7,995	$11,011	$65,577	$142,297	$46,629	($18,948)	$5,631	$2,364	$2,218	$1,421	$2,218	$897	$20	$27,419	$1,001	$19,211
27	$21,340	$7,995	$11,245	$71,660	$144,209	$47,844	($23,816)	$6,083	$1,912	$2,274	$1,298	$2,274	$920	$17	$27,626	$1,007	$20,218
28	$14,769	$7,995	$11,492	$78,231	$145,633	$49,036	($29,195)	$6,571	$1,424	$2,330	$1,164	$2,330	$943	$15	$27,806	$1,013	$21,230
29	$7,669	$7,995	$11,754	$85,331	$146,529	$50,212	($35,119)	$7,099	$896	$2,389	$1,018	$2,389	$966	$13	$27,964	$1,017	$22,248
30	$0	$7,995	$12,032	$93,000	$146,855	$51,379	($41,621)	$7,669	$326	$2,448	$860	$2,448	$990	$12	$28,111	$1,021	$23,269

* Represents the approximate amount of money which should be saved monthly
** After Tax Down Payment is the initial principal plus the after-tax value of the closing cost

Copyright © Myth Breakers - 1993

Figure 20 - Page 109

Chicago, IL

Using the Median Home Price and the Average Monthly Rent

HOME:

Purchase Price:	$138,100
Closing Cost:	$4,600
+Total Home Cost:	$142,700
+After-tax Cost:	$141,274
Down Payment:	$13,800
+Initial Principal:	$9,200
+Starting Loan:	$128,900

Mortgage Rate:	7.750%
Loan Length (in Yrs):	30
+Monthly Payment:	$923
Real Estate Tax:	2.050%
Add Repair/Utility Cost:	0.10%
Closing Commission Rate:	6.0%

GENERAL:

Tax Bracket:	31.0%
Savings Rate:	4.0%

RENT:

Starting Rental Amount:	$540
Monthly Rental Incr./Yr (in %):	2.5%
+Initial Monthly Savings Amt:	$427

COMPARISON (3 YRS):

+Principal Paid:	$3,674
+Interest Paid:	$29,570
+Amount Renter Can Save:	$16,928
+Amount Difference Rent/Own:	$13,254
+Appr. Required to Break Even:	$26,292
+Required Home Sales Price:	$164,392
+Yearly % Appr. to Break Even:	6.0%
+Total % Appr. to Break Even:	19.0%

COMPARISON (5 YRS):

+Principal Paid:	$6,641
+Interest Paid:	$48,766
+Amount Renter Can Save:	$28,695
+Amount Difference Rent/Own:	$22,054
+Appr. Required to Break Even:	$35,653
+Required Home Sales Price:	$173,753
+Yearly % Appr. to Break Even:	4.7%
+Total % Appr. to Break Even:	25.8%

COMPARISON (10 YRS):

+Principal Paid:	$16,414
+Interest Paid:	$94,401
+Amount Renter Can Save:	$59,784
+Amount Difference Rent/Own:	$43,371
+Appr. Required to Break Even:	$58,331
+Required Home Sales Price:	$196,431
+Yearly % Appr. to Break Even:	3.6%
+Total % Appr. to Break Even:	42.2%

Figure 21

Myth Breakers®

Summary Information | Home Ownership | Rental Difference

Yr	Current Loan	Mortgage Payment	After Tax Layout	Cumulative Principal Paid	Cumulative Interest Paid	Amount Renter Can Save	Amount Diff Rent/Own	Annual Principal Paid	Annual Interest Paid	Real Estate Tax	Income Tax Break	Repairs + Add Utils	Mthly Rent*	Ave Mthly Savings Amount	Before Int Diff Rent/Own	Int on Diff	**ATDP
0	$128,900																
1	$127,769	$11,081	$11,608	$1,131	$9,950	$5,546	$4,414	$1,131	$9,950	$2,831	$3,962	$1,657	$540	$427	$5,128	$418	$418
2	$126,546	$11,081	$11,726	$2,354	$19,809	$11,189	$8,835	$1,222	$9,859	$2,902	$3,956	$1,699	$554	$424	$10,212	$559	$977
3	$125,226	$11,081	$11,849	$3,674	$29,570	$16,928	$13,254	$1,320	$9,761	$2,974	$3,948	$1,741	$567	$420	$15,252	$699	$1,676
4	$123,800	$11,081	$11,977	$5,100	$39,226	$22,764	$17,663	$1,426	$9,655	$3,049	$3,938	$1,785	$582	$417	$20,251	$837	$2,513
5	$122,259	$11,081	$12,109	$6,641	$48,766	$28,695	$22,054	$1,541	$9,541	$3,125	$3,926	$1,829	$596	$413	$25,207	$974	$3,487
6	$120,594	$11,081	$12,247	$8,306	$58,183	$34,721	$26,415	$1,665	$9,417	$3,203	$3,912	$1,875	$611	$410	$30,123	$1,111	$4,598
7	$118,796	$11,081	$12,391	$10,104	$67,466	$40,843	$30,739	$1,798	$9,283	$3,283	$3,896	$1,922	$626	$406	$34,999	$1,246	$5,844
8	$116,853	$11,081	$12,540	$12,047	$76,604	$47,061	$35,013	$1,943	$9,139	$3,365	$3,876	$1,970	$642	$403	$39,837	$1,380	$7,223
9	$114,754	$11,081	$12,696	$14,146	$85,587	$53,374	$39,228	$2,099	$8,983	$3,449	$3,854	$2,019	$658	$400	$44,638	$1,513	$8,736
10	$112,486	$11,081	$12,858	$16,414	$94,401	$59,784	$43,371	$2,267	$8,814	$3,536	$3,828	$2,070	$674	$397	$49,404	$1,645	$10,381
11	$110,037	$11,081	$13,027	$18,863	$103,033	$66,293	$47,429	$2,450	$8,632	$3,624	$3,799	$2,121	$691	$394	$54,136	$1,776	$12,156
12	$107,391	$11,081	$13,204	$21,509	$111,468	$72,900	$51,391	$2,646	$8,435	$3,715	$3,766	$2,174	$709	$392	$58,838	$1,906	$14,062
13	$104,532	$11,081	$13,388	$24,368	$119,691	$79,609	$55,240	$2,859	$8,223	$3,807	$3,729	$2,229	$726	$389	$63,511	$2,035	$16,097
14	$101,443	$11,081	$13,581	$27,457	$127,684	$86,421	$58,964	$3,088	$7,993	$3,903	$3,688	$2,284	$744	$387	$68,159	$2,164	$18,261
15	$98,107	$11,081	$13,782	$30,793	$135,429	$93,339	$62,545	$3,336	$7,745	$4,000	$3,641	$2,342	$763	$386	$72,786	$2,292	$20,553
16	$94,502	$11,081	$13,993	$34,398	$142,906	$100,366	$65,968	$3,604	$7,477	$4,100	$3,589	$2,400	$782	$384	$77,393	$2,419	$22,972
17	$90,608	$11,081	$14,213	$38,292	$150,093	$107,505	$69,214	$3,894	$7,188	$4,203	$3,531	$2,460	$802	$383	$81,987	$2,546	$25,518
18	$86,402	$11,081	$14,444	$42,498	$156,968	$114,762	$72,264	$4,207	$6,875	$4,308	$3,467	$2,522	$822	$382	$86,571	$2,673	$28,191
19	$81,857	$11,081	$14,686	$47,043	$163,505	$122,141	$75,098	$4,544	$6,537	$4,415	$3,395	$2,585	$842	$382	$91,151	$2,799	$30,990
20	$76,948	$11,081	$14,940	$51,952	$169,677	$129,648	$77,695	$4,909	$6,172	$4,526	$3,316	$2,649	$863	$382	$95,732	$2,926	$33,915
21	$71,644	$11,081	$15,207	$57,256	$175,455	$137,288	$80,032	$5,304	$5,778	$4,639	$3,229	$2,716	$885	$382	$100,321	$3,052	$36,967
22	$65,914	$11,081	$15,487	$62,986	$180,807	$145,070	$82,084	$5,730	$5,352	$4,755	$3,133	$2,783	$907	$384	$104,924	$3,179	$40,146
23	$59,724	$11,081	$15,781	$69,176	$185,698	$153,002	$83,826	$6,190	$4,892	$4,874	$3,027	$2,853	$930	$385	$109,549	$3,306	$43,452
24	$53,037	$11,081	$16,091	$75,863	$190,092	$161,092	$85,229	$6,687	$4,394	$4,996	$2,911	$2,924	$953	$388	$114,205	$3,434	$46,887
25	$45,813	$11,081	$16,416	$83,087	$193,950	$169,351	$86,264	$7,224	$3,857	$5,121	$2,783	$2,997	$977	$391	$118,901	$3,563	$50,450
26	$38,009	$11,081	$16,759	$90,891	$197,227	$177,790	$86,899	$7,804	$3,277	$5,249	$2,643	$3,072	$1,001	$395	$123,647	$3,694	$54,144
27	$29,578	$11,081	$17,121	$99,322	$199,877	$186,423	$87,101	$8,431	$2,650	$5,380	$2,489	$3,149	$1,026	$401	$128,454	$3,826	$57,969
28	$20,470	$11,081	$17,503	$108,430	$201,851	$195,263	$86,833	$9,108	$1,973	$5,514	$2,321	$3,228	$1,052	$407	$133,335	$3,959	$61,929
29	$10,630	$11,081	$17,905	$118,270	$203,092	$204,326	$86,056	$9,840	$1,242	$5,652	$2,137	$3,309	$1,078	$414	$138,302	$4,095	$66,024
30	$0	$11,081	$18,330	$128,900	$203,544	$213,630	$84,730	$10,630	$452	$5,793	$1,936	$3,391	$1,105	$422	$143,372	$4,234	$70,258

* Represents the approximate amount of money which should be saved monthly

** After Tax Down Payment is the initial principal plus the after-tax value of the closing cost

Figure 22 - Page 111

Copyright © Myth Breakers - 1993

Cleveland, OH

Using the Median Home Price and the Average Monthly Rent

HOME:

Purchase Price:	$92,300
Closing Cost:	$3,000
+Total Home Cost:	$95,300
+After-tax Cost:	$94,370
Down Payment:	$9,200
+Initial Principal:	$6,200
+Starting Loan:	$86,100

Mortgage Rate:	7.750%
Loan Length (in Yrs):	30
+Monthly Payment:	$617
Real Estate Tax:	2.000%
Add Repair/Utility Cost:	0.10%
Closing Commission Rate:	6.0%

GENERAL:

Tax Bracket:	31.0%
Savings Rate:	4.0%

RENT:

Starting Rental Amount:	$586
Monthly Rental Incr./Yr (in %):	2.5%
+Initial Monthly Savings Amt:	$58

COMPARISON (3 YRS):

+Principal Paid:	$2,454
+Interest Paid:	$19,752
+Amount Renter Can Save:	$2,545
+Amount Difference Rent/Own:	$91
+Appr. Required to Break Even:	$8,190
+Required Home Sales Price:	$100,490
+Yearly % Appr. to Break Even:	2.9%
+Total % Appr. to Break Even:	8.9%

COMPARISON (5 YRS):

+Principal Paid:	$4,436
+Interest Paid:	$32,574
+Amount Renter Can Save:	$3,808
+Amount Difference Rent/Own:	($628)
+Appr. Required to Break Even:	$7,426
+Required Home Sales Price:	$99,726
+Yearly % Appr. to Break Even:	1.6%
+Total % Appr. to Break Even:	8.0%

COMPARISON (10 YRS):

+Principal Paid:	$10,964
+Interest Paid:	$63,056
+Amount Renter Can Save:	$5,214
+Amount Difference Rent/Own:	($5,749)
+Appr. Required to Break Even:	$1,977
+Required Home Sales Price:	$94,277
+Yearly % Appr. to Break Even:	0.2%
+Total % Appr. to Break Even:	2.1%

Figure 23

Myth Breakers

		Summary Information						Home Ownership						Rental Difference			
	Current Loan	Mortgage Payment	After Tax Layout	Cumulative Principal Paid	Interest Paid	Amount Renter Can Save	Amount Diff Rent/Own	Annual Principal Paid	Annual Interest Paid	Real Estate Tax	Income Tax Break	Repairs + Add Utils	Mthly Rent*	Ave Mthly Savings Amount	Before Int Diff Rent/Own	Int on Diff & **ATDP	
Yr 0	$86,100																
Yr 1	$85,344	$7,402	$7,723	$756	$6,646	$930	$174	$756	$6,646	$1,846	$2,633	$1,108	$586	$58	$691	$239	$239
Yr 2	$84,528	$7,402	$7,801	$1,572	$13,232	$1,779	$207	$816	$6,586	$1,892	$2,628	$1,135	$601	$49	$1,284	$256	$495
Yr 3	$83,646	$7,402	$7,883	$2,454	$19,752	$2,545	$91	$882	$6,520	$1,939	$2,622	$1,164	$616	$41	$1,779	$271	$766
Yr 4	$82,693	$7,402	$7,967	$3,407	$26,201	$3,223	($184)	$953	$6,449	$1,988	$2,616	$1,193	$631	$33	$2,174	$283	$1,049
Yr 5	$81,664	$7,402	$8,055	$4,436	$32,574	$3,808	($628)	$1,029	$6,373	$2,038	$2,607	$1,223	$647	$24	$2,467	$293	$1,342
Yr 6	$80,552	$7,402	$8,146	$5,548	$38,864	$4,297	($1,251)	$1,112	$6,290	$2,089	$2,597	$1,253	$663	$16	$2,657	$299	$1,641
Yr 7	$79,351	$7,402	$8,241	$6,749	$45,064	$4,687	($2,063)	$1,201	$6,201	$2,141	$2,586	$1,284	$680	$7	$2,743	$303	$1,943
Yr 8	$78,053	$7,402	$8,340	$8,047	$51,169	$4,972	($3,075)	$1,298	$6,104	$2,194	$2,573	$1,317	$697	($2)	$2,725	$304	$2,247
Yr 9	$76,651	$7,402	$8,443	$9,449	$57,169	$5,149	($4,300)	$1,402	$6,000	$2,249	$2,557	$1,350	$714	($10)	$2,600	$302	$2,549
Yr 10	$75,136	$7,402	$8,551	$10,964	$63,056	$5,214	($5,749)	$1,515	$5,887	$2,305	$2,540	$1,383	$732	($19)	$2,369	$296	$2,845
Yr 11	$73,500	$7,402	$8,663	$12,600	$68,822	$5,164	($7,436)	$1,636	$5,766	$2,363	$2,520	$1,418	$750	($28)	$2,031	$288	$3,134
Yr 12	$71,733	$7,402	$8,780	$14,367	$74,456	$4,995	($9,373)	$1,768	$5,634	$2,422	$2,498	$1,453	$769	($37)	$1,584	$278	$3,411
Yr 13	$69,823	$7,402	$8,902	$16,277	$79,949	$4,703	($11,574)	$1,910	$5,492	$2,483	$2,472	$1,490	$788	($46)	$1,029	$264	$3,675
Yr 14	$67,760	$7,402	$9,030	$18,340	$85,288	$4,286	($14,054)	$2,063	$5,339	$2,545	$2,444	$1,527	$808	($55)	$364	$247	$3,921
Yr 15	$65,531	$7,402	$9,163	$20,569	$90,461	$3,739	($16,829)	$2,229	$5,173	$2,608	$2,412	$1,565	$828	($64)	($409)	$227	$4,148
Yr 16	$63,124	$7,402	$9,303	$22,976	$95,455	$3,061	($19,915)	$2,408	$4,994	$2,674	$2,377	$1,604	$849	($73)	($1,290)	$204	$4,352
Yr 17	$60,523	$7,402	$9,449	$25,577	$100,256	$2,248	($23,329)	$2,601	$4,801	$2,740	$2,338	$1,644	$870	($83)	($2,281)	$178	$4,529
Yr 18	$57,713	$7,402	$9,602	$28,387	$104,848	$1,299	($27,088)	$2,810	$4,592	$2,809	$2,294	$1,685	$892	($92)	($3,379)	$149	$4,678
Yr 19	$54,677	$7,402	$9,762	$31,423	$109,215	$211	($31,212)	$3,036	$4,366	$2,879	$2,246	$1,727	$914	($100)	($4,584)	$117	$4,795
Yr 20	$51,398	$7,402	$9,931	$34,702	$113,337	($1,018)	($35,720)	$3,279	$4,123	$2,951	$2,193	$1,771	$937	($109)	($5,895)	$82	$4,877
Yr 21	$47,855	$7,402	$10,108	$38,245	$117,197	($2,389)	($40,634)	$3,543	$3,859	$3,025	$2,134	$1,815	$960	($118)	($7,310)	$44	$4,921
Yr 22	$44,028	$7,402	$10,293	$42,072	$120,771	($3,903)	($45,975)	$3,827	$3,575	$3,101	$2,069	$1,860	$984	($126)	($8,827)	$4	$4,925
Yr 23	$39,893	$7,402	$10,489	$46,207	$124,039	($5,560)	($51,766)	$4,135	$3,267	$3,178	$1,998	$1,907	$1,009	($135)	($10,444)	($40)	$4,885
Yr 24	$35,427	$7,402	$10,694	$50,673	$126,974	($7,360)	($58,033)	$4,467	$2,935	$3,257	$1,920	$1,954	$1,034	($143)	($12,159)	($86)	$4,799
Yr 25	$30,601	$7,402	$10,910	$55,499	$129,551	($9,303)	($64,802)	$4,825	$2,577	$3,339	$1,834	$2,003	$1,060	($151)	($13,968)	($135)	$4,664
Yr 26	$25,388	$7,402	$11,138	$60,712	$131,740	($11,388)	($72,100)	$5,213	$2,189	$3,422	$1,740	$2,053	$1,086	($158)	($15,866)	($186)	$4,478
Yr 27	$19,757	$7,402	$11,378	$66,343	$133,510	($13,612)	($79,955)	$5,632	$1,770	$3,508	$1,636	$2,105	$1,114	($165)	($17,851)	($240)	$4,239
Yr 28	$13,673	$7,402	$11,632	$72,427	$134,828	($15,973)	($88,400)	$6,084	$1,318	$3,596	$1,523	$2,157	$1,141	($172)	($19,916)	($296)	$3,943
Yr 29	$7,100	$7,402	$11,899	$79,000	$135,658	($18,467)	($97,466)	$6,573	$829	$3,686	$1,400	$2,211	$1,170	($178)	($22,056)	($354)	$3,589
Yr 30	$0	$7,402	$12,182	$86,100	$135,959	($21,089)	($107,189)	$7,100	$302	$3,778	$1,265	$2,267	$1,199	($184)	($24,265)	($414)	$3,175

* Represents the approximate amount of money which should be saved monthly

** After Tax Down Payment is the initial principal plus the after-tax value of the closing cost

Figure 24 - Page 113

Rent vs Buy Analysis for Various Metropolitan Cities

Denver, CO

Using the Median Home Price and the Average Monthly Rent

HOME:

Purchase Price:	$95,500
Closing Cost:	$3,200
+Total Home Cost:	$98,700
+After-tax Cost:	$97,708
Down Payment:	$9,600
+Initial Principal:	$6,400
+Starting Loan:	$89,100

Mortgage Rate:	7.750%
Loan Length (in Yrs):	30
+Monthly Payment:	$638
Real Estate Tax:	0.970%
Add Repair/Utility Cost:	0.10%
Closing Commission Rate:	6.0%

GENERAL:

Tax Bracket:	31.0%
Savings Rate:	4.0%

RENT:

Starting Rental Amount:	$404
Monthly Rental Incr./Yr (in %):	2.5%
+Initial Monthly Savings Amt:	$205

COMPARISON (3 YRS):

+Principal Paid:	$2,540
+Interest Paid:	$20,440
+Amount Renter Can Save:	$8,246
+Amount Difference Rent/Own:	$5,707
+Appr. Required to Break Even:	$14,516
+Required Home Sales Price:	$110,016
+Yearly % Appr. to Break Even:	4.8%
+Total % Appr. to Break Even:	15.2%

COMPARISON (5 YRS):

+Principal Paid:	$4,591
+Interest Paid:	$33,709
+Amount Renter Can Save:	$13,778
+Amount Difference Rent/Own:	$9,188
+Appr. Required to Break Even:	$18,219
+Required Home Sales Price:	$113,719
+Yearly % Appr. to Break Even:	3.6%
+Total % Appr. to Break Even:	19.1%

COMPARISON (10 YRS):

+Principal Paid:	$11,346
+Interest Paid:	$65,253
+Amount Renter Can Save:	$27,632
+Amount Difference Rent/Own:	$16,287
+Appr. Required to Break Even:	$25,771
+Required Home Sales Price:	$121,271
+Yearly % Appr. to Break Even:	2.4%
+Total % Appr. to Break Even:	27.0%

Figure 25

Myth Breakers®

			Summary Information					Home Ownership					Rental Difference			
	Current Loan	Mortgage Payment	After Tax Layout	Cumulative Principal Paid	Cumulative Interest Paid	Amount Renter Can Save	Amount Diff Rent/Own	Annual Principal Paid	Annual Interest Paid	Real Estate Tax	Income Tax Break	Repairs + Add Utils	Mthly Rent	Ave Mthly Savings Amount	Before Int Diff Rent/Own	Int on Diff &	**ATDP
Yr 0	$89,100																
Yr 1	$88,318	$7,660	$7,313	$782	$6,878	$2,739	$1,957	$782	$6,878	$926	$2,419	$1,146	$404	$205	$2,465	$274	$274
Yr 2	$87,473	$7,660	$7,377	$1,627	$13,693	$5,489	$3,862	$845	$6,815	$950	$2,407	$1,175	$414	$201	$4,873	$342	$616
Yr 3	$86,560	$7,660	$7,444	$2,540	$20,440	$8,246	$5,707	$913	$6,747	$973	$2,393	$1,204	$424	$196	$7,223	$407	$1,023
Yr 4	$85,574	$7,660	$7,513	$3,526	$27,114	$11,010	$7,485	$986	$6,674	$998	$2,378	$1,234	$435	$191	$9,516	$471	$1,494
Yr 5	$84,509	$7,660	$7,586	$4,591	$33,709	$13,778	$9,188	$1,065	$6,595	$1,023	$2,361	$1,265	$446	$186	$11,751	$534	$2,028
Yr 6	$83,359	$7,660	$7,662	$5,741	$40,218	$16,549	$10,808	$1,151	$6,509	$1,048	$2,343	$1,297	$457	$181	$13,927	$594	$2,622
Yr 7	$82,115	$7,660	$7,741	$6,985	$46,635	$19,322	$12,337	$1,243	$6,417	$1,074	$2,322	$1,329	$469	$177	$16,046	$654	$3,276
Yr 8	$80,773	$7,660	$7,824	$8,327	$52,952	$22,094	$13,766	$1,343	$6,317	$1,101	$2,300	$1,362	$480	$172	$18,107	$711	$3,987
Yr 9	$79,322	$7,660	$7,910	$9,778	$59,161	$24,864	$15,086	$1,451	$6,209	$1,129	$2,275	$1,396	$492	$167	$20,110	$767	$4,754
Yr 10	$77,754	$7,660	$8,001	$11,346	$65,253	$27,632	$16,287	$1,567	$6,093	$1,157	$2,247	$1,431	$505	$162	$22,056	$822	$5,576
Yr 11	$76,061	$7,660	$8,095	$13,039	$71,220	$30,396	$17,357	$1,693	$5,967	$1,186	$2,217	$1,467	$517	$157	$23,946	$874	$6,450
Yr 12	$74,232	$7,660	$8,195	$14,868	$77,050	$33,156	$18,288	$1,829	$5,831	$1,215	$2,184	$1,504	$530	$153	$25,780	$926	$7,376
Yr 13	$72,256	$7,660	$8,299	$16,844	$82,734	$35,910	$19,066	$1,976	$5,684	$1,246	$2,148	$1,541	$543	$148	$27,558	$976	$8,352
Yr 14	$70,121	$7,660	$8,408	$18,979	$88,259	$38,659	$19,680	$2,135	$5,525	$1,277	$2,109	$1,580	$557	$144	$29,283	$1,024	$9,376
Yr 15	$67,815	$7,660	$8,523	$21,285	$93,613	$41,402	$20,117	$2,306	$5,354	$1,309	$2,065	$1,619	$571	$139	$30,956	$1,071	$10,446
Yr 16	$65,323	$7,660	$8,643	$23,777	$98,781	$44,140	$20,363	$2,492	$5,168	$1,342	$2,018	$1,660	$585	$135	$32,578	$1,116	$11,562
Yr 17	$62,632	$7,660	$8,770	$26,468	$103,750	$46,873	$20,405	$2,692	$4,968	$1,375	$1,966	$1,701	$600	$131	$34,151	$1,160	$12,722
Yr 18	$59,724	$7,660	$8,903	$29,376	$108,502	$49,602	$20,226	$2,908	$4,752	$1,410	$1,910	$1,744	$615	$127	$35,677	$1,203	$13,925
Yr 19	$56,582	$7,660	$9,043	$32,518	$113,020	$52,329	$19,811	$3,141	$4,519	$1,445	$1,849	$1,787	$630	$124	$37,159	$1,244	$15,169
Yr 20	$53,189	$7,660	$9,191	$35,911	$117,286	$55,054	$19,143	$3,394	$4,266	$1,481	$1,782	$1,832	$646	$120	$38,600	$1,285	$16,454
Yr 21	$49,523	$7,660	$9,347	$39,577	$121,280	$57,781	$18,204	$3,666	$3,994	$1,518	$1,709	$1,878	$662	$117	$40,003	$1,324	$17,778
Yr 22	$45,562	$7,660	$9,511	$43,538	$124,980	$60,512	$16,974	$3,961	$3,699	$1,556	$1,629	$1,925	$679	$114	$41,372	$1,362	$19,140
Yr 23	$41,283	$7,660	$9,685	$47,817	$128,361	$63,250	$15,433	$4,279	$3,381	$1,595	$1,543	$1,973	$696	$112	$42,711	$1,399	$20,539
Yr 24	$36,661	$7,660	$9,868	$52,439	$131,398	$65,999	$13,560	$4,622	$3,038	$1,635	$1,448	$2,022	$713	$109	$44,024	$1,436	$21,975
Yr 25	$31,668	$7,660	$10,062	$57,432	$134,065	$68,764	$11,332	$4,994	$2,666	$1,676	$1,346	$2,073	$731	$108	$45,318	$1,472	$23,446
Yr 26	$26,273	$7,660	$10,267	$62,827	$136,330	$71,551	$8,724	$5,395	$2,265	$1,717	$1,235	$2,125	$749	$107	$46,597	$1,507	$24,954
Yr 27	$20,445	$7,660	$10,484	$68,655	$138,162	$74,365	$5,710	$5,828	$1,832	$1,760	$1,114	$2,178	$768	$106	$47,869	$1,542	$26,496
Yr 28	$14,149	$7,660	$10,714	$74,951	$139,526	$77,214	$2,263	$6,296	$1,364	$1,804	$982	$2,232	$787	$106	$49,140	$1,577	$28,073
Yr 29	$7,348	$7,660	$10,958	$81,752	$140,384	$80,105	($1,647)	$6,802	$858	$1,849	$839	$2,288	$807	$107	$50,419	$1,613	$29,686
Yr 30	$0	$7,660	$11,216	$89,100	$140,696	$83,049	($6,051)	$7,348	$312	$1,896	$684	$2,345	$827	$108	$51,714	$1,648	$31,334

* Represents the approximate amount of money which should be saved monthly
** After Tax Down Payment is the initial principal plus the after-tax value of the closing cost

Copyright © Myth Breakers - 1993

Figure 26 - Page 115

Detroit, MI

Using the Median Home Price and the Average Monthly Rent

HOME:

Purchase Price:	$79,400
Closing Cost:	$2,600
+Total Home Cost:	$82,000
+After-tax Cost:	$81,194
Down Payment:	$7,900
+Initial Principal:	$5,300
+Starting Loan:	$74,100
Mortgage Rate:	7.750%
Loan Length (in Yrs):	30
+Monthly Payment:	$531
Real Estate Tax:	4.400%
Add Repair/Utility Cost:	0.10%
Closing Commission Rate:	6.0%

GENERAL:

Tax Bracket:	31.0%
Savings Rate:	4.0%

RENT:

Starting Rental Amount:	$552
Monthly Rental Incr./Yr (in %):	2.5%
+Initial Monthly Savings Amt:	$111

COMPARISON (3 YRS):

+Principal Paid:	$2,112
+Interest Paid:	$16,999
+Amount Renter Can Save:	$4,566
+Amount Difference Rent/Own:	$2,454
+Appr. Required to Break Even:	$9,587
+Required Home Sales Price:	$88,987
+Yearly % Appr. to Break Even:	3.9%
+Total % Appr. to Break Even:	12.1%

COMPARISON (5 YRS):

+Principal Paid:	$3,818
+Interest Paid:	$28,034
+Amount Renter Can Save:	$7,442
+Amount Difference Rent/Own:	$3,624
+Appr. Required to Break Even:	$10,832
+Required Home Sales Price:	$90,232
+Yearly % Appr. to Break Even:	2.6%
+Total % Appr. to Break Even:	13.6%

COMPARISON (10 YRS):

+Principal Paid:	$9,436
+Interest Paid:	$54,268
+Amount Renter Can Save:	$13,902
+Amount Difference Rent/Own:	$4,467
+Appr. Required to Break Even:	$11,728
+Required Home Sales Price:	$91,128
+Yearly % Appr. to Break Even:	1.4%
+Total % Appr. to Break Even:	14.8%

Figure 27

Myth Breakers®

Yr	Summary Information							Home Ownership						Rental Difference			
	Current Loan	Mortgage Payment	After Tax Layout	Cumulative Principal Paid	Cumulative Interest Paid	Amount Renter Can Save	Amount Diff Rent/Own	Annual Principal Paid	Annual Interest Paid	Real Estate Tax	Income Tax Break	Repairs + Add Utils	Mthly Rent *	Ave Mthly Savings Amount	Before Int Diff Rent/Own	Int on Diff & **ATDP	
0	$74,100																
1	$73,450	$6,370	$7,961	$650	$5,720	$1,552	$902	$650	$5,720	$3,494	$2,856	$953	$552	$111	$1,337	$216	$216
2	$72,747	$6,370	$8,061	$1,353	$11,388	$3,075	$1,722	$703	$5,668	$3,581	$2,867	$977	$566	$106	$2,608	$252	$467
3	$71,988	$6,370	$8,164	$2,112	$16,999	$4,566	$2,454	$759	$5,611	$3,670	$2,877	$1,001	$580	$100	$3,813	$286	$753
4	$71,168	$6,370	$8,272	$2,932	$22,549	$6,022	$3,090	$820	$5,550	$3,762	$2,887	$1,026	$594	$95	$4,951	$318	$1,071
5	$70,282	$6,370	$8,383	$3,818	$28,034	$7,442	$3,624	$886	$5,484	$3,856	$2,896	$1,052	$609	$89	$6,022	$348	$1,420
6	$69,325	$6,370	$8,498	$4,775	$33,447	$8,822	$4,047	$957	$5,413	$3,953	$2,903	$1,078	$625	$84	$7,025	$377	$1,797
7	$68,291	$6,370	$8,617	$5,809	$38,784	$10,160	$4,352	$1,034	$5,336	$4,052	$2,910	$1,105	$640	$78	$7,960	$404	$2,200
8	$67,174	$6,370	$8,740	$6,926	$44,037	$11,455	$4,529	$1,117	$5,253	$4,153	$2,916	$1,133	$656	$72	$8,826	$428	$2,628
9	$65,968	$6,370	$8,868	$8,132	$49,201	$12,703	$4,571	$1,207	$5,164	$4,257	$2,920	$1,161	$673	$66	$9,623	$451	$3,080
10	$64,664	$6,370	$9,000	$9,436	$54,268	$13,902	$4,467	$1,303	$5,067	$4,363	$2,923	$1,190	$689	$61	$10,350	$472	$3,552
11	$63,256	$6,370	$9,137	$10,844	$59,230	$15,052	$4,208	$1,408	$4,962	$4,472	$2,925	$1,220	$707	$55	$11,009	$491	$4,043
12	$61,735	$6,370	$9,280	$12,365	$64,079	$16,149	$3,784	$1,521	$4,849	$4,584	$2,924	$1,250	$724	$49	$11,598	$508	$4,552
13	$60,092	$6,370	$9,428	$14,008	$68,806	$17,192	$3,184	$1,643	$4,727	$4,699	$2,922	$1,281	$742	$43	$12,117	$524	$5,075
14	$58,316	$6,370	$9,582	$15,784	$73,401	$18,180	$2,397	$1,775	$4,595	$4,816	$2,917	$1,313	$761	$38	$12,569	$537	$5,612
15	$56,398	$6,370	$9,742	$17,702	$77,853	$19,112	$1,410	$1,918	$4,452	$4,936	$2,910	$1,346	$780	$32	$12,951	$548	$6,160
16	$54,326	$6,370	$9,909	$19,774	$82,151	$19,985	$211	$2,072	$4,298	$5,060	$2,901	$1,380	$799	$26	$13,267	$558	$6,718
17	$52,088	$6,370	$10,082	$22,012	$86,283	$20,800	($1,213)	$2,238	$4,132	$5,186	$2,889	$1,414	$819	$21	$13,516	$566	$7,284
18	$49,669	$6,370	$10,263	$24,431	$90,235	$21,555	($2,876)	$2,418	$3,952	$5,316	$2,873	$1,450	$840	$15	$13,700	$571	$7,855
19	$47,057	$6,370	$10,451	$27,043	$93,993	$22,250	($4,793)	$2,612	$3,758	$5,449	$2,854	$1,486	$861	$10	$13,820	$576	$8,431
20	$44,235	$6,370	$10,647	$29,865	$97,541	$22,886	($6,979)	$2,822	$3,548	$5,585	$2,831	$1,523	$882	$5	$13,878	$578	$9,009
21	$41,186	$6,370	$10,852	$32,914	$100,863	$23,463	($9,452)	$3,049	$3,321	$5,725	$2,804	$1,561	$905	$0	$13,875	$579	$9,587
22	$37,892	$6,370	$11,066	$36,208	$103,939	$23,981	($12,228)	$3,294	$3,077	$5,868	$2,773	$1,600	$927	($5)	$13,816	$578	$10,165
23	$34,333	$6,370	$11,289	$39,767	$106,751	$24,441	($15,326)	$3,558	$2,812	$6,014	$2,736	$1,640	$950	($10)	$13,701	$575	$10,740
24	$30,489	$6,370	$11,522	$43,611	$109,277	$24,846	($18,765)	$3,844	$2,526	$6,165	$2,694	$1,681	$974	($14)	$13,534	$571	$11,311
25	$26,336	$6,370	$11,766	$47,764	$111,495	$25,197	($22,567)	$4,153	$2,217	$6,319	$2,646	$1,723	$998	($18)	$13,320	$566	$11,877
26	$21,850	$6,370	$12,022	$52,250	$113,379	$25,498	($26,752)	$4,486	$1,884	$6,477	$2,592	$1,766	$1,023	($22)	$13,061	$559	$12,437
27	$17,003	$6,370	$12,289	$57,097	$114,902	$25,751	($31,346)	$4,847	$1,524	$6,639	$2,530	$1,811	$1,049	($25)	$12,763	$552	$12,988
28	$11,767	$6,370	$12,570	$62,333	$116,037	$25,961	($36,371)	$5,236	$1,134	$6,805	$2,461	$1,856	$1,075	($28)	$12,431	$543	$13,531
29	$6,111	$6,370	$12,864	$67,989	$116,751	$26,134	($41,855)	$5,656	$714	$6,975	$2,384	$1,902	$1,102	($30)	$12,070	$533	$14,064
30	$0	$6,370	$13,173	$74,100	$117,010	$26,274	($47,826)	$6,111	$260	$7,149	$2,297	$1,950	$1,130	($32)	$11,687	$523	$14,587

* Represents the approximate amount of money which should be saved monthly
** After Tax Down Payment is the initial principal plus the after-tax value of the closing cost

Figure 28 - Page 117

Rent vs Buy Analysis for Various Metropolitan Cities

Honolulu, HI

Using the Median Home Price and the Average Monthly Rent

HOME:

Purchase Price:	$339,500
Closing Cost:	$10,000
+Total Home Cost:	$349,500
+After-tax Cost:	$346,400
Down Payment:	$34,000
+Initial Principal:	$24,000
+Starting Loan:	$315,500

Mortgage Rate:	8.250%
Loan Length (in Yrs):	30
+Monthly Payment:	$2,370
Real Estate Tax:	0.370%
Add Repair/Utility Cost:	0.10%
Closing Commission Rate:	6.0%

GENERAL:

Tax Bracket:	31.0%
Savings Rate:	4.0%

RENT:

Starting Rental Amount:	$1,200
Monthly Rental Incr./Yr (in %):	2.5%
+Initial Monthly Savings Amt:	$912

COMPARISON (3 YRS):

+Principal Paid:	$8,186
+Interest Paid:	$77,143
+Amount Renter Can Save:	$36,264
+Amount Difference Rent/Own:	$28,078
+Appr. Required to Break Even:	$58,881
+Required Home Sales Price:	$398,381
+Yearly % Appr. to Break Even:	5.5%
+Total % Appr. to Break Even:	17.3%

COMPARISON (5 YRS):

+Principal Paid:	$14,879
+Interest Paid:	$127,336
+Amount Renter Can Save:	$61,049
+Amount Difference Rent/Own:	$46,170
+Appr. Required to Break Even:	$78,128
+Required Home Sales Price:	$417,628
+Yearly % Appr. to Break Even:	4.2%
+Total % Appr. to Break Even:	23.0%

COMPARISON (10 YRS):

+Principal Paid:	$37,324
+Interest Paid:	$247,106
+Amount Renter Can Save:	$124,931
+Amount Difference Rent/Own:	$87,607
+Appr. Required to Break Even:	$122,210
+Required Home Sales Price:	$461,710
+Yearly % Appr. to Break Even:	3.1%
+Total % Appr. to Break Even:	36.0%

Figure 29

![Myth Breakers logo]

Summary Information · Home Ownership · Rental Difference

Yr	Current Loan	Mortgage Payment	After Tax Layout	Cumulative Principal Paid	Cumulative Interest Paid	Amount Renter Can Save	Amount Diff Rent/Own	Annual Principal Paid	Annual Interest Paid	Real Estate Tax	Income Tax Break	Repairs + Add Utils	Mthly Rent *	Ave Mthly Savings Amount	Before Int Diff Rent/Own	Int on Diff	Int on Diff & **ATDP
0	$315,500																
1	$312,992	$28,443	$25,344	$2,508	$25,935	$11,960	$9,452	$2,508	$25,935	$1,256	$8,429	$4,074	$1,200	$912	$10,944	$1,016	$1,016
2	$310,270	$28,443	$25,534	$5,230	$51,656	$24,050	$18,820	$2,722	$25,720	$1,288	$8,372	$4,176	$1,230	$898	$21,718	$1,316	$2,332
3	$307,314	$28,443	$25,733	$8,186	$77,143	$36,264	$28,078	$2,956	$25,487	$1,320	$8,310	$4,280	$1,261	$884	$32,321	$1,611	$3,943
4	$304,105	$28,443	$25,941	$11,395	$102,377	$48,599	$37,204	$3,209	$25,234	$1,353	$8,242	$4,387	$1,292	$869	$42,755	$1,901	$5,843
5	$300,621	$28,443	$26,159	$14,879	$127,336	$61,049	$46,170	$3,484	$24,959	$1,387	$8,167	$4,497	$1,325	$855	$53,020	$2,186	$8,030
6	$296,838	$28,443	$26,388	$18,662	$151,996	$73,612	$54,950	$3,783	$24,660	$1,421	$8,085	$4,609	$1,358	$841	$63,116	$2,467	$10,496
7	$292,732	$28,443	$26,628	$22,768	$176,332	$86,284	$63,516	$4,107	$24,336	$1,457	$7,996	$4,725	$1,392	$827	$73,045	$2,743	$13,239
8	$288,273	$28,443	$26,881	$27,227	$200,316	$99,062	$71,835	$4,459	$23,984	$1,493	$7,898	$4,843	$1,426	$814	$82,808	$3,015	$16,254
9	$283,432	$28,443	$27,146	$32,068	$223,919	$111,945	$79,877	$4,841	$23,603	$1,530	$7,791	$4,964	$1,462	$800	$92,409	$3,282	$19,536
10	$278,176	$28,443	$27,425	$37,324	$247,106	$124,931	$87,607	$5,256	$23,187	$1,569	$7,674	$5,088	$1,499	$787	$101,851	$3,544	$23,080
11	$272,471	$28,443	$27,719	$43,029	$269,843	$138,019	$94,990	$5,706	$22,737	$1,608	$7,547	$5,215	$1,536	$774	$111,137	$3,802	$26,882
12	$266,276	$28,443	$28,029	$49,224	$292,091	$151,210	$101,986	$6,195	$22,248	$1,648	$7,408	$5,345	$1,575	$761	$120,272	$4,056	$30,939
13	$259,550	$28,443	$28,355	$55,950	$313,808	$164,506	$108,555	$6,726	$21,717	$1,689	$7,256	$5,479	$1,614	$749	$129,261	$4,306	$35,245
14	$252,248	$28,443	$28,700	$63,252	$334,949	$177,907	$114,655	$7,302	$21,141	$1,732	$7,090	$5,616	$1,654	$737	$138,110	$4,552	$39,797
15	$244,320	$28,443	$29,064	$71,180	$355,464	$191,420	$120,239	$7,928	$20,515	$1,775	$6,910	$5,756	$1,696	$726	$146,828	$4,795	$44,592
16	$235,713	$28,443	$29,450	$79,787	$375,300	$205,047	$125,260	$8,607	$19,836	$1,819	$6,713	$5,900	$1,738	$716	$155,422	$5,033	$49,625
17	$226,368	$28,443	$29,857	$89,132	$394,398	$218,796	$129,664	$9,345	$19,098	$1,865	$6,499	$6,048	$1,781	$707	$163,902	$5,269	$54,894
18	$216,222	$28,443	$30,289	$99,278	$412,696	$232,674	$133,397	$10,146	$18,297	$1,911	$6,265	$6,199	$1,826	$698	$172,279	$5,501	$60,395
19	$205,208	$28,443	$30,746	$110,292	$430,124	$246,692	$136,400	$11,015	$17,428	$1,959	$6,010	$6,354	$1,872	$691	$180,566	$5,731	$66,126
20	$193,249	$28,443	$31,231	$122,251	$446,608	$260,862	$138,610	$11,959	$16,484	$2,008	$5,733	$6,513	$1,918	$684	$188,777	$5,959	$72,085
21	$180,265	$28,443	$31,747	$135,235	$462,067	$275,196	$139,962	$12,984	$15,459	$2,058	$5,430	$6,676	$1,966	$679	$196,928	$6,184	$78,269
22	$166,169	$28,443	$32,294	$149,331	$476,414	$289,713	$140,382	$14,096	$14,347	$2,110	$5,102	$6,843	$2,015	$676	$205,036	$6,408	$84,677
23	$150,865	$28,443	$32,876	$164,635	$489,553	$304,430	$139,794	$15,304	$13,139	$2,163	$4,743	$7,014	$2,066	$674	$213,121	$6,632	$91,309
24	$134,249	$28,443	$33,495	$181,251	$501,380	$319,369	$138,118	$16,616	$11,827	$2,217	$4,354	$7,189	$2,118	$674	$221,205	$6,855	$98,164
25	$116,210	$28,443	$34,154	$199,290	$511,784	$334,556	$135,266	$18,039	$10,404	$2,272	$3,929	$7,369	$2,170	$676	$229,314	$7,078	$105,242
26	$96,625	$28,443	$34,857	$218,875	$520,641	$350,019	$131,144	$19,585	$8,858	$2,329	$3,468	$7,553	$2,225	$680	$237,474	$7,303	$112,545
27	$75,361	$28,443	$35,606	$240,139	$527,821	$365,790	$125,651	$21,264	$7,179	$2,387	$2,966	$7,742	$2,280	$687	$245,716	$7,529	$120,074
28	$52,276	$28,443	$36,406	$263,224	$533,178	$381,906	$118,681	$23,086	$5,357	$2,447	$2,419	$7,935	$2,337	$696	$254,073	$7,758	$127,832
29	$27,212	$28,443	$37,260	$288,288	$536,557	$398,407	$110,118	$25,064	$3,379	$2,508	$1,825	$8,134	$2,396	$709	$262,583	$7,991	$135,823
30	$0	$28,443	$38,172	$315,500	$537,789	$415,339	$99,839	$27,212	$1,231	$2,571	$1,179	$8,337	$2,456	$725	$271,287	$8,229	$144,052

* Represents the approximate amount of money which should be saved monthly
** After Tax Down Payment is the initial principal plus the after-tax value of the closing cost

Copyright © Myth Breakers - 1993

Figure 30 - Page 119

Rent vs Buy Analysis for Various Metropolitan Cities

Houston, TX

Using the Median Home Price and the Average Monthly Rent

HOME:

Purchase Price:	$79,700
Closing Cost:	$2,700
+Total Home Cost:	$82,400
+After-tax Cost:	$81,563
Down Payment:	$8,000
+Initial Principal:	$5,300
+Starting Loan:	$74,400
Mortgage Rate:	7.750%
Loan Length (in Yrs):	30
+Monthly Payment:	$533
Real Estate Tax:	2.000%
Add Repair/Utility Cost:	0.10%
Closing Commission Rate:	6.0%

GENERAL:

Tax Bracket:	31.0%
Savings Rate:	4.0%

RENT:

Starting Rental Amount:	$372
Monthly Rental Incr./Yr (in %):	2.5%
+Initial Monthly Savings Amt:	$184

COMPARISON (3 YRS):

+Principal Paid:	$2,121
+Interest Paid:	$17,068
+Amount Renter Can Save:	$7,364
+Amount Difference Rent/Own:	$5,243
+Appr. Required to Break Even:	$12,647
+Required Home Sales Price:	$92,347
+Yearly % Appr. to Break Even:	5.0%
+Total % Appr. to Break Even:	15.9%

COMPARISON (5 YRS):

+Principal Paid:	$3,833
+Interest Paid:	$28,147
+Amount Renter Can Save:	$12,343
+Amount Difference Rent/Own:	$8,510
+Appr. Required to Break Even:	$16,122
+Required Home Sales Price:	$95,822
+Yearly % Appr. to Break Even:	3.8%
+Total % Appr. to Break Even:	20.2%

COMPARISON (10 YRS):

+Principal Paid:	$9,474
+Interest Paid:	$54,487
+Amount Renter Can Save:	$24,968
+Amount Difference Rent/Own:	$15,495
+Appr. Required to Break Even:	$23,553
+Required Home Sales Price:	$103,253
+Yearly % Appr. to Break Even:	2.6%
+Total % Appr. to Break Even:	29.6%

Figure 31

Myth Breakers

			Summary Information					Home Ownership						Rental Difference			
Yr	Current Loan	Mortgage Payment	After Tax Layout	Cumulative Principal Paid	Cumulative Interest Paid	Amount Renter Can Save	Amount Diff Rent/Own	Annual Principal Paid	Annual Interest Paid	Real Estate Tax	Income Tax Break	Repairs + Add Utils	Mthly Rent *	Ave Mthly Savings Amount	Before Int Diff Rent/Own	Int on Diff & **ATDP	
0	$74,400	$6,396															
1	$73,747	$6,396	$6,672	$653	$5,743	$2,439	$1,786	$653	$5,743	$1,594	$2,275	$956	$372	$184	$2,208	$231	$231
2	$73,042	$6,396	$6,740	$1,358	$11,434	$4,894	$3,535	$705	$5,691	$1,634	$2,271	$980	$381	$180	$4,372	$291	$522
3	$72,279	$6,396	$6,810	$2,121	$17,068	$7,364	$5,243	$762	$5,634	$1,675	$2,266	$1,005	$391	$177	$6,492	$350	$872
4	$71,456	$6,396	$6,883	$2,944	$22,641	$9,847	$6,903	$823	$5,573	$1,717	$2,260	$1,030	$401	$173	$8,568	$408	$1,280
5	$70,567	$6,396	$6,959	$3,833	$28,147	$12,343	$8,510	$889	$5,507	$1,759	$2,253	$1,056	$411	$169	$10,599	$464	$1,744
6	$69,606	$6,396	$7,038	$4,794	$33,583	$14,850	$10,056	$961	$5,435	$1,803	$2,244	$1,082	$421	$166	$12,586	$520	$2,264
7	$68,568	$6,396	$7,120	$5,832	$38,941	$17,367	$11,535	$1,038	$5,358	$1,849	$2,234	$1,109	$431	$162	$14,529	$574	$2,838
8	$67,446	$6,396	$7,205	$6,954	$44,215	$19,893	$12,939	$1,121	$5,275	$1,895	$2,223	$1,137	$442	$158	$16,428	$627	$3,465
9	$66,235	$6,396	$7,294	$8,165	$49,400	$22,427	$14,262	$1,211	$5,185	$1,942	$2,209	$1,165	$453	$155	$18,283	$679	$4,144
10	$64,926	$6,396	$7,387	$9,474	$54,487	$24,968	$15,495	$1,309	$5,087	$1,991	$2,194	$1,194	$465	$151	$20,095	$729	$4,873
11	$63,512	$6,396	$7,484	$10,888	$59,470	$27,517	$16,629	$1,414	$4,982	$2,040	$2,177	$1,224	$476	$147	$21,865	$779	$5,652
12	$61,985	$6,396	$7,585	$12,415	$64,338	$30,071	$17,656	$1,527	$4,869	$2,091	$2,158	$1,255	$488	$144	$23,593	$827	$6,479
13	$60,335	$6,396	$7,690	$14,065	$69,084	$32,632	$18,567	$1,650	$4,746	$2,144	$2,136	$1,286	$500	$141	$25,279	$874	$7,353
14	$58,552	$6,396	$7,801	$15,848	$73,698	$35,199	$19,351	$1,783	$4,614	$2,197	$2,111	$1,318	$513	$137	$26,926	$920	$8,273
15	$56,626	$6,396	$7,916	$17,774	$78,168	$37,772	$19,998	$1,926	$4,470	$2,252	$2,084	$1,351	$526	$134	$28,534	$965	$9,237
16	$54,546	$6,396	$8,036	$19,854	$82,484	$40,352	$20,497	$2,080	$4,316	$2,309	$2,054	$1,385	$539	$131	$30,105	$1,009	$10,246
17	$52,298	$6,396	$8,163	$22,102	$86,633	$42,939	$20,837	$2,248	$4,149	$2,366	$2,020	$1,420	$552	$128	$31,641	$1,051	$11,297
18	$49,870	$6,396	$8,295	$24,530	$90,601	$45,534	$21,005	$2,428	$3,968	$2,425	$1,982	$1,455	$566	$125	$33,144	$1,093	$12,391
19	$47,247	$6,396	$8,434	$27,153	$94,374	$48,140	$20,987	$2,623	$3,773	$2,486	$1,940	$1,492	$580	$123	$34,615	$1,134	$13,525
20	$44,414	$6,396	$8,579	$29,986	$97,936	$50,757	$20,771	$2,834	$3,562	$2,548	$1,894	$1,529	$595	$120	$36,057	$1,174	$14,700
21	$41,352	$6,396	$8,732	$33,048	$101,271	$53,388	$20,340	$3,061	$3,335	$2,612	$1,844	$1,567	$610	$118	$37,474	$1,214	$15,914
22	$38,045	$6,396	$8,892	$36,355	$104,360	$56,035	$19,680	$3,307	$3,089	$2,677	$1,788	$1,606	$625	$116	$38,869	$1,253	$17,166
23	$34,472	$6,396	$9,061	$39,928	$107,183	$58,702	$18,774	$3,573	$2,823	$2,744	$1,726	$1,647	$640	$115	$40,245	$1,291	$18,457
24	$30,613	$6,396	$9,238	$43,787	$109,720	$61,391	$17,604	$3,860	$2,536	$2,813	$1,658	$1,688	$656	$113	$41,606	$1,329	$19,786
25	$26,443	$6,396	$9,425	$47,957	$111,946	$64,108	$16,151	$4,170	$2,226	$2,883	$1,584	$1,730	$673	$113	$42,957	$1,366	$21,152
26	$21,938	$6,396	$9,622	$52,462	$113,838	$66,858	$14,396	$4,505	$1,892	$2,955	$1,502	$1,773	$690	$112	$44,303	$1,403	$22,555
27	$17,072	$6,396	$9,829	$57,328	$115,368	$69,644	$12,316	$4,866	$1,530	$3,029	$1,413	$1,817	$707	$112	$45,649	$1,440	$23,995
28	$11,815	$6,396	$10,048	$62,585	$116,507	$72,475	$9,890	$5,257	$1,139	$3,105	$1,316	$1,863	$725	$113	$47,003	$1,478	$25,473
29	$6,136	$6,396	$10,279	$68,264	$117,223	$75,357	$7,093	$5,679	$717	$3,182	$1,209	$1,909	$743	$114	$48,369	$1,515	$26,988
30	$0	$6,396	$10,523	$74,400	$117,484	$78,298	$3,898	$6,136	$261	$3,262	$1,092	$1,957	$761	$116	$49,758	$1,553	$28,541

* Represents the approximate amount of money which should be saved monthly
** After Tax Down Payment is the initial principal plus the after-tax value of the closing cost

Figure 32 - Page 121

Indianapolis, IN

Using the Median Home Price and the Average Monthly Rent

HOME:

Purchase Price:	$84,100
Closing Cost:	$2,800
+Total Home Cost:	$86,900
+After-tax Cost:	$86,032
Down Payment:	$8,400
+Initial Principal:	$5,600
+Starting Loan:	$78,500

Mortgage Rate:	7.750%
Loan Length (in Yrs):	30
+Monthly Payment:	$562
Real Estate Tax:	1.750%
Add Repair/Utility Cost:	0.10%
Closing Commission Rate:	6.0%

GENERAL:

Tax Bracket:	31.0%
Savings Rate:	4.0%

RENT:

Starting Rental Amount:	$461
Monthly Rental Incr./Yr (in %):	2.5%
+Initial Monthly Savings Amt:	$114

COMPARISON (3 YRS):

+Principal Paid:	$2,237
+Interest Paid:	$18,008
+Amount Renter Can Save:	$4,668
+Amount Difference Rent/Own:	$2,431
+Appr. Required to Break Even:	$10,010
+Required Home Sales Price:	$94,110
+Yearly % Appr. to Break Even:	3.8%
+Total % Appr. to Break Even:	11.9%

COMPARISON (5 YRS):

+Principal Paid:	$4,045
+Interest Paid:	$29,698
+Amount Renter Can Save:	$7,588
+Amount Difference Rent/Own:	$3,543
+Appr. Required to Break Even:	$11,193
+Required Home Sales Price:	$95,293
+Yearly % Appr. to Break Even:	2.5%
+Total % Appr. to Break Even:	13.3%

COMPARISON (10 YRS):

+Principal Paid:	$9,996
+Interest Paid:	$57,490
+Amount Renter Can Save:	$14,059
+Amount Difference Rent/Own:	$4,063
+Appr. Required to Break Even:	$11,745
+Required Home Sales Price:	$95,845
+Yearly % Appr. to Break Even:	1.3%
+Total % Appr. to Break Even:	14.0%

Figure 33

Myth Breakers®

Summary Information / Home Ownership / Rental Difference

Yr	Current Loan	Mortgage Payment	After Tax Layout	Cumulative Principal Paid	Cumulative Interest Paid	Amount Renter Can Save	Amount Diff Rent/Own	Annual Principal Paid	Annual Interest Paid	Real Estate Tax	Income Tax Break	Repairs + Add Utils	Mthly Rent*	Ave Mthly Savings Amount	Before Int Diff Rent/Own	Int on Diff & **ATDP
0	$78,500															
1	$77,811	$6,749	$6,895	$689	$6,060	$1,591	$902	$689	$6,060	$1,472	$2,335	$1,009	$461	$114	$1,363	$228 $228
2	$77,067	$6,749	$6,963	$1,433	$12,064	$3,148	$1,715	$744	$6,004	$1,509	$2,329	$1,034	$473	$108	$2,655	$265 $493
3	$76,263	$6,749	$7,033	$2,237	$18,008	$4,668	$2,431	$804	$5,945	$1,546	$2,322	$1,060	$484	$102	$3,876	$299 $792
4	$75,394	$6,749	$7,106	$3,106	$23,888	$6,149	$3,043	$869	$5,880	$1,585	$2,314	$1,087	$496	$96	$5,025	$332 $1,124
5	$74,455	$6,749	$7,182	$4,045	$29,698	$7,588	$3,543	$938	$5,810	$1,625	$2,305	$1,114	$509	$90	$6,101	$363 $1,487
6	$73,442	$6,749	$7,262	$5,058	$35,433	$8,982	$3,923	$1,014	$5,735	$1,665	$2,294	$1,142	$522	$84	$7,104	$391 $1,878
7	$72,346	$6,749	$7,344	$6,154	$41,087	$10,328	$4,175	$1,095	$5,653	$1,707	$2,282	$1,170	$535	$77	$8,032	$418 $2,296
8	$71,163	$6,749	$7,430	$7,337	$46,652	$11,625	$4,288	$1,183	$5,565	$1,749	$2,268	$1,200	$548	$71	$8,887	$442 $2,738
9	$69,885	$6,749	$7,520	$8,615	$52,122	$12,869	$4,254	$1,278	$5,470	$1,793	$2,252	$1,230	$562	$65	$9,666	$465 $3,203
10	$68,504	$6,749	$7,613	$9,996	$57,490	$14,059	$4,063	$1,381	$5,368	$1,838	$2,234	$1,260	$576	$59	$10,371	$485 $3,688
11	$67,012	$6,749	$7,711	$11,488	$62,747	$15,191	$3,704	$1,492	$5,257	$1,884	$2,214	$1,292	$590	$52	$11,000	$503 $4,192
12	$65,401	$6,749	$7,813	$13,099	$67,884	$16,265	$3,166	$1,612	$5,137	$1,931	$2,191	$1,324	$605	$46	$11,554	$520 $4,711
13	$63,660	$6,749	$7,919	$14,840	$72,892	$17,279	$2,438	$1,741	$5,008	$1,979	$2,166	$1,357	$620	$40	$12,034	$534 $5,245
14	$61,779	$6,749	$8,031	$16,721	$77,759	$18,229	$1,508	$1,881	$4,868	$2,029	$2,138	$1,391	$635	$34	$12,438	$546 $5,791
15	$59,747	$6,749	$8,147	$18,753	$82,476	$19,116	$363	$2,032	$4,717	$2,080	$2,107	$1,426	$651	$28	$12,769	$556 $6,347
16	$57,552	$6,749	$8,269	$20,948	$87,030	$19,937	($1,011)	$2,195	$4,554	$2,132	$2,072	$1,462	$668	$21	$13,026	$564 $6,911
17	$55,180	$6,749	$8,397	$23,320	$91,407	$20,693	($2,627)	$2,371	$4,377	$2,185	$2,034	$1,498	$684	$15	$13,211	$570 $7,481
18	$52,619	$6,749	$8,532	$25,881	$95,593	$21,381	($4,501)	$2,562	$4,187	$2,239	$1,992	$1,536	$701	$9	$13,325	$574 $8,055
19	$49,851	$6,749	$8,672	$28,649	$99,574	$22,001	($6,648)	$2,768	$3,981	$2,295	$1,946	$1,574	$719	$4	$13,370	$576 $8,631
20	$46,861	$6,749	$8,820	$31,639	$103,333	$22,554	($9,085)	$2,990	$3,759	$2,353	$1,895	$1,613	$737	($2)	$13,346	$576 $9,208
21	$43,631	$6,749	$8,976	$34,869	$106,852	$23,039	($11,829)	$3,230	$3,519	$2,412	$1,838	$1,654	$755	($7)	$13,257	$575 $9,782
22	$40,142	$6,749	$9,139	$38,358	$110,111	$23,458	($14,900)	$3,489	$3,259	$2,472	$1,777	$1,695	$774	($13)	$13,104	$571 $10,354
23	$36,372	$6,749	$9,311	$42,128	$113,090	$23,811	($18,317)	$3,770	$2,979	$2,534	$1,709	$1,737	$794	($18)	$12,891	$566 $10,920
24	$32,300	$6,749	$9,492	$46,200	$115,766	$24,101	($22,100)	$4,072	$2,676	$2,597	$1,635	$1,781	$813	($23)	$12,621	$559 $11,479
25	$27,900	$6,749	$9,683	$50,600	$118,115	$24,329	($26,271)	$4,399	$2,349	$2,662	$1,553	$1,825	$834	($27)	$12,298	$551 $12,031
26	$23,147	$6,749	$9,884	$55,353	$120,111	$24,498	($30,855)	$4,753	$1,996	$2,729	$1,465	$1,871	$855	($31)	$11,926	$541 $12,572
27	$18,013	$6,749	$10,096	$60,487	$121,725	$24,612	($35,876)	$5,135	$1,614	$2,797	$1,367	$1,918	$876	($35)	$11,509	$531 $13,103
28	$12,466	$6,749	$10,320	$66,034	$122,927	$24,675	($41,359)	$5,547	$1,202	$2,867	$1,261	$1,966	$898	($38)	$11,054	$518 $13,621
29	$6,474	$6,749	$10,556	$72,026	$123,683	$24,692	($47,335)	$5,992	$756	$2,938	$1,145	$2,015	$920	($41)	$10,565	$505 $14,126
30	$0	$6,474	$10,807	$78,500	$123,958	$24,669	($53,831)	$6,474	$275	$3,012	$1,019	$2,065	$943	($43)	$10,051	$491 $14,618

* Represents the approximate amount of money which should be saved monthly
** After Tax Down Payment is the initial principal plus the after-tax value of the closing cost

Figure 34 - Page 123

Rent vs Buy Analysis for Various Metropolitan Cities

Jacksonville, FL

Using the Median Home Price and the Average Monthly Rent

HOME:

Purchase Price:	$74,700
Closing Cost:	$2,200
+Total Home Cost:	$76,900
+After-tax Cost:	$76,218
Down Payment:	$7,500
+Initial Principal:	$5,300
+Starting Loan:	$69,400

Mortgage Rate:	7.750%
Loan Length (in Yrs):	30
+Monthly Payment:	$497
Real Estate Tax:	2.150%
Add Repair/Utility Cost:	0.10%
Closing Commission Rate:	6.0%

GENERAL:

Tax Bracket:	31.0%
Savings Rate:	4.0%

RENT:

Starting Rental Amount:	$471
Monthly Rental Incr./Yr (in %):	2.5%
+Initial Monthly Savings Amt:	$55

COMPARISON (3 YRS):

+Principal Paid:	$1,978
+Interest Paid:	$15,921
+Amount Renter Can Save:	$2,388
+Amount Difference Rent/Own:	$410
+Appr. Required to Break Even:	$6,819
+Required Home Sales Price:	$81,519
+Yearly % Appr. to Break Even:	3.0%
+Total % Appr. to Break Even:	9.1%

COMPARISON (5 YRS):

+Principal Paid:	$3,576
+Interest Paid:	$26,256
+Amount Renter Can Save:	$3,659
+Amount Difference Rent/Own:	$83
+Appr. Required to Break Even:	$6,472
+Required Home Sales Price:	$81,172
+Yearly % Appr. to Break Even:	1.7%
+Total % Appr. to Break Even:	8.7%

COMPARISON (10 YRS):

+Principal Paid:	$8,837
+Interest Paid:	$50,826
+Amount Renter Can Save:	$5,530
+Amount Difference Rent/Own:	($3,307)
+Appr. Required to Break Even:	$2,865
+Required Home Sales Price:	$77,565
+Yearly % Appr. to Break Even:	0.4%
+Total % Appr. to Break Even:	3.8%

Figure 35

Myth Breakers®

Figure 36 - Page 125

				Summary Information				Home Ownership						Rental Difference			
Yr	Current Loan	Mortgage Payment	After Tax Layout	Cumulative Principal Paid	Interest Paid	Amount Renter Can Save	Amount Diff Rent/Own	Annual Principal Paid	Annual Interest Paid	Real Estate Tax	Income Tax Break	Repairs + Add Utils	* Mthly Rent	Ave Mthly Savings Amount	Before Int Diff Rent/Own	Int on Diff & **ATDP	
0	$69,400																
1	$68,791	$5,966	$6,310	$609	$5,357	$856	$247	$609	$5,357	$1,606	$2,159	$896	$471	$55	$658	$198	$198
2	$68,133	$5,966	$6,375	$1,267	$10,665	$1,653	$386	$658	$5,308	$1,646	$2,156	$919	$483	$49	$1,240	$215	$413
3	$67,422	$5,966	$6,443	$1,978	$15,921	$2,388	$410	$711	$5,255	$1,687	$2,152	$942	$495	$42	$1,745	$230	$643
4	$66,654	$5,966	$6,514	$2,746	$21,119	$3,058	$312	$768	$5,198	$1,730	$2,148	$965	$507	$36	$2,172	$243	$886
5	$65,824	$5,966	$6,587	$3,576	$26,256	$3,659	$83	$830	$5,137	$1,773	$2,142	$989	$520	$29	$2,520	$253	$1,139
6	$64,928	$5,966	$6,663	$4,472	$31,326	$4,188	($283)	$896	$5,070	$1,817	$2,135	$1,014	$533	$22	$2,788	$262	$1,401
7	$63,960	$5,966	$6,742	$5,440	$36,324	$4,643	($797)	$968	$4,998	$1,863	$2,127	$1,040	$546	$16	$2,975	$268	$1,668
8	$62,914	$5,966	$6,824	$6,486	$41,244	$5,021	($1,466)	$1,046	$4,920	$1,909	$2,117	$1,066	$560	$9	$3,080	$272	$1,940
9	$61,784	$5,966	$6,909	$7,616	$46,080	$5,317	($2,299)	$1,130	$4,836	$1,957	$2,106	$1,092	$574	$2	$3,103	$273	$2,214
10	$60,563	$5,966	$6,999	$8,837	$50,826	$5,530	($3,307)	$1,221	$4,745	$2,006	$2,093	$1,119	$588	($5)	$3,043	$273	$2,487
11	$59,244	$5,966	$7,092	$10,156	$55,473	$5,656	($4,500)	$1,319	$4,647	$2,056	$2,078	$1,147	$603	($12)	$2,900	$270	$2,757
12	$57,819	$5,966	$7,189	$11,581	$60,015	$5,694	($5,887)	$1,425	$4,542	$2,107	$2,061	$1,176	$618	($19)	$2,673	$265	$3,021
13	$56,280	$5,966	$7,290	$13,120	$64,442	$5,640	($7,480)	$1,539	$4,427	$2,160	$2,042	$1,206	$633	($26)	$2,361	$257	$3,278
14	$54,617	$5,966	$7,396	$14,783	$68,745	$5,491	($9,292)	$1,663	$4,303	$2,214	$2,020	$1,236	$649	($33)	$1,965	$247	$3,526
15	$52,821	$5,966	$7,506	$16,579	$72,915	$5,246	($11,333)	$1,796	$4,170	$2,269	$1,996	$1,267	$666	($40)	$1,485	$235	$3,761
16	$50,880	$5,966	$7,622	$18,520	$76,941	$4,903	($13,617)	$1,941	$4,026	$2,326	$1,969	$1,298	$682	($47)	$921	$221	$3,982
17	$48,784	$5,966	$7,742	$20,616	$80,811	$4,458	($16,158)	$2,096	$3,870	$2,384	$1,939	$1,331	$699	($54)	$273	$204	$4,185
18	$46,519	$5,966	$7,869	$22,881	$84,512	$3,912	($18,969)	$2,265	$3,701	$2,444	$1,905	$1,364	$717	($61)	($458)	$185	$4,370
19	$44,072	$5,966	$8,002	$25,328	$88,031	$3,262	($22,066)	$2,447	$3,520	$2,505	$1,868	$1,398	$735	($68)	($1,272)	$163	$4,533
20	$41,429	$5,966	$8,141	$27,971	$91,354	$2,506	($25,465)	$2,643	$3,323	$2,568	$1,826	$1,433	$753	($75)	($2,166)	$140	$4,673
21	$38,573	$5,966	$8,287	$30,827	$94,465	$1,645	($29,182)	$2,856	$3,111	$2,632	$1,780	$1,469	$772	($81)	($3,141)	$114	$4,786
22	$35,488	$5,966	$8,440	$33,912	$97,347	$678	($33,234)	$3,085	$2,881	$2,697	$1,729	$1,506	$791	($88)	($4,194)	$86	$4,872
23	$32,156	$5,966	$8,601	$37,244	$99,980	($396)	($37,641)	$3,333	$2,634	$2,765	$1,674	$1,543	$811	($94)	($5,324)	$55	$4,927
24	$28,555	$5,966	$8,770	$40,845	$102,346	($1,577)	($42,421)	$3,600	$2,366	$2,834	$1,612	$1,582	$831	($100)	($6,527)	$23	$4,950
25	$24,666	$5,966	$8,948	$44,734	$104,423	($2,863)	($47,597)	$3,889	$2,077	$2,905	$1,544	$1,621	$852	($106)	($7,802)	($11)	$4,939
26	$20,464	$5,966	$9,136	$48,936	$106,187	($4,253)	($53,189)	$4,202	$1,764	$2,978	$1,470	$1,662	$873	($112)	($9,145)	($47)	$4,892
27	$15,925	$5,966	$9,333	$53,475	$107,614	($5,746)	($59,221)	$4,539	$1,427	$3,052	$1,388	$1,703	$895	($117)	($10,552)	($86)	$4,806
28	$11,021	$5,966	$9,541	$58,379	$108,677	($7,339)	($65,718)	$4,904	$1,062	$3,128	$1,299	$1,746	$917	($122)	($12,020)	($125)	$4,681
29	$5,723	$5,966	$9,761	$63,677	$109,345	($9,028)	($72,705)	$5,298	$669	$3,206	$1,201	$1,790	$940	($127)	($13,543)	($167)	$4,514
30	$0	$5,966	$9,993	$69,400	$109,588	($10,811)	($80,211)	$5,723	$243	$3,287	$1,094	$1,834	$964	($131)	($15,116)	($209)	$4,305

* Represents the approximate amount of money which should be saved monthly

** After Tax Down Payment is the initial principal plus the after-tax value of the closing cost

Rent vs Buy Analysis for Various Metropolitan Cities

Las Vegas, NV

Using the Median Home Price and the Average Monthly Rent

HOME:

Purchase Price:	$105,600
Closing Cost:	$3,500
+Total Home Cost:	$109,100
+After-tax Cost:	$108,015
Down Payment:	$10,600
+Initial Principal:	$7,100
+Starting Loan:	$98,500
Mortgage Rate:	7.750%
Loan Length (in Yrs):	30
+Monthly Payment:	$706
Real Estate Tax:	1.020%
Add Repair/Utility Cost:	0.10%
Closing Commission Rate:	6.0%

GENERAL:

Tax Bracket:	31.0%
Savings Rate:	4.0%

RENT:

Starting Rental Amount:	$541
Monthly Rental Incr./Yr (in %):	2.5%
+Initial Monthly Savings Amt:	$136

COMPARISON (3 YRS):

+Principal Paid:	$2,807
+Interest Paid:	$22,597
+Amount Renter Can Save:	$5,604
+Amount Difference Rent/Own:	$2,797
+Appr. Required to Break Even:	$12,285
+Required Home Sales Price:	$117,885
+Yearly % Appr. to Break Even:	3.7%
+Total % Appr. to Break Even:	11.6%

COMPARISON (5 YRS):

+Principal Paid:	$5,075
+Interest Paid:	$37,265
+Amount Renter Can Save:	$9,077
+Amount Difference Rent/Own:	$4,002
+Appr. Required to Break Even:	$13,567
+Required Home Sales Price:	$119,167
+Yearly % Appr. to Break Even:	2.4%
+Total % Appr. to Break Even:	12.8%

COMPARISON (10 YRS):

+Principal Paid:	$12,543
+Interest Paid:	$72,137
+Amount Renter Can Save:	$16,633
+Amount Difference Rent/Own:	$4,090
+Appr. Required to Break Even:	$13,661
+Required Home Sales Price:	$119,261
+Yearly % Appr. to Break Even:	1.2%
+Total % Appr. to Break Even:	12.9%

Figure 37

Myth Breakers®

Summary Information / Home Ownership / Rental Difference

Yr	Current Loan	Mortgage Payment	After Tax Layout	Cumulative Principal Paid	Cumulative Interest Paid	Amount Renter Can Save	Amount Diff Rent/Own	Annual Principal Paid	Annual Interest Paid	Real Estate Tax	Income Tax Break	Repairs + Add Utils	Mthly Rent *	Ave Mthly Savings Amount	Before Int Diff Rent/Own	Int on Diff & **ATDP	
0	$98,500																
1	$97,635	$8,468	$8,121	$865	$7,603	$1,916	$1,052	$865	$7,603	$1,077	$2,691	$1,267	$541	$136	$1,629	$287	$287
2	$96,702	$8,468	$8,193	$1,798	$15,138	$3,786	$1,987	$934	$7,534	$1,104	$2,678	$1,299	$555	$128	$3,168	$331	$617
3	$95,693	$8,468	$8,268	$2,807	$22,597	$5,604	$2,797	$1,009	$7,459	$1,132	$2,663	$1,331	$568	$121	$4,615	$372	$989
4	$94,603	$8,468	$8,346	$3,897	$29,975	$7,369	$3,472	$1,090	$7,378	$1,160	$2,647	$1,365	$583	$113	$5,970	$410	$1,399
5	$93,425	$8,468	$8,427	$5,075	$37,265	$9,077	$4,002	$1,178	$7,290	$1,189	$2,629	$1,399	$597	$105	$7,231	$446	$1,845
6	$92,153	$8,468	$8,512	$6,347	$44,461	$10,723	$4,376	$1,272	$7,196	$1,219	$2,609	$1,434	$612	$97	$8,398	$480	$2,325
7	$90,779	$8,468	$8,600	$7,721	$51,555	$12,305	$4,584	$1,374	$7,094	$1,249	$2,586	$1,470	$627	$89	$9,470	$510	$2,835
8	$89,294	$8,468	$8,693	$9,206	$58,538	$13,819	$4,613	$1,485	$6,983	$1,280	$2,562	$1,506	$643	$81	$10,446	$538	$3,374
9	$87,690	$8,468	$8,790	$10,810	$65,402	$15,263	$4,453	$1,604	$6,864	$1,312	$2,535	$1,544	$659	$73	$11,325	$564	$3,938
10	$85,957	$8,468	$8,891	$12,543	$72,137	$16,633	$4,090	$1,733	$6,735	$1,345	$2,505	$1,583	$676	$65	$12,108	$587	$4,525
11	$84,086	$8,468	$8,997	$14,414	$78,733	$17,926	$3,512	$1,872	$6,596	$1,379	$2,472	$1,622	$693	$57	$12,795	$607	$5,132
12	$82,063	$8,468	$9,108	$16,437	$85,179	$19,140	$2,704	$2,022	$6,446	$1,413	$2,436	$1,663	$710	$49	$13,384	$624	$5,756
13	$79,879	$8,468	$9,224	$18,621	$91,463	$20,273	$1,651	$2,185	$6,283	$1,449	$2,397	$1,704	$728	$41	$13,877	$639	$6,395
14	$77,519	$8,468	$9,346	$20,981	$97,571	$21,321	$339	$2,360	$6,108	$1,485	$2,354	$1,747	$746	$33	$14,274	$661	$7,047
15	$74,969	$8,468	$9,474	$23,531	$103,489	$22,282	($1,248)	$2,550	$5,918	$1,522	$2,307	$1,791	$764	$25	$14,575	$661	$7,708
16	$72,215	$8,468	$9,608	$26,285	$109,203	$23,156	($3,129)	$2,754	$5,714	$1,560	$2,255	$1,835	$784	$17	$14,781	$668	$8,375
17	$69,239	$8,468	$9,750	$29,261	$114,695	$23,941	($5,320)	$2,976	$5,492	$1,599	$2,198	$1,881	$803	$9	$14,893	$672	$9,048
18	$66,025	$8,468	$9,899	$32,475	$119,949	$24,635	($7,841)	$3,215	$5,253	$1,639	$2,137	$1,928	$823	$2	$14,913	$674	$9,721
19	$62,552	$8,468	$10,055	$35,948	$124,944	$25,238	($10,711)	$3,473	$4,995	$1,680	$2,069	$1,976	$844	($6)	$14,843	$673	$10,394
20	$58,800	$8,468	$10,220	$39,700	$129,660	$25,749	($13,951)	$3,752	$4,716	$1,722	$1,996	$2,026	$865	($13)	$14,685	$670	$11,064
21	$54,747	$8,468	$10,394	$43,753	$134,075	$26,168	($17,584)	$4,053	$4,415	$1,765	$1,916	$2,076	$886	($20)	$14,440	$664	$11,728
22	$50,369	$8,468	$10,577	$48,131	$138,165	$26,497	($21,634)	$4,378	$4,090	$1,809	$1,829	$2,128	$909	($27)	$14,113	$656	$12,384
23	$45,639	$8,468	$10,770	$52,861	$141,903	$26,737	($26,124)	$4,730	$3,738	$1,854	$1,734	$2,182	$931	($34)	$13,707	$646	$13,030
24	$40,529	$8,468	$10,975	$57,971	$145,261	$26,889	($31,082)	$5,110	$3,358	$1,901	$1,630	$2,236	$955	($40)	$13,226	$633	$13,663
25	$35,009	$8,468	$11,191	$63,491	$148,208	$26,957	($36,535)	$5,520	$2,948	$1,948	$1,518	$2,292	$979	($46)	$12,674	$619	$14,283
26	$29,045	$8,468	$11,419	$69,455	$150,713	$26,943	($42,512)	$5,964	$2,504	$1,997	$1,395	$2,349	$1,003	($51)	$12,057	$603	$14,885
27	$22,602	$8,468	$11,661	$75,898	$152,738	$26,851	($49,046)	$6,443	$2,025	$2,047	$1,262	$2,408	$1,028	($56)	$11,381	$585	$15,470
28	$15,642	$8,468	$11,916	$82,858	$154,246	$26,688	($56,170)	$6,960	$1,508	$2,098	$1,118	$2,468	$1,054	($61)	$10,652	$565	$16,036
29	$8,123	$8,468	$12,188	$90,377	$155,195	$26,459	($63,918)	$7,519	$949	$2,150	$961	$2,530	$1,080	($64)	$9,879	$545	$16,580
30	$0	$8,123	$12,475	$98,500	$155,540	$26,172	($72,328)	$8,123	$345	$2,204	$790	$2,593	$1,107	($68)	$9,069	$523	$17,103

* Represents the approximate amount of money which should be saved monthly

** After Tax Down Payment is the initial principal plus the after-tax value of the closing cost

Copyright © Myth Breakers - 1993

Figure 38 - Page 127

Los Angeles, CA

Using the Median Home Price and the Average Monthly Rent

HOME:

Purchase Price:	$216,600
Closing Cost:	$7,200
+Total Home Cost:	$223,800
+After-tax Cost:	$221,568
Down Payment:	$21,700
+Initial Principal:	$14,500
+Starting Loan:	$202,100
Mortgage Rate:	7.750%
Loan Length (in Yrs):	30
+Monthly Payment:	$1,448
Real Estate Tax:	0.630%
Add Repair/Utility Cost:	0.10%
Closing Commission Rate:	6.0%

GENERAL:

Tax Bracket:	31.0%
Savings Rate:	4.0%

RENT:

Starting Rental Amount:	$685
Monthly Rental Incr./Yr (in %):	2.5%
+Initial Monthly Savings Amt:	$655

COMPARISON (3 YRS):

+Principal Paid:	$5,760
+Interest Paid:	$46,363
+Amount Renter Can Save:	$25,969
+Amount Difference Rent/Own:	$20,208
+Appr. Required to Break Even:	$40,609
+Required Home Sales Price:	$257,209
+Yearly % Appr. to Break Even:	5.9%
+Total % Appr. to Break Even:	18.7%

COMPARISON (5 YRS):

+Principal Paid:	$10,413
+Interest Paid:	$76,459
+Amount Renter Can Save:	$43,986
+Amount Difference Rent/Own:	$33,573
+Appr. Required to Break Even:	$54,827
+Required Home Sales Price:	$271,427
+Yearly % Appr. to Break Even:	4.6%
+Total % Appr. to Break Even:	25.3%

COMPARISON (10 YRS):

+Principal Paid:	$25,735
+Interest Paid:	$148,010
+Amount Renter Can Save:	$91,462
+Amount Difference Rent/Own:	$65,728
+Appr. Required to Break Even:	$89,034
+Required Home Sales Price:	$305,634
+Yearly % Appr. to Break Even:	3.5%
+Total % Appr. to Break Even:	41.1%

Figure 39

Myth Breakers®

Column groups: *Summary Information* (After Tax Layout, Cumulative Principal Paid, Interest Paid, Amount Renter Can Save, Amount Diff Rent/Own) · *Home Ownership* (Annual Principal Paid, Annual Interest Paid, Real Estate Tax, Income Tax Break, Repairs + Add Utils, * Mthly Rent) · *Rental Difference* (Ave Mthly Savings Amount, Before Int Diff Rent/Own, Int on Diff & **ATDP)

Yr	Current Loan	Mortgage Payment	After Tax Layout	Cumulative Principal Paid	Interest Paid	Amount Renter Can Save	Amount Diff Rent/Own	Annual Principal Paid	Annual Interest Paid	Real Estate Tax	Income Tax Break	Repairs + Add Utils	* Mthly Rent	Ave Mthly Savings Amount	Before Int Diff Rent/Own	Int on Diff & **ATDP	Int on Diff & **ATDP (cum)
0	$202,100																
1	$200,326	$17,374	$16,079	$1,774	$15,601	$8,514	$6,740	$1,774	$15,601	$1,365	$5,259	$2,599	$685	$655	$7,859	$655	$655
2	$198,410	$17,374	$16,212	$3,690	$31,059	$17,170	$13,480	$1,916	$15,458	$1,399	$5,226	$2,664	$702	$649	$15,645	$871	$1,525
3	$196,340	$17,374	$16,350	$5,760	$46,363	$25,969	$20,208	$2,070	$15,304	$1,434	$5,189	$2,731	$720	$643	$23,359	$1,084	$2,610
4	$194,103	$17,374	$16,495	$7,997	$61,501	$34,908	$26,911	$2,236	$15,138	$1,470	$5,148	$2,799	$738	$637	$31,002	$1,296	$3,906
5	$191,687	$17,374	$16,646	$10,413	$76,459	$43,986	$33,573	$2,416	$14,958	$1,506	$5,104	$2,869	$756	$631	$38,574	$1,506	$5,412
6	$189,077	$17,374	$16,804	$13,023	$91,224	$53,203	$40,180	$2,610	$14,764	$1,544	$5,056	$2,941	$775	$625	$46,077	$1,714	$7,126
7	$186,257	$17,374	$16,969	$15,843	$105,778	$62,559	$46,717	$2,820	$14,555	$1,582	$5,003	$3,014	$794	$620	$53,513	$1,920	$9,046
8	$183,211	$17,374	$17,142	$18,889	$120,107	$72,054	$53,165	$3,046	$14,328	$1,622	$4,945	$3,090	$814	$614	$60,884	$2,124	$11,170
9	$179,921	$17,374	$17,323	$22,179	$134,190	$81,688	$59,509	$3,291	$14,084	$1,663	$4,881	$3,167	$835	$609	$68,191	$2,327	$13,497
10	$176,365	$17,374	$17,512	$25,735	$148,010	$91,462	$65,728	$3,555	$13,819	$1,704	$4,812	$3,246	$855	$604	$75,438	$2,528	$16,024
11	$172,525	$17,374	$17,711	$29,575	$161,543	$101,378	$71,803	$3,841	$13,534	$1,747	$4,737	$3,327	$877	$599	$82,627	$2,727	$18,751
12	$168,376	$17,374	$17,920	$33,724	$174,769	$111,438	$77,713	$4,149	$13,225	$1,790	$4,655	$3,410	$899	$595	$89,762	$2,924	$21,675
13	$163,893	$17,374	$18,140	$38,207	$187,661	$121,643	$83,436	$4,482	$12,892	$1,835	$4,565	$3,496	$921	$590	$96,847	$3,120	$24,796
14	$159,051	$17,374	$18,370	$43,049	$200,193	$131,997	$88,948	$4,842	$12,532	$1,881	$4,468	$3,583	$944	$587	$103,886	$3,315	$28,111
15	$153,820	$17,374	$18,613	$48,280	$212,336	$142,504	$94,224	$5,231	$12,143	$1,928	$4,362	$3,673	$968	$583	$110,884	$3,509	$31,620
16	$148,169	$17,374	$18,868	$53,931	$224,059	$153,169	$99,238	$5,651	$11,723	$1,976	$4,247	$3,764	$992	$580	$117,848	$3,702	$35,322
17	$142,063	$17,374	$19,137	$60,037	$235,329	$163,997	$103,960	$6,105	$11,269	$2,026	$4,121	$3,859	$1,017	$578	$124,782	$3,893	$39,215
18	$135,468	$17,374	$19,421	$66,632	$246,108	$174,994	$108,362	$6,596	$10,779	$2,076	$3,985	$3,955	$1,042	$576	$131,695	$4,084	$43,299
19	$128,343	$17,374	$19,720	$73,757	$256,357	$186,168	$112,411	$7,125	$10,249	$2,128	$3,837	$4,054	$1,068	$575	$138,594	$4,275	$47,574
20	$120,645	$17,374	$20,035	$81,455	$266,034	$197,528	$116,073	$7,697	$9,677	$2,181	$3,676	$4,155	$1,095	$575	$145,489	$4,465	$52,039
21	$112,329	$17,374	$20,368	$89,771	$275,092	$209,082	$119,311	$8,316	$9,059	$2,236	$3,501	$4,259	$1,122	$575	$152,387	$4,655	$56,695
22	$103,346	$17,374	$20,720	$98,754	$283,483	$220,842	$122,088	$8,984	$8,391	$2,292	$3,312	$4,366	$1,151	$576	$159,301	$4,846	$61,541
23	$93,641	$17,374	$21,093	$108,459	$291,153	$232,821	$124,361	$9,705	$7,669	$2,349	$3,106	$4,475	$1,179	$578	$166,243	$5,037	$66,578
24	$83,156	$17,374	$21,487	$118,944	$298,043	$245,032	$126,088	$10,484	$6,890	$2,408	$2,882	$4,587	$1,209	$582	$173,224	$5,229	$71,807
25	$71,830	$17,374	$21,904	$130,270	$304,090	$257,491	$127,220	$11,327	$6,048	$2,468	$2,640	$4,701	$1,239	$586	$180,260	$5,423	$77,230
26	$59,594	$17,374	$22,346	$142,506	$309,229	$270,215	$127,709	$12,236	$5,138	$2,530	$2,377	$4,819	$1,270	$592	$187,367	$5,618	$82,848
27	$46,375	$17,374	$22,815	$155,725	$313,384	$283,225	$127,500	$13,219	$4,156	$2,593	$2,092	$4,939	$1,302	$600	$194,561	$5,815	$88,664
28	$32,094	$17,374	$23,312	$170,006	$316,478	$296,542	$126,536	$14,281	$3,094	$2,658	$1,783	$5,063	$1,334	$608	$201,862	$6,016	$94,679
29	$16,667	$17,374	$23,840	$185,433	$318,425	$310,189	$124,756	$15,427	$1,947	$2,724	$1,448	$5,189	$1,368	$619	$209,291	$6,219	$100,898
30	$0	$17,374	$24,401	$202,100	$319,133	$324,195	$122,095	$16,667	$708	$2,792	$1,085	$5,319	$1,402	$632	$216,870	$6,426	$107,324

* Represents the approximate amount of money which should be saved monthly
** After Tax Down Payment is the initial principal plus the after-tax value of the closing cost

Figure 40 - Page 129

Memphis, TN

Using the Median Home Price and the Average Monthly Rent

HOME:

Purchase Price:	$85,500
Closing Cost:	$2,800
+Total Home Cost:	$88,300
+After-tax Cost:	$87,432
Down Payment:	$8,600
+Initial Principal:	$5,800
+Starting Loan:	$79,700
Mortgage Rate:	7.750%
Loan Length (in Yrs):	30
+Monthly Payment:	$571
Real Estate Tax:	0.540%
Add Repair/Utility Cost:	0.10%
Closing Commission Rate:	6.0%

GENERAL:

Tax Bracket:	31.0%
Savings Rate:	4.0%

RENT:

Starting Rental Amount:	$447
Monthly Rental Incr./Yr (in %):	2.5%
+Initial Monthly Savings Amt:	$77

COMPARISON (3 YRS):

+Principal Paid:	$2,272
+Interest Paid:	$18,284
+Amount Renter Can Save:	$3,277
+Amount Difference Rent/Own:	$1,006
+Appr. Required to Break Even:	$8,583
+Required Home Sales Price:	$94,083
+Yearly % Appr. to Break Even:	3.2%
+Total % Appr. to Break Even:	10.0%

COMPARISON (5 YRS):

+Principal Paid:	$4,106
+Interest Paid:	$30,152
+Amount Renter Can Save:	$5,140
+Amount Difference Rent/Own:	$1,033
+Appr. Required to Break Even:	$8,612
+Required Home Sales Price:	$94,112
+Yearly % Appr. to Break Even:	1.9%
+Total % Appr. to Break Even:	10.1%

COMPARISON (10 YRS):

+Principal Paid:	$10,149
+Interest Paid:	$58,369
+Amount Renter Can Save:	$8,474
+Amount Difference Rent/Own:	($1,675)
+Appr. Required to Break Even:	$5,731
+Required Home Sales Price:	$91,231
+Yearly % Appr. to Break Even:	0.7%
+Total % Appr. to Break Even:	6.7%

Figure 41

Myth Breakers®

			Summary Information					Home Ownership						Rental Difference			
Yr	Current Loan	Mortgage Payment	After Tax Layout	Cumulative Principal Paid	Interest Paid	Amount Renter Can Save	Amount Diff Rent/Own	Annual Principal Paid	Annual Interest Paid	Real Estate Tax	Income Tax Break	Repairs + Add Utils	Mthly Rent*	Ave Mthly Savings Amount	Before Int Diff Rent/Own	Int on Diff & **ATDP	
0	$79,700																
1	$79,000	$6,852	$6,289	$700	$6,152	$1,152	$453	$700	$6,152	$462	$2,050	$1,026	$447	$77	$925	$227	$227
2	$78,245	$6,852	$6,340	$1,455	$12,248	$2,246	$791	$756	$6,096	$473	$2,036	$1,052	$458	$70	$1,767	$251	$479
3	$77,428	$6,852	$6,393	$2,272	$18,284	$3,277	$1,006	$816	$6,035	$485	$2,021	$1,078	$470	$63	$2,525	$273	$752
4	$76,546	$6,852	$6,449	$3,154	$24,254	$4,243	$1,089	$882	$5,970	$497	$2,005	$1,105	$481	$56	$3,198	$293	$1,045
5	$75,594	$6,852	$6,507	$4,106	$30,152	$5,140	$1,033	$953	$5,899	$510	$1,987	$1,133	$493	$49	$3,784	$310	$1,356
6	$74,564	$6,852	$6,568	$5,136	$35,975	$5,964	$829	$1,029	$5,822	$522	$1,967	$1,161	$506	$42	$4,283	$325	$1,681
7	$73,452	$6,852	$6,632	$6,248	$41,715	$6,713	$465	$1,112	$5,740	$535	$1,945	$1,190	$518	$34	$4,694	$338	$2,019
8	$72,251	$6,852	$6,698	$7,449	$47,365	$7,383	($66)	$1,201	$5,650	$549	$1,922	$1,220	$531	$27	$5,017	$348	$2,366
9	$70,953	$6,852	$6,768	$8,747	$52,919	$7,971	($776)	$1,298	$5,554	$563	$1,896	$1,250	$545	$19	$5,249	$355	$2,722
10	$69,551	$6,852	$6,842	$10,149	$58,369	$8,474	($1,675)	$1,402	$5,450	$577	$1,868	$1,281	$558	$12	$5,392	$360	$3,082
11	$68,037	$6,852	$6,918	$11,663	$63,706	$8,889	($2,774)	$1,515	$5,337	$591	$1,838	$1,313	$572	$4	$5,444	$363	$3,445
12	$66,401	$6,852	$6,999	$13,299	$68,922	$9,213	($4,086)	$1,636	$5,216	$606	$1,805	$1,346	$587	($3)	$5,405	$363	$3,808
13	$64,633	$6,852	$7,084	$15,067	$74,006	$9,444	($5,623)	$1,768	$5,084	$621	$1,769	$1,380	$601	($11)	$5,275	$361	$4,168
14	$62,723	$6,852	$7,173	$16,977	$78,948	$9,578	($7,399)	$1,910	$4,942	$636	$1,729	$1,414	$616	($18)	$5,054	$356	$4,524
15	$60,660	$6,852	$7,267	$19,040	$83,737	$9,614	($9,426)	$2,063	$4,789	$652	$1,687	$1,450	$632	($26)	$4,742	$348	$4,872
16	$58,432	$6,852	$7,366	$21,268	$88,360	$9,550	($11,719)	$2,229	$4,623	$669	$1,640	$1,486	$647	($34)	$4,339	$338	$5,210
17	$56,024	$6,852	$7,470	$23,676	$92,804	$9,382	($14,294)	$2,408	$4,444	$685	$1,590	$1,523	$664	($41)	$3,847	$326	$5,536
18	$53,423	$6,852	$7,580	$26,277	$97,055	$9,111	($17,166)	$2,601	$4,251	$703	$1,536	$1,561	$680	($49)	$3,265	$311	$5,847
19	$50,613	$6,852	$7,696	$29,087	$101,097	$8,734	($20,353)	$2,810	$4,042	$720	$1,476	$1,600	$697	($56)	$2,594	$293	$6,140
20	$47,577	$6,852	$7,818	$32,123	$104,913	$8,251	($23,872)	$3,036	$3,816	$738	$1,412	$1,640	$715	($63)	$1,837	$274	$6,413
21	$44,298	$6,852	$7,948	$35,402	$108,485	$7,660	($27,742)	$3,279	$3,572	$757	$1,342	$1,681	$732	($70)	$995	$251	$6,665
22	$40,755	$6,852	$8,084	$38,945	$111,794	$6,962	($31,982)	$3,543	$3,309	$775	$1,266	$1,723	$751	($77)	$71	$227	$6,892
23	$36,928	$6,852	$8,229	$42,772	$114,819	$6,157	($36,615)	$3,827	$3,024	$795	$1,184	$1,766	$770	($84)	($935)	$200	$7,092
24	$32,793	$6,852	$8,382	$46,907	$117,536	$5,245	($41,662)	$4,135	$2,717	$815	$1,095	$1,810	$789	($90)	($2,018)	$171	$7,263
25	$28,327	$6,852	$8,544	$51,373	$119,921	$4,227	($47,146)	$4,467	$2,385	$835	$998	$1,856	$809	($96)	($3,176)	$140	$7,403
26	$23,501	$6,852	$8,716	$56,199	$121,947	$3,106	($53,093)	$4,825	$2,026	$856	$894	$1,902	$829	($102)	($4,404)	$107	$7,510
27	$18,288	$6,852	$8,899	$61,412	$123,586	$1,884	($59,528)	$5,213	$1,639	$877	$780	$1,950	$849	($108)	($5,698)	$72	$7,582
28	$12,657	$6,852	$9,092	$67,043	$124,806	$564	($66,479)	$5,632	$1,220	$899	$657	$1,998	$871	($113)	($7,054)	$36	$7,618
29	$6,573	$6,852	$9,298	$73,127	$125,574	($850)	($73,977)	$6,084	$768	$922	$524	$2,048	$892	($118)	($8,465)	($3)	$7,615
30	$0	$6,852	$9,517	$79,700	$125,853	($2,352)	($82,052)	$6,573	$279	$945	$379	$2,100	$915	($122)	($9,925)	($42)	$7,573

* Represents the approximate amount of money which should be saved monthly
** After Tax Down Payment is the initial principal plus the after-tax value of the closing cost

Copyright © Myth Breakers - 1993

Figure 42 - Page 131

Rent vs Buy Analysis for Various Metropolitan Cities

Milwaukee, WI

Using the Median Home Price and the Average Monthly Rent

HOME:

Purchase Price:	$95,700
Closing Cost:	$3,200
+Total Home Cost:	$98,900
+After-tax Cost:	$97,908
Down Payment:	$9,600
+Initial Principal:	$6,400
+Starting Loan:	$89,300
Mortgage Rate:	7.750%
Loan Length (in Yrs):	30
+Monthly Payment:	$640
Real Estate Tax:	3.750%
Add Repair/Utility Cost:	0.10%
Closing Commission Rate:	6.0%

GENERAL:

Tax Bracket:	31.0%
Savings Rate:	4.0%

RENT:

Starting Rental Amount:	$625
Monthly Rental Incr./Yr (in %):	2.5%
+Initial Monthly Savings Amt:	$139

COMPARISON (3 YRS):

+Principal Paid:	$2,545
+Interest Paid:	$20,486
+Amount Renter Can Save:	$5,681
+Amount Difference Rent/Own:	$3,136
+Appr. Required to Break Even:	$11,793
+Required Home Sales Price:	$107,493
+Yearly % Appr. to Break Even:	3.9%
+Total % Appr. to Break Even:	12.3%

COMPARISON (5 YRS):

+Principal Paid:	$4,601
+Interest Paid:	$33,784
+Amount Renter Can Save:	$9,280
+Amount Difference Rent/Own:	$4,679
+Appr. Required to Break Even:	$13,436
+Required Home Sales Price:	$109,136
+Yearly % Appr. to Break Even:	2.7%
+Total % Appr. to Break Even:	14.0%

COMPARISON (10 YRS):

+Principal Paid:	$11,371
+Interest Paid:	$65,400
+Amount Renter Can Save:	$17,457
+Amount Difference Rent/Own:	$6,086
+Appr. Required to Break Even:	$14,932
+Required Home Sales Price:	$110,632
+Yearly % Appr. to Break Even:	1.5%
+Total % Appr. to Break Even:	15.6%

Figure 43

Myth Breakers

Yr	Current Loan	Mortgage Payment	After Tax Layout	Cumulative Principal Paid	Interest Paid	Amount Renter Can Save	Amount Diff Rent/Own	Annual Principal Paid	Annual Interest Paid	Real Estate Tax	Income Tax Break	Repairs + Add Utils	Mthly Rent*	Ave Mthly Savings Amount	Before Int Diff Rent/Own	Int on Diff & **ATDP	(Cumulative)
0	$89,300																
1	$88,516	$7,677	$9,165	$784	$6,893	$1,927	$1,143	$784	$6,893	$3,589	$3,249	$1,148	$625	$139	$1,665	$262	$262
2	$87,670	$7,677	$9,275	$1,630	$13,724	$3,822	$2,191	$847	$6,830	$3,678	$3,258	$1,177	$641	$132	$3,252	$307	$570
3	$86,755	$7,677	$9,389	$2,545	$20,486	$5,681	$3,136	$915	$6,762	$3,770	$3,265	$1,207	$657	$126	$4,761	$350	$919
4	$85,767	$7,677	$9,507	$3,533	$27,175	$7,501	$3,968	$988	$6,689	$3,865	$3,272	$1,237	$673	$119	$6,192	$390	$1,310
5	$84,699	$7,677	$9,629	$4,601	$33,784	$9,280	$4,679	$1,068	$6,610	$3,961	$3,277	$1,268	$690	$113	$7,542	$429	$1,738
6	$83,546	$7,677	$9,756	$5,754	$40,308	$11,015	$5,261	$1,153	$6,524	$4,060	$3,281	$1,299	$707	$106	$8,812	$465	$2,203
7	$82,300	$7,677	$9,887	$7,000	$46,739	$12,703	$5,703	$1,246	$6,431	$4,162	$3,284	$1,332	$725	$99	$10,001	$499	$2,702
8	$80,954	$7,677	$10,023	$8,346	$53,070	$14,341	$5,995	$1,346	$6,331	$4,266	$3,285	$1,365	$743	$92	$11,109	$530	$3,232
9	$79,500	$7,677	$10,164	$9,800	$59,293	$15,926	$6,126	$1,454	$6,223	$4,373	$3,285	$1,399	$762	$86	$12,135	$559	$3,791
10	$77,929	$7,677	$10,311	$11,371	$65,400	$17,457	$6,086	$1,571	$6,106	$4,482	$3,282	$1,434	$781	$79	$13,080	$587	$4,378
11	$76,232	$7,677	$10,463	$13,068	$71,380	$18,931	$5,863	$1,697	$5,980	$4,594	$3,278	$1,470	$800	$72	$13,942	$611	$4,989
12	$74,399	$7,677	$10,621	$14,901	$77,223	$20,346	$5,444	$1,833	$5,844	$4,709	$3,271	$1,507	$820	$65	$14,723	$634	$5,623
13	$72,418	$7,677	$10,786	$16,882	$82,920	$21,699	$4,817	$1,981	$5,697	$4,826	$3,262	$1,544	$841	$58	$15,422	$654	$6,277
14	$70,278	$7,677	$10,957	$19,022	$88,457	$22,990	$3,968	$2,140	$5,537	$4,947	$3,250	$1,583	$862	$52	$16,040	$672	$6,950
15	$67,967	$7,677	$11,135	$21,333	$93,823	$24,216	$2,883	$2,311	$5,366	$5,071	$3,235	$1,623	$883	$45	$16,578	$688	$7,638
16	$65,470	$7,677	$11,321	$23,830	$99,003	$25,377	$1,546	$2,497	$5,180	$5,198	$3,217	$1,663	$905	$38	$17,037	$702	$8,340
17	$62,772	$7,677	$11,514	$26,528	$103,982	$26,470	($57)	$2,698	$4,979	$5,328	$3,195	$1,705	$928	$32	$17,417	$713	$9,053
18	$59,858	$7,677	$11,716	$29,442	$108,745	$27,497	($1,945)	$2,914	$4,763	$5,461	$3,169	$1,747	$951	$25	$17,721	$723	$9,776
19	$56,710	$7,677	$11,926	$32,590	$113,274	$28,456	($4,135)	$3,148	$4,529	$5,597	$3,139	$1,791	$975	$19	$17,950	$730	$10,506
20	$53,308	$7,677	$12,146	$35,992	$117,550	$29,347	($6,645)	$3,401	$4,276	$5,737	$3,104	$1,836	$999	$13	$18,106	$735	$11,241
21	$49,634	$7,677	$12,376	$39,666	$121,552	$30,171	($9,495)	$3,674	$4,003	$5,881	$3,064	$1,882	$1,024	$7	$18,192	$738	$11,979
22	$45,664	$7,677	$12,616	$43,636	$125,260	$30,930	($12,706)	$3,969	$3,708	$6,028	$3,018	$1,929	$1,050	$2	$18,211	$740	$12,719
23	$41,376	$7,677	$12,867	$47,924	$128,649	$31,624	($16,300)	$4,288	$3,389	$6,178	$2,966	$1,977	$1,076	($4)	$18,166	$739	$13,458
24	$36,743	$7,677	$13,129	$52,557	$131,693	$32,256	($20,301)	$4,633	$3,044	$6,333	$2,907	$2,026	$1,103	($9)	$18,061	$737	$14,195
25	$31,739	$7,677	$13,405	$57,561	$134,366	$32,829	($24,733)	$5,005	$2,672	$6,491	$2,841	$2,077	$1,130	($13)	$17,900	$733	$14,929
26	$26,332	$7,677	$13,693	$62,968	$136,636	$33,345	($29,623)	$5,407	$2,270	$6,653	$2,766	$2,129	$1,159	($18)	$17,688	$728	$15,657
27	$20,491	$7,677	$13,996	$68,809	$138,472	$33,810	($34,998)	$5,841	$1,836	$6,820	$2,683	$2,182	$1,188	($21)	$17,432	$722	$16,379
28	$14,181	$7,677	$14,313	$75,119	$139,839	$34,229	($40,890)	$6,310	$1,367	$6,990	$2,591	$2,237	$1,217	($25)	$17,137	$714	$17,093
29	$7,364	$7,677	$14,647	$81,936	$140,699	$34,608	($47,328)	$6,817	$860	$7,165	$2,488	$2,293	$1,248	($27)	$16,810	$705	$17,798
30	$0	$7,677	$14,998	$89,300	$141,012	$34,953	($54,347)	$7,364	$313	$7,344	$2,374	$2,350	$1,279	($29)	$16,460	$696	$18,494

Column groups: Summary Information (Current Loan … Amount Diff Rent/Own); Home Ownership (Annual Principal Paid … Repairs + Add Utils); Rental Difference (Mthly Rent … cumulative).

* Represents the approximate amount of money which should be saved monthly
** After Tax Down Payment is the initial principal plus the after-tax value of the closing cost

Copyright © Myth Breakers - 1993

Figure 44 - Page 133

Rent vs Buy Analysis for Various Metropolitan Cities

Minneapolis, MN

Using the Median Home Price and the Average Monthly Rent

HOME:

Purchase Price:	$95,100
Closing Cost:	$3,200
+Total Home Cost:	$98,300
+After-tax Cost:	$97,308
Down Payment:	$9,500
+Initial Principal:	$6,300
+Starting Loan:	$88,800
Mortgage Rate:	7.750%
Loan Length (in Yrs):	30
+Monthly Payment:	$636
Real Estate Tax:	1.390%
Add Repair/Utility Cost:	0.10%
Closing Commission Rate:	6.0%

GENERAL:

Tax Bracket:	31.0%
Savings Rate:	4.0%

RENT:

Starting Rental Amount:	$632
Monthly Rental Incr./Yr (in %):	2.5%
+Initial Monthly Savings Amt:	($2)

COMPARISON (3 YRS):

+Principal Paid:	$2,531
+Interest Paid:	$20,371
+Amount Renter Can Save:	$270
+Amount Difference Rent/Own:	($2,261)
+Appr. Required to Break Even:	$6,014
+Required Home Sales Price:	$101,114
+Yearly % Appr. to Break Even:	2.1%
+Total % Appr. to Break Even:	6.3%

COMPARISON (5 YRS):

+Principal Paid:	$4,575
+Interest Paid:	$33,595
+Amount Renter Can Save:	($200)
+Amount Difference Rent/Own:	($4,775)
+Appr. Required to Break Even:	$3,339
+Required Home Sales Price:	$98,439
+Yearly % Appr. to Break Even:	0.7%
+Total % Appr. to Break Even:	3.5%

COMPARISON (10 YRS):

+Principal Paid:	$11,307
+Interest Paid:	$65,033
+Amount Renter Can Save:	($3,952)
+Amount Difference Rent/Own:	($15,259)
+Appr. Required to Break Even:	($7,814)
+Required Home Sales Price:	$87,286
+Yearly % Appr. to Break Even:	-0.9%
+Total % Appr. to Break Even:	-8.2%

Figure 45

	Summary Information							Home Ownership					Rental Difference				
Year	Current Loan	Mortgage Payment	After Tax Layout	Cumulative Principal Paid	Cumulative Interest Paid	Amount Diff Rent/Own	Amount Renter Can Save	Annual Principal Paid	Annual Interest Paid	Real Estate Tax	Income Tax Break	Repairs + Add Utils	* Mthly Rent	Ave Mthly Savings Amount	Before Int Diff Rent/Own	Int on Diff & **ATDP	Int on Diff & **ATDP
Yr 0	$88,800																
Yr 1	$88,021	$7,634	$7,562	$779	$6,855	($566)	$213	$779	$6,855	$1,322	$2,535	$1,141	$632	($2)	($22)	$234	$234
Yr 2	$87,179	$7,634	$7,633	$1,621	$13,647	($1,317)	$305	$842	$6,792	$1,355	$2,526	$1,170	$648	($12)	($162)	$467	$232
Yr 3	$86,269	$7,634	$7,707	$2,531	$20,371	($2,261)	$270	$910	$6,724	$1,389	$2,515	$1,199	$664	($22)	($423)	$693	$226
Yr 4	$85,286	$7,634	$7,783	$3,514	$27,023	($3,410)	$103	$983	$6,651	$1,424	$2,503	$1,229	$681	($32)	($807)	$910	$217
Yr 5	$84,225	$7,634	$7,863	$4,575	$33,595	($4,775)	($200)	$1,062	$6,573	$1,459	$2,490	$1,260	$698	($42)	($1,315)	$1,115	$205
Yr 6	$83,078	$7,634	$7,946	$5,722	$40,082	($6,368)	($646)	$1,147	$6,487	$1,496	$2,475	$1,291	$715	($53)	($1,950)	$1,304	$189
Yr 7	$81,839	$7,634	$8,033	$6,961	$46,478	($8,199)	($1,238)	$1,239	$6,395	$1,533	$2,458	$1,323	$733	($64)	($2,712)	$1,474	$170
Yr 8	$80,501	$7,634	$8,123	$8,299	$52,773	($10,283)	($1,984)	$1,338	$6,296	$1,571	$2,439	$1,357	$751	($74)	($3,604)	$1,620	$147
Yr 9	$79,055	$7,634	$8,218	$9,745	$58,961	($12,632)	($2,886)	$1,446	$6,188	$1,611	$2,418	$1,390	$770	($85)	($4,627)	$1,740	$120
Yr 10	$77,493	$7,634	$8,316	$11,307	$65,033	($15,259)	($3,952)	$1,562	$6,072	$1,651	$2,394	$1,425	$789	($96)	($5,782)	$1,830	$90
Yr 11	$75,805	$7,634	$8,419	$12,995	$70,980	($18,180)	($5,185)	$1,688	$5,947	$1,692	$2,368	$1,461	$809	($107)	($7,071)	$1,886	$56
Yr 12	$73,982	$7,634	$8,527	$14,818	$76,791	($21,409)	($6,591)	$1,823	$5,811	$1,734	$2,339	$1,497	$829	($119)	($8,495)	$1,904	$18
Yr 13	$72,013	$7,634	$8,640	$16,787	$82,456	($24,962)	($8,174)	$1,969	$5,665	$1,778	$2,307	$1,535	$850	($130)	($10,055)	$1,881	($23)
Yr 14	$69,885	$7,634	$8,758	$18,915	$87,962	($28,855)	($9,939)	$2,128	$5,506	$1,822	$2,272	$1,573	$871	($141)	($11,752)	$1,813	($68)
Yr 15	$67,586	$7,634	$8,881	$21,214	$93,298	($33,105)	($11,891)	$2,299	$5,336	$1,868	$2,233	$1,612	$893	($153)	($13,587)	$1,696	($117)
Yr 16	$65,103	$7,634	$9,011	$23,697	$98,449	($37,731)	($14,034)	$2,483	$5,151	$1,914	$2,190	$1,653	$915	($164)	($15,560)	$1,526	($170)
Yr 17	$62,421	$7,634	$9,147	$26,379	$103,400	($42,751)	($16,371)	$2,683	$4,952	$1,962	$2,143	$1,694	$938	($176)	($17,671)	$1,300	($226)
Yr 18	$59,523	$7,634	$9,290	$29,277	$108,136	($48,185)	($18,908)	$2,898	$4,736	$2,011	$2,092	$1,736	$962	($187)	($19,921)	$1,013	($287)
Yr 19	$56,392	$7,634	$9,441	$32,408	$112,640	($54,055)	($21,647)	$3,131	$4,503	$2,062	$2,035	$1,780	$986	($199)	($22,309)	$662	($351)
Yr 20	$53,010	$7,634	$9,599	$35,790	$116,892	($60,381)	($24,591)	$3,382	$4,252	$2,113	$1,973	$1,824	$1,010	($210)	($24,834)	$243	($419)
Yr 21	$49,356	$7,634	$9,765	$39,444	$120,872	($67,188)	($27,744)	$3,654	$3,980	$2,166	$1,905	$1,870	$1,036	($222)	($27,497)	($247)	($491)
Yr 22	$45,409	$7,634	$9,940	$43,391	$124,559	($74,500)	($31,108)	$3,947	$3,687	$2,220	$1,831	$1,917	$1,061	($233)	($30,295)	($814)	($566)
Yr 23	$41,144	$7,634	$10,124	$47,656	$127,929	($82,341)	($34,686)	$4,264	$3,370	$2,276	$1,750	$1,965	$1,088	($244)	($33,227)	($1,459)	($645)
Yr 24	$36,538	$7,634	$10,319	$52,262	$130,956	($90,740)	($38,478)	$4,607	$3,027	$2,333	$1,662	$2,014	$1,115	($255)	($36,291)	($2,187)	($728)
Yr 25	$31,561	$7,634	$10,524	$57,239	$133,613	($99,725)	($42,486)	$4,977	$2,657	$2,391	$1,565	$2,064	$1,143	($266)	($39,484)	($3,002)	($815)
Yr 26	$26,185	$7,634	$10,741	$62,615	$135,871	($109,326)	($46,710)	$5,376	$2,258	$2,451	$1,460	$2,116	$1,172	($277)	($42,803)	($3,907)	($905)
Yr 27	$20,376	$7,634	$10,970	$68,424	$137,697	($119,574)	($51,151)	$5,808	$1,826	$2,512	$1,345	$2,169	$1,201	($287)	($46,245)	($4,905)	($998)
Yr 28	$14,102	$7,634	$11,212	$74,698	$139,056	($130,504)	($55,806)	$6,275	$1,359	$2,575	$1,220	$2,223	$1,231	($297)	($49,805)	($6,000)	($1,095)
Yr 29	$7,323	$7,634	$11,468	$81,477	$139,912	($142,151)	($60,674)	$6,779	$855	$2,639	$1,083	$2,278	$1,262	($306)	($53,478)	($7,195)	($1,195)
Yr 30	$0	$7,634	$11,740	$88,800	$140,223	($154,552)	($65,752)	$7,323	$311	$2,705	$935	$2,335	$1,293	($315)	($57,259)	($8,494)	($1,298)

* Represents the approximate amount of money which should be saved monthly

** After Tax Down Payment is the initial principal plus the after-tax value of the closing cost

Figure 46 - Page 135

Newark, NJ

Using the Median Home Price and the Average Monthly Rent

HOME:

Purchase Price:	$188,900
Closing Cost:	$6,300
+Total Home Cost:	$195,200
+After-tax Cost:	$193,247
Down Payment:	$18,900
+Initial Principal:	$12,600
+Starting Loan:	$176,300

Mortgage Rate:	7.750%
Loan Length (in Yrs):	30
+Monthly Payment:	$1,263
Real Estate Tax:	3.140%
Add Repair/Utility Cost:	0.10%
Closing Commission Rate:	6.0%

GENERAL:

Tax Bracket:	31.0%
Savings Rate:	4.0%

RENT:

Starting Rental Amount:	$525*
Monthly Rental Incr./Yr (in %):	2.5%
+Initial Monthly Savings Amt:	$916

COMPARISON (3 YRS):

+Principal Paid:	$5,025
+Interest Paid:	$40,444
+Amount Renter Can Save:	$35,924
+Amount Difference Rent/Own:	$30,899
+Appr. Required to Break Even:	$49,554
+Required Home Sales Price:	$238,454
+Yearly % Appr. to Break Even:	8.1%
+Total % Appr. to Break Even:	26.2%

COMPARISON (5 YRS):

+Principal Paid:	$9,083
+Interest Paid:	$66,699
+Amount Renter Can Save:	$61,632
+Amount Difference Rent/Own:	$52,548
+Appr. Required to Break Even:	$72,584
+Required Home Sales Price:	$261,484
+Yearly % Appr. to Break Even:	6.7%
+Total % Appr. to Break Even:	38.4%

COMPARISON (10 YRS):

+Principal Paid:	$22,449
+Interest Paid:	$129,115
+Amount Renter Can Save:	$132,370
+Amount Difference Rent/Own:	$109,920
+Appr. Required to Break Even:	$133,619
+Required Home Sales Price:	$322,519
+Yearly % Appr. to Break Even:	5.5%
+Total % Appr. to Break Even:	70.7%

* Rent is low because of rent control   Figure 47

Myth Breakers®

Summary Information / Home Ownership / Rental Difference

Yr	Current Loan	Mortgage Payment	Summary Information					Home Ownership					Rental Difference				
			After Tax Layout	Cumulative Principal Paid	Cumulative Interest Paid	Amount Renter Can Save	Amount Diff Rent/Own	Annual Principal Paid	Annual Interest Paid	Real Estate Tax	Income Tax Break	Repairs + Add Utils	Mthly Rent	Ave Mthly Savings Amount*	Before Int Diff Rent/Own	Int on Diff	**ATDP
Yr 0	$176,300																
Yr 1	$174,753	$15,156	$17,297	$1,547	$13,609	$11,629	$10,082	$1,547	$13,609	$5,931	$6,058	$2,267	$525	$916	$10,997	$632	$632
Yr 2	$173,081	$15,156	$17,495	$3,219	$27,094	$23,602	$20,383	$1,672	$13,485	$6,080	$6,065	$2,323	$538	$920	$22,034	$936	$1,568
Yr 3	$171,275	$15,156	$17,699	$5,025	$40,444	$35,924	$30,899	$1,806	$13,351	$6,232	$6,071	$2,382	$552	$923	$33,115	$1,241	$2,810
Yr 4	$169,324	$15,156	$17,911	$6,976	$53,650	$48,599	$41,623	$1,951	$13,205	$6,388	$6,074	$2,441	$565	$927	$44,241	$1,548	$4,358
Yr 5	$167,217	$15,156	$18,131	$9,083	$66,699	$61,632	$52,548	$2,108	$13,049	$6,547	$6,075	$2,502	$580	$931	$55,418	$1,856	$6,213
Yr 6	$164,940	$15,156	$18,359	$11,360	$79,578	$75,028	$63,668	$2,277	$12,880	$6,711	$6,073	$2,565	$594	$936	$66,649	$2,165	$8,378
Yr 7	$162,480	$15,156	$18,596	$13,820	$92,275	$88,793	$74,973	$2,460	$12,697	$6,879	$6,068	$2,629	$609	$941	$77,939	$2,476	$10,854
Yr 8	$159,823	$15,156	$18,841	$16,477	$104,774	$102,934	$86,457	$2,657	$12,499	$7,051	$6,060	$2,695	$624	$946	$89,291	$2,788	$13,643
Yr 9	$156,952	$15,156	$19,096	$19,348	$117,457	$117,060	$98,109	$2,871	$12,286	$7,227	$6,049	$2,762	$640	$952	$100,712	$3,103	$16,746
Yr 10	$153,851	$15,156	$19,361	$22,449	$129,115	$132,370	$109,920	$3,101	$12,055	$7,408	$6,033	$2,831	$656	$958	$112,205	$3,419	$20,165
Yr 11	$150,500	$15,156	$19,637	$25,800	$140,921	$147,680	$121,880	$3,350	$11,806	$7,593	$6,014	$2,902	$672	$964	$123,778	$3,737	$23,902
Yr 12	$146,881	$15,156	$19,924	$29,419	$152,458	$163,396	$133,977	$3,619	$11,537	$7,783	$5,989	$2,974	$689	$972	$135,436	$4,058	$27,960
Yr 13	$142,971	$15,156	$20,223	$33,329	$163,704	$179,527	$146,198	$3,910	$11,246	$7,977	$5,959	$3,049	$706	$979	$147,186	$4,381	$32,341
Yr 14	$138,747	$15,156	$20,534	$37,553	$174,637	$196,084	$158,531	$4,224	$10,932	$8,177	$5,924	$3,125	$724	$987	$159,036	$4,707	$37,048
Yr 15	$134,183	$15,156	$20,858	$42,117	$185,230	$213,076	$170,959	$4,563	$10,593	$8,381	$5,882	$3,203	$742	$996	$170,992	$5,036	$42,084
Yr 16	$129,253	$15,156	$21,197	$47,047	$195,456	$230,516	$183,469	$4,930	$10,227	$8,591	$5,833	$3,283	$760	$1,006	$183,065	$5,367	$47,451
Yr 17	$123,928	$15,156	$21,550	$52,372	$205,287	$248,415	$196,043	$5,326	$9,831	$8,805	$5,777	$3,365	$779	$1,016	$195,262	$5,702	$53,154
Yr 18	$118,174	$15,156	$21,918	$58,126	$214,690	$266,789	$208,663	$5,754	$9,403	$9,025	$5,713	$3,449	$799	$1,028	$207,594	$6,041	$59,195
Yr 19	$111,958	$15,156	$22,303	$64,342	$223,630	$285,650	$221,308	$6,216	$8,941	$9,251	$5,639	$3,535	$819	$1,040	$220,071	$6,384	$65,578
Yr 20	$105,244	$15,156	$22,706	$71,056	$232,072	$305,015	$233,958	$6,715	$8,442	$9,482	$5,556	$3,624	$839	$1,053	$232,706	$6,730	$72,308
Yr 21	$97,989	$15,156	$23,127	$78,311	$239,974	$324,900	$246,590	$7,254	$7,902	$9,719	$5,463	$3,714	$860	$1,067	$245,510	$7,081	$79,390
Yr 22	$90,153	$15,156	$23,569	$86,147	$247,294	$345,325	$259,178	$7,837	$7,320	$9,962	$5,357	$3,807	$882	$1,082	$258,498	$7,438	$86,827
Yr 23	$81,687	$15,156	$24,031	$94,613	$253,984	$366,309	$271,695	$8,466	$6,690	$10,211	$5,240	$3,902	$904	$1,099	$271,682	$7,799	$94,626
Yr 24	$72,541	$15,156	$24,515	$103,759	$259,995	$387,873	$284,114	$9,146	$6,010	$10,467	$5,108	$4,000	$926	$1,117	$285,081	$8,166	$102,792
Yr 25	$62,660	$15,156	$25,024	$113,640	$265,270	$410,041	$296,401	$9,881	$5,276	$10,728	$4,961	$4,100	$950	$1,136	$298,709	$8,539	$111,331
Yr 26	$51,986	$15,156	$25,557	$124,314	$269,753	$432,837	$308,523	$10,674	$4,482	$10,997	$4,798	$4,203	$973	$1,156	$312,586	$8,919	$120,250
Yr 27	$40,454	$15,156	$26,118	$135,846	$273,378	$456,289	$320,443	$11,531	$3,625	$11,272	$4,618	$4,308	$998	$1,179	$326,732	$9,306	$129,556
Yr 28	$27,997	$15,156	$26,707	$148,303	$276,077	$480,425	$332,122	$12,458	$2,699	$11,553	$4,418	$4,415	$1,023	$1,203	$341,168	$9,701	$139,257
Yr 29	$14,539	$15,156	$27,327	$161,761	$277,775	$505,277	$343,516	$13,458	$1,698	$11,842	$4,198	$4,526	$1,048	$1,229	$355,917	$10,104	$149,361
Yr 30	$0	$15,156	$27,979	$176,300	$278,393	$530,880	$354,580	$14,539	$618	$12,138	$3,954	$4,639	$1,074	$1,257	$371,003	$10,516	$159,877

* Represents the approximate amount of money which should be saved monthly
** After Tax Down Payment is the initial principal plus the after-tax value of the closing cost

Figure 48 - Page 137

Rent vs Buy Analysis for Various Metropolitan Cities

New Orleans, LA

Using the Median Home Price and the Average Monthly Rent

HOME:

Purchase Price:	$73,700
Closing Cost:	$2,500
+Total Home Cost:	$76,200
+After-tax Cost:	$75,425
Down Payment:	$7,400
+Initial Principal:	$4,900
+Starting Loan:	$68,800

Mortgage Rate:	7.750%
Loan Length (in Yrs):	30
+Monthly Payment:	$493
Real Estate Tax:	1.610%
Add Repair/Utility Cost:	0.10%
Closing Commission Rate:	6.0%

GENERAL:

Tax Bracket:	31.0%
Savings Rate:	4.0%

RENT:

Starting Rental Amount:	$500
Monthly Rental Incr./Yr (in %):	2.5%
+Initial Monthly Savings Amt:	($2)

COMPARISON (3 YRS):

+Principal Paid:	$1,961
+Interest Paid:	$15,783
+Amount Renter Can Save:	$174
+Amount Difference Rent/Own:	($1,787)
+Appr. Required to Break Even:	$4,638
+Required Home Sales Price:	$78,338
+Yearly % Appr. to Break Even:	2.1%
+Total % Appr. to Break Even:	6.3%

COMPARISON (5 YRS):

+Principal Paid:	$3,545
+Interest Paid:	$26,029
+Amount Renter Can Save:	($217)
+Amount Difference Rent/Own:	($3,762)
+Appr. Required to Break Even:	$2,538
+Required Home Sales Price:	$76,238
+Yearly % Appr. to Break Even:	0.7%
+Total % Appr. to Break Even:	3.4%

COMPARISON (10 YRS):

+Principal Paid:	$8,761
+Interest Paid:	$50,386
+Amount Renter Can Save:	($3,203)
+Amount Difference Rent/Own:	($11,964)
+Appr. Required to Break Even:	($6,188)
+Required Home Sales Price:	$67,512
+Yearly % Appr. to Break Even:	-0.9%
+Total % Appr. to Break Even:	-8.4%

Figure 49

Myth Breakers®

Summary Information / Home Ownership / Rental Difference

Yr	Current Loan	Mortgage Payment	After Tax Layout	Cumulative Principal Paid	Interest Paid	Amount Renter Can Save	Amount Diff Rent/Own	Annual Principal Paid	Annual Interest Paid	Real Estate Tax	Income Tax Break	Repairs + Add Utils	*Mthly Rent	Ave Mthly Savings Amount	Before Int Diff Rent/Own	Int on Diff	& **ATDP
Yr 0	$68,800																
Yr 1	$68,196	$5,915	$5,971	$604	$5,311	$154	($450)	$604	$5,311	$1,187	$2,014	$884	$500	($2)	($29)	$182	$182
Yr 2	$67,544	$5,915	$6,029	$1,256	$10,573	$213	($1,043)	$652	$5,262	$1,216	$2,008	$907	$513	($10)	($149)	$182	$363
Yr 3	$66,839	$5,915	$6,089	$1,961	$15,783	$174	($1,787)	$705	$5,210	$1,247	$2,002	$929	$525	($18)	($364)	$180	$538
Yr 4	$66,078	$5,915	$6,151	$2,722	$20,937	$32	($2,690)	$761	$5,153	$1,278	$1,994	$952	$538	($26)	($674)	$175	$706
Yr 5	$65,255	$5,915	$6,216	$3,545	$26,029	($217)	($3,762)	$822	$5,092	$1,310	$1,985	$976	$552	($34)	($1,081)	$168	$864
Yr 6	$64,367	$5,915	$6,284	$4,433	$31,055	($576)	($5,010)	$889	$5,026	$1,342	$1,974	$1,001	$566	($42)	($1,586)	$158	$1,010
Yr 7	$63,407	$5,915	$6,354	$5,393	$36,010	($1,051)	($6,444)	$960	$4,955	$1,376	$1,963	$1,026	$580	($50)	($2,190)	$145	$1,140
Yr 8	$62,370	$5,915	$6,427	$6,430	$40,887	($1,644)	($8,074)	$1,037	$4,878	$1,410	$1,949	$1,051	$594	($59)	($2,895)	$130	$1,252
Yr 9	$61,250	$5,915	$6,504	$7,550	$45,682	($2,360)	($9,910)	$1,120	$4,794	$1,446	$1,934	$1,078	$609	($67)	($3,702)	$112	$1,342
Yr 10	$60,039	$5,915	$6,583	$8,761	$50,386	($3,203)	($11,964)	$1,210	$4,704	$1,482	$1,918	$1,104	$624	($76)	($4,612)	$91	$1,409
Yr 11	$58,732	$5,915	$6,667	$10,068	$54,994	($4,176)	($14,245)	$1,307	$4,607	$1,519	$1,899	$1,132	$640	($84)	($5,626)	$67	$1,450
Yr 12	$57,319	$5,915	$6,754	$11,481	$59,496	($5,285)	($16,765)	$1,412	$4,502	$1,557	$1,878	$1,160	$656	($93)	($6,745)	$40	$1,460
Yr 13	$55,793	$5,915	$6,845	$13,007	$63,885	($6,531)	($19,537)	$1,526	$4,389	$1,596	$1,855	$1,189	$672	($102)	($7,970)	$11	$1,439
Yr 14	$54,145	$5,915	$6,940	$14,655	$68,151	($7,919)	($22,574)	$1,648	$4,266	$1,636	$1,830	$1,219	$689	($111)	($9,301)	($22)	$1,382
Yr 15	$52,364	$5,915	$7,040	$16,436	$72,285	($9,453)	($25,888)	$1,781	$4,134	$1,677	$1,801	$1,250	$706	($120)	($10,739)	($57)	$1,286
Yr 16	$50,440	$5,915	$7,144	$18,360	$76,276	($11,135)	($29,495)	$1,924	$3,991	$1,719	$1,770	$1,281	$724	($129)	($12,284)	($95)	$1,149
Yr 17	$48,362	$5,915	$7,254	$20,438	$80,112	($12,969)	($33,407)	$2,078	$3,836	$1,761	$1,735	$1,313	$742	($138)	($13,938)	($137)	$968
Yr 18	$46,117	$5,915	$7,369	$22,683	$83,781	($14,959)	($37,642)	$2,245	$3,669	$1,806	$1,697	$1,346	$761	($147)	($15,699)	($181)	$740
Yr 19	$43,691	$5,915	$7,489	$25,109	$87,270	($17,106)	($42,215)	$2,426	$3,489	$1,851	$1,655	$1,379	$780	($156)	($17,567)	($228)	$462
Yr 20	$41,071	$5,915	$7,616	$27,729	$90,565	($19,413)	($47,142)	$2,620	$3,294	$1,897	$1,609	$1,414	$799	($165)	($19,543)	($279)	$130
Yr 21	$38,240	$5,915	$7,749	$30,560	$93,648	($21,883)	($52,443)	$2,831	$3,084	$1,944	$1,559	$1,449	$819	($174)	($21,625)	($332)	($258)
Yr 22	$35,182	$5,915	$7,890	$33,618	$96,505	($24,518)	($58,136)	$3,058	$2,856	$1,993	$1,503	$1,485	$840	($182)	($23,813)	($388)	($705)
Yr 23	$31,878	$5,915	$8,037	$36,922	$99,116	($27,319)	($64,241)	$3,304	$2,611	$2,043	$1,443	$1,523	$861	($191)	($26,105)	($447)	($1,214)
Yr 24	$28,309	$5,915	$8,193	$40,491	$101,461	($30,287)	($70,778)	$3,569	$2,346	$2,094	$1,376	$1,561	$882	($200)	($28,500)	($509)	($1,787)
Yr 25	$24,453	$5,915	$8,357	$44,347	$103,520	($33,424)	($77,771)	$3,856	$2,059	$2,146	$1,304	$1,600	$904	($208)	($30,995)	($574)	($2,429)
Yr 26	$20,287	$5,915	$8,530	$48,513	$105,269	($36,729)	($85,242)	$4,166	$1,749	$2,200	$1,224	$1,640	$927	($216)	($33,589)	($641)	($3,140)
Yr 27	$15,787	$5,915	$8,713	$53,013	$106,684	($40,203)	($93,216)	$4,500	$1,415	$2,255	$1,138	$1,681	$950	($224)	($36,278)	($712)	($3,925)
Yr 28	$10,926	$5,915	$8,906	$57,874	$107,737	($43,844)	($101,719)	$4,861	$1,053	$2,311	$1,043	$1,723	$974	($232)	($39,059)	($785)	($4,785)
Yr 29	$5,674	$5,915	$9,110	$63,126	$108,400	($47,652)	($110,778)	$5,252	$663	$2,369	$940	$1,766	$998	($239)	($41,929)	($860)	($5,723)
Yr 30	$0	$5,915	$9,325	$68,800	$108,641	($51,624)	($120,424)	$5,674	$241	$2,428	$827	$1,810	$1,023	($246)	($44,882)	($938)	($6,742)

* Represents the approximate amount of money which should be saved monthly
** After Tax Down Payment is the initial principal plus the after-tax value of the closing cost

Figure 50 - Page 139

NYC (Average of the 5 Boroughs), NY

Using the Median Home Price and the Average Monthly Rent

HOME:

Purchase Price:	$174,800
Closing Cost:	$5,800
+Total Home Cost:	$180,600
+After-tax Cost:	$178,802
Down Payment:	$17,500
+Initial Principal:	$11,700
+Starting Loan:	$163,100

Mortgage Rate:	7.750%
Loan Length (in Yrs):	30
+Monthly Payment:	$1,168
Real Estate Tax:	0.870%
Add Repair/Utility Cost:	0.10%
Closing Commission Rate:	6.0%

GENERAL:

Tax Bracket:	31.0%
Savings Rate:	4.0%

RENT:

Starting Rental Amount:	$542*
Monthly Rental Incr./Yr (in %):	2.5%
+Initial Monthly Savings Amt:	$563

COMPARISON (3 YRS):

+Principal Paid:	$4,649
+Interest Paid:	$37,416
+Amount Renter Can Save:	$22,300
+Amount Difference Rent/Own:	$17,652
+Appr. Required to Break Even:	$34,193
+Required Home Sales Price:	$208,993
+Yearly % Appr. to Break Even:	6.1%
+Total % Appr. to Break Even:	19.6%

COMPARISON (5 YRS):

+Principal Paid:	$8,403
+Interest Paid:	$61,705
+Amount Renter Can Save:	$37,851
+Amount Difference Rent/Own:	$29,448
+Appr. Required to Break Even:	$46,743
+Required Home Sales Price:	$221,543
+Yearly % Appr. to Break Even:	4.9%
+Total % Appr. to Break Even:	26.7%

COMPARISON (10 YRS):

+Principal Paid:	$20,769
+Interest Paid:	$119,448
+Amount Renter Can Save:	$79,134
+Amount Difference Rent/Own:	$58,365
+Appr. Required to Break Even:	$77,505
+Required Home Sales Price:	$252,305
+Yearly % Appr. to Break Even:	3.7%
+Total % Appr. to Break Even:	44.3%

* Rent is low because of rent control   Figure 51

Summary Information | Home Ownership | Rental Difference

Yr	Current Loan	Mortgage Payment	After Tax Layout	Cumulative Principal Paid	Cumulative Interest Paid	Amount Renter Can Save	Amount Diff Rent/Own	Annual Principal Paid	Annual Interest Paid	Real Estate Tax	Income Tax Break	Repairs + Add Utils	Mthly Rent	Ave Mthly Savings Amount	Before Int Diff Rent/Own	Int on Diff & **ATDP	
0	$163,100																$534
1	$161,668	$14,022	$13,266	$1,432	$12,590	$7,296	$5,864	$1,432	$12,590	$1,521	$4,374	$2,098	$542	$563	$6,762	$534	$1,255
2	$160,122	$14,022	$13,380	$2,978	$25,065	$14,730	$11,752	$1,546	$12,475	$1,559	$4,351	$2,150	$556	$559	$13,475	$720	$2,160
3	$158,451	$14,022	$13,499	$4,649	$37,416	$22,300	$17,652	$1,671	$12,351	$1,598	$4,324	$2,204	$569	$555	$20,141	$905	$3,248
4	$156,646	$14,022	$13,623	$6,454	$49,633	$30,008	$23,554	$1,805	$12,217	$1,638	$4,295	$2,259	$584	$552	$26,760	$1,088	$4,518
5	$154,697	$14,022	$13,753	$8,403	$61,705	$37,851	$29,448	$1,950	$12,072	$1,679	$4,263	$2,315	$598	$548	$33,334	$1,270	
6	$152,590	$14,022	$13,888	$10,510	$73,620	$45,832	$35,322	$2,106	$11,915	$1,721	$4,227	$2,373	$613	$544	$39,863	$1,451	$5,969
7	$150,315	$14,022	$14,030	$12,785	$85,366	$53,950	$41,164	$2,276	$11,746	$1,764	$4,188	$2,433	$629	$541	$46,351	$1,630	$7,599
8	$147,856	$14,022	$14,178	$15,244	$96,929	$62,205	$46,961	$2,458	$11,563	$1,808	$4,145	$2,493	$644	$537	$52,797	$1,809	$9,408
9	$145,201	$14,022	$14,332	$17,899	$108,295	$70,599	$52,700	$2,656	$11,366	$1,853	$4,098	$2,556	$660	$534	$59,205	$1,986	$11,394
10	$142,331	$14,022	$14,494	$20,769	$119,448	$79,134	$58,365	$2,869	$11,153	$1,899	$4,046	$2,620	$677	$531	$65,577	$2,163	$13,557
11	$139,232	$14,022	$14,664	$23,868	$130,370	$87,810	$63,942	$3,099	$10,922	$1,947	$3,989	$2,685	$694	$528	$71,915	$2,338	$15,895
12	$135,884	$14,022	$14,842	$27,216	$141,043	$96,630	$69,414	$3,348	$10,673	$1,995	$3,927	$2,752	$711	$526	$78,223	$2,512	$18,407
13	$132,266	$14,022	$15,029	$30,834	$151,447	$105,598	$74,764	$3,617	$10,404	$2,045	$3,859	$2,821	$729	$523	$84,505	$2,686	$21,093
14	$128,358	$14,022	$15,224	$34,742	$161,561	$114,715	$79,974	$3,908	$10,114	$2,096	$3,785	$2,892	$747	$522	$90,763	$2,859	$23,952
15	$124,137	$14,022	$15,430	$38,963	$171,361	$123,987	$85,024	$4,222	$9,800	$2,149	$3,704	$2,964	$766	$520	$97,004	$3,032	$26,984
16	$119,576	$14,022	$15,646	$43,524	$180,822	$133,417	$89,893	$4,561	$9,461	$2,203	$3,616	$3,038	$785	$519	$103,230	$3,204	$30,187
17	$114,649	$14,022	$15,874	$48,451	$189,916	$143,011	$94,560	$4,927	$9,095	$2,258	$3,519	$3,114	$805	$518	$109,449	$3,375	$33,562
18	$109,326	$14,022	$16,113	$53,774	$198,615	$152,775	$99,001	$5,323	$8,699	$2,314	$3,414	$3,192	$825	$518	$115,666	$3,547	$37,109
19	$103,576	$14,022	$16,366	$59,524	$206,887	$162,715	$103,191	$5,750	$8,271	$2,372	$3,299	$3,272	$845	$518	$121,887	$3,718	$40,828
20	$97,364	$14,022	$16,631	$65,736	$214,696	$172,839	$107,103	$6,212	$7,810	$2,431	$3,175	$3,353	$866	$519	$128,121	$3,890	$44,718
21	$90,653	$14,022	$16,912	$72,447	$222,007	$183,156	$110,709	$6,711	$7,311	$2,492	$3,039	$3,437	$888	$521	$134,376	$4,063	$48,781
22	$83,403	$14,022	$17,208	$79,697	$228,778	$193,676	$113,979	$7,250	$6,772	$2,554	$2,891	$3,523	$910	$524	$140,660	$4,236	$53,016
23	$75,571	$14,022	$17,521	$87,529	$234,968	$204,409	$116,880	$7,832	$6,189	$2,618	$2,730	$3,611	$933	$527	$146,983	$4,410	$57,426
24	$67,109	$14,022	$17,851	$95,991	$240,528	$215,368	$119,377	$8,461	$5,560	$2,684	$2,556	$3,701	$956	$531	$153,357	$4,585	$62,011
25	$57,968	$14,022	$18,200	$105,132	$245,409	$226,566	$121,435	$9,141	$4,881	$2,751	$2,366	$3,794	$980	$536	$159,794	$4,762	$66,773
26	$48,094	$14,022	$18,570	$115,006	$249,556	$238,019	$123,013	$9,875	$4,147	$2,819	$2,159	$3,889	$1,005	$543	$166,306	$4,940	$71,713
27	$37,426	$14,022	$18,962	$125,674	$252,909	$249,743	$124,069	$10,668	$3,354	$2,890	$1,935	$3,986	$1,030	$550	$172,908	$5,122	$76,835
28	$25,901	$14,022	$19,377	$137,199	$255,406	$261,757	$124,558	$11,525	$2,497	$2,962	$1,692	$4,086	$1,056	$559	$179,617	$5,305	$82,140
29	$13,450	$14,022	$19,817	$149,650	$256,977	$274,082	$124,432	$12,450	$1,571	$3,036	$1,428	$4,188	$1,082	$569	$186,449	$5,492	$87,632
30	$0	$14,022	$20,284	$163,100	$257,549	$286,739	$123,639	$13,450	$571	$3,112	$1,142	$4,293	$1,109	$581	$193,424	$5,683	$93,315

* Represents the approximate amount of money which should be saved monthly

** After Tax Down Payment is the initial principal plus the after-tax value of the closing cost

Copyright © Myth Breakers - 1993

Figure 52 - Page 141

Phildelphia, PA

Using the Median Home Price and the Average Monthly Rent

HOME:

Purchase Price:	$120,700
Closing Cost:	$4,000
+Total Home Cost:	$124,700
+After-tax Cost:	$123,460
Down Payment:	$12,100
+Initial Principal:	$8,100
+Starting Loan:	$112,600
Mortgage Rate:	7.750%
Loan Length (in Yrs):	30
+Monthly Payment:	$807
Real Estate Tax:	2.640%
Add Repair/Utility Cost:	0.10%
Closing Commission Rate:	6.0%

GENERAL:

Tax Bracket:	31.0%
Savings Rate:	4.0%

RENT:

Starting Rental Amount:	$716
Monthly Rental Incr./Yr (in %):	2.5%
+Initial Monthly Savings Amt:	$170

COMPARISON (3 YRS):

+Principal Paid:	$3,209
+Interest Paid:	$25,831
+Amount Renter Can Save:	$6,976
+Amount Difference Rent/Own:	$3,767
+Appr. Required to Break Even:	$14,648
+Required Home Sales Price:	$135,348
+Yearly % Appr. to Break Even:	3.9%
+Total % Appr. to Break Even:	12.1%

COMPARISON (5 YRS):

+Principal Paid:	$5,801
+Interest Paid:	$42,599
+Amount Renter Can Save:	$11,375
+Amount Difference Rent/Own:	$5,573
+Appr. Required to Break Even:	$16,569
+Required Home Sales Price:	$137,269
+Yearly % Appr. to Break Even:	2.6%
+Total % Appr. to Break Even:	13.7%

COMPARISON (10 YRS):

+Principal Paid:	$14,338
+Interest Paid:	$82,464
+Amount Renter Can Save:	$21,272
+Amount Difference Rent/Own:	$6,934
+Appr. Required to Break Even:	$18,017
+Required Home Sales Price:	$138,717
+Yearly % Appr. to Break Even:	1.4%
+Total % Appr. to Break Even:	14.9%

Figure 53

Myth Breakers®

Yr	Current Loan	Mortgage Payment	After Tax Layout	Cumulative Principal Paid	Cumulative Interest Paid	Amount Renter Can Save	Amount Diff Rent/Own	Annual Principal Paid	Annual Interest Paid	Real Estate Tax	Income Tax Break	Repairs + Add Utils	Mthly Rent	Ave Mthly Savings Amount *	Before Int Diff Rent/Own	Int on Diff & **ATDP	
0	$112,600																
1	$111,612	$9,680	$10,633	$988	$8,692	$2,371	$1,383	$988	$8,692	$3,186	$3,682	$1,448	$716	$170	$2,041	$330	$330
2	$110,544	$9,680	$10,749	$2,056	$17,304	$4,698	$2,642	$1,068	$8,613	$3,266	$3,682	$1,485	$734	$162	$3,982	$365	$715
3	$109,391	$9,680	$10,869	$3,209	$25,831	$6,976	$3,767	$1,153	$8,527	$3,348	$3,681	$1,522	$752	$153	$5,824	$437	$1,152
4	$108,145	$9,680	$10,993	$4,455	$34,265	$9,203	$4,748	$1,246	$8,434	$3,431	$3,678	$1,560	$771	$145	$7,565	$486	$1,639
5	$106,799	$9,680	$11,122	$5,801	$42,599	$11,375	$5,573	$1,346	$8,334	$3,517	$3,674	$1,599	$790	$137	$9,203	$533	$2,172
6	$105,344	$9,680	$11,256	$7,256	$50,825	$13,487	$6,231	$1,454	$8,226	$3,605	$3,668	$1,639	$810	$128	$10,738	$577	$2,748
7	$103,773	$9,680	$11,396	$8,827	$58,934	$15,536	$6,709	$1,571	$8,109	$3,695	$3,659	$1,680	$830	$119	$12,170	$617	$3,366
8	$102,076	$9,680	$11,541	$10,524	$66,917	$17,519	$6,995	$1,697	$7,983	$3,788	$3,649	$1,722	$851	$111	$13,497	$655	$4,021
9	$100,243	$9,680	$11,691	$12,357	$74,764	$19,432	$7,074	$1,833	$7,847	$3,882	$3,636	$1,765	$872	$102	$14,720	$690	$4,712
10	$98,262	$9,680	$11,848	$14,338	$82,464	$21,272	$6,934	$1,981	$7,699	$3,979	$3,620	$1,809	$894	$93	$15,838	$723	$5,434
11	$96,122	$9,680	$12,011	$16,478	$90,004	$23,037	$6,559	$2,140	$7,540	$4,079	$3,602	$1,854	$917	$84	$16,851	$752	$6,186
12	$93,810	$9,680	$12,181	$18,790	$97,372	$24,723	$5,933	$2,312	$7,369	$4,181	$3,580	$1,900	$939	$76	$17,758	$778	$6,964
13	$91,313	$9,680	$12,358	$21,287	$104,555	$26,328	$5,041	$2,497	$7,183	$4,285	$3,555	$1,948	$963	$67	$18,562	$802	$7,766
14	$88,615	$9,680	$12,543	$23,985	$111,538	$27,849	$3,864	$2,698	$6,982	$4,393	$3,526	$1,997	$987	$58	$19,261	$822	$8,588
15	$85,701	$9,680	$12,736	$26,899	$118,303	$29,285	$2,386	$2,915	$6,766	$4,502	$3,493	$2,047	$1,012	$50	$19,856	$840	$9,428
16	$82,552	$9,680	$12,937	$30,048	$124,835	$30,633	$586	$3,149	$6,532	$4,615	$3,455	$2,098	$1,037	$41	$20,350	$855	$10,283
17	$79,151	$9,680	$13,148	$33,449	$131,113	$31,894	($1,556)	$3,402	$6,279	$4,730	$3,413	$2,150	$1,063	$33	$20,743	$867	$11,151
18	$75,476	$9,680	$13,368	$37,124	$137,119	$33,064	($4,060)	$3,675	$6,005	$4,849	$3,365	$2,204	$1,089	$25	$21,037	$876	$12,027
19	$71,506	$9,680	$13,598	$41,094	$142,829	$34,145	($6,949)	$3,970	$5,710	$4,970	$3,311	$2,259	$1,117	$16	$21,235	$883	$12,910
20	$67,217	$9,680	$13,839	$45,383	$148,221	$35,136	($10,247)	$4,289	$5,392	$5,094	$3,251	$2,315	$1,145	$9	$21,338	$887	$13,797
21	$62,584	$9,680	$14,092	$50,016	$153,268	$36,037	($13,979)	$4,633	$5,047	$5,221	$3,183	$2,373	$1,173	$1	$21,351	$889	$14,686
22	$57,579	$9,680	$14,356	$55,021	$157,943	$36,850	($18,171)	$5,005	$4,675	$5,352	$3,108	$2,433	$1,203	($6)	$21,277	$888	$15,573
23	$52,172	$9,680	$14,634	$60,428	$162,216	$37,577	($22,851)	$5,407	$4,273	$5,486	$3,025	$2,494	$1,233	($13)	$21,119	$884	$16,458
24	$46,331	$9,680	$14,926	$66,269	$166,054	$38,220	($28,050)	$5,841	$3,839	$5,623	$2,933	$2,556	$1,263	($20)	$20,883	$879	$17,337
25	$40,020	$9,680	$15,232	$72,580	$169,424	$38,783	($33,797)	$6,311	$3,370	$5,763	$2,831	$2,620	$1,295	($26)	$20,575	$871	$18,208
26	$33,203	$9,680	$15,554	$79,397	$172,287	$39,269	($40,128)	$6,817	$2,863	$5,908	$2,719	$2,685	$1,327	($31)	$20,200	$862	$19,069
27	$25,838	$9,680	$15,893	$86,762	$174,602	$39,685	($47,077)	$7,365	$2,315	$6,055	$2,595	$2,752	$1,361	($36)	$19,766	$850	$19,920
28	$17,881	$9,680	$16,250	$94,719	$176,326	$40,037	($54,682)	$7,956	$1,724	$6,207	$2,458	$2,821	$1,395	($40)	$19,280	$838	$20,757
29	$9,286	$9,680	$16,625	$103,314	$177,410	$40,332	($62,982)	$8,595	$1,085	$6,362	$2,308	$2,892	$1,429	($44)	$18,751	$823	$21,581
30	$0	$9,680	$17,021	$112,600	$177,805	$40,579	($72,021)	$9,286	$394	$6,521	$2,144	$2,964	$1,465	($47)	$18,190	$808	$22,389

* Represents the approximate amount of money which should be saved monthly
** After Tax Down Payment is the initial principal plus the after-tax value of the closing cost

Figure 54 - Page 143

Rent vs Buy Analysis for Various Metropolitan Cities

Phoenix, AZ

Using the Median Home Price and the Average Monthly Rent

HOME:

Purchase Price:	$87,200
Closing Cost:	$2,900
+Total Home Cost:	$90,100
+After-tax Cost:	$89,201
Down Payment:	$8,700
+Initial Principal:	$5,800
+Starting Loan:	$81,400

Mortgage Rate:	7.750%
Loan Length (in Yrs):	30
+Monthly Payment:	$583
Real Estate Tax:	1.470%
Add Repair/Utility Cost:	0.10%
Closing Commission Rate:	6.0%

GENERAL:

Tax Bracket:	31.0%
Savings Rate:	4.0%

RENT:

Starting Rental Amount:	$414
Monthly Rental Incr./Yr (in %):	2.5%
+Initial Monthly Savings Amt:	$168

COMPARISON (3 YRS):

+Principal Paid:	$2,320
+Interest Paid:	$18,674
+Amount Renter Can Save:	$6,762
+Amount Difference Rent/Own:	$4,442
+Appr. Required to Break Even:	$12,421
+Required Home Sales Price:	$99,621
+Yearly % Appr. to Break Even:	4.5%
+Total % Appr. to Break Even:	14.2%

COMPARISON (5 YRS):

+Principal Paid:	$4,194
+Interest Paid:	$30,796
+Amount Renter Can Save:	$11,236
+Amount Difference Rent/Own:	$7,042
+Appr. Required to Break Even:	$15,186
+Required Home Sales Price:	$102,386
+Yearly % Appr. to Break Even:	3.3%
+Total % Appr. to Break Even:	17.4%

COMPARISON (10 YRS):

+Principal Paid:	$10,365
+Interest Paid:	$59,614
+Amount Renter Can Save:	$22,192
+Amount Difference Rent/Own:	$11,827
+Appr. Required to Break Even:	$20,276
+Required Home Sales Price:	$107,476
+Yearly % Appr. to Break Even:	2.1%
+Total % Appr. to Break Even:	23.3%

Figure 55

Myth Breakers®

			Summary Information					Home Ownership					Rental Difference				
Yr	Current Loan	Mortgage Payment	After Tax Layout	Cumulative Principal Paid	Cumulative Interest Paid	Amount Renter Can Save	Amount Diff Rent/Own	Annual Principal Paid	Annual Interest Paid	Real Estate Tax	Income Tax Break	Repairs + Add Utils	Mthly Rent*	Ave Mthly Savings Amount	Before Int Diff Rent/Own	Int on Diff	& **ATDP
0	$81,400																
1	$80,686	$6,998	$6,981	$714	$6,283	$2,258	$1,544	$714	$6,283	$1,282	$2,345	$1,046	$414	$168	$2,013	$245	$245
2	$79,914	$6,998	$7,047	$1,486	$12,510	$4,513	$3,027	$772	$6,226	$1,314	$2,337	$1,073	$424	$163	$3,968	$300	$545
3	$79,080	$6,998	$7,116	$2,320	$18,674	$6,762	$4,442	$834	$6,164	$1,347	$2,328	$1,099	$435	$158	$5,864	$353	$899
4	$78,179	$6,998	$7,187	$3,221	$24,771	$9,004	$5,783	$901	$6,097	$1,380	$2,318	$1,127	$446	$153	$7,701	$405	$1,303
5	$77,206	$6,998	$7,262	$4,194	$30,796	$11,236	$7,042	$973	$6,025	$1,415	$2,306	$1,155	$457	$148	$9,479	$454	$1,757
6	$76,155	$6,998	$7,339	$5,245	$36,742	$13,457	$8,212	$1,051	$5,947	$1,450	$2,293	$1,184	$468	$143	$11,197	$503	$2,260
7	$75,019	$6,998	$7,420	$6,381	$42,604	$15,665	$9,284	$1,136	$5,862	$1,487	$2,278	$1,214	$480	$138	$12,855	$549	$2,809
8	$73,792	$6,998	$7,504	$7,608	$48,376	$17,857	$10,249	$1,227	$5,771	$1,524	$2,261	$1,244	$492	$133	$14,454	$594	$3,403
9	$72,467	$6,998	$7,592	$8,933	$54,048	$20,033	$11,100	$1,325	$5,672	$1,562	$2,243	$1,275	$504	$128	$15,993	$637	$4,040
10	$71,035	$6,998	$7,684	$10,365	$59,614	$22,192	$11,827	$1,432	$5,566	$1,601	$2,222	$1,307	$517	$123	$17,473	$679	$4,719
11	$69,488	$6,998	$7,780	$11,912	$65,065	$24,331	$12,419	$1,547	$5,451	$1,641	$2,198	$1,339	$530	$118	$18,893	$719	$5,438
12	$67,817	$6,998	$7,880	$13,583	$70,392	$26,449	$12,866	$1,671	$5,327	$1,682	$2,173	$1,373	$543	$113	$20,255	$757	$6,195
13	$66,011	$6,998	$7,985	$15,389	$75,584	$28,547	$13,158	$1,805	$5,193	$1,724	$2,144	$1,407	$557	$108	$21,558	$794	$6,988
14	$64,061	$6,998	$8,095	$17,339	$80,632	$30,622	$13,283	$1,950	$5,048	$1,767	$2,113	$1,442	$571	$104	$22,805	$829	$7,817
15	$61,954	$6,998	$8,210	$19,446	$85,523	$32,675	$13,229	$2,107	$4,891	$1,811	$2,078	$1,479	$585	$99	$23,995	$862	$8,680
16	$59,678	$6,998	$8,331	$21,722	$90,245	$34,705	$12,983	$2,276	$4,722	$1,856	$2,039	$1,515	$600	$95	$25,131	$894	$9,574
17	$57,219	$6,998	$8,457	$24,181	$94,784	$36,712	$12,531	$2,459	$4,539	$1,903	$1,997	$1,553	$615	$90	$26,213	$925	$10,499
18	$54,562	$6,998	$8,590	$26,838	$99,125	$38,697	$11,859	$2,656	$4,341	$1,950	$1,950	$1,592	$630	$86	$27,243	$954	$11,453
19	$51,693	$6,998	$8,730	$29,707	$103,253	$40,660	$10,952	$2,870	$4,128	$1,999	$1,899	$1,632	$646	$82	$28,225	$982	$12,435
20	$48,592	$6,998	$8,876	$32,808	$107,151	$42,602	$9,794	$3,100	$3,898	$2,049	$1,844	$1,673	$662	$78	$29,159	$1,008	$13,443
21	$45,243	$6,998	$9,031	$36,157	$110,799	$44,525	$8,368	$3,349	$3,649	$2,100	$1,782	$1,715	$678	$74	$30,049	$1,033	$14,476
22	$41,625	$6,998	$9,193	$39,775	$114,179	$46,432	$6,656	$3,618	$3,380	$2,153	$1,715	$1,758	$695	$71	$30,898	$1,057	$15,533
23	$37,716	$6,998	$9,364	$43,684	$117,268	$48,323	$4,639	$3,909	$3,089	$2,207	$1,642	$1,801	$713	$68	$31,710	$1,080	$16,613
24	$33,493	$6,998	$9,545	$47,907	$120,043	$50,204	$2,297	$4,223	$2,775	$2,262	$1,561	$1,846	$731	$65	$32,488	$1,102	$17,715
25	$28,931	$6,998	$9,735	$52,469	$122,479	$52,076	($393)	$4,562	$2,436	$2,318	$1,474	$1,893	$749	$62	$33,238	$1,123	$18,838
26	$24,003	$6,998	$9,936	$57,397	$124,548	$53,945	($3,452)	$4,928	$2,070	$2,376	$1,378	$1,940	$768	$60	$33,964	$1,143	$19,981
27	$18,678	$6,998	$10,148	$62,722	$126,222	$55,816	($6,906)	$5,324	$1,674	$2,436	$1,274	$1,988	$787	$59	$34,671	$1,163	$21,144
28	$12,927	$6,998	$10,373	$68,473	$127,468	$57,694	($10,780)	$5,752	$1,246	$2,497	$1,160	$2,038	$806	$58	$35,367	$1,182	$22,327
29	$6,713	$6,998	$10,610	$74,687	$128,252	$59,586	($15,101)	$6,214	$784	$2,559	$1,036	$2,089	$827	$58	$36,058	$1,201	$23,528
30	$0	$6,998	$10,861	$81,400	$128,537	$61,501	($19,899)	$6,713	$285	$2,623	$902	$2,141	$847	$58	$36,753	$1,221	$24,749

* Represents the approximate amount of money which should be saved monthly
** After Tax Down Payment is the initial principal plus the after-tax value of the closing cost

Figure 56 - Page 145

Portland, OR

Using the Median Home Price and the Average Monthly Rent

HOME:

Purchase Price:	$97,400
Closing Cost:	$3,200
+Total Home Cost:	$100,600
+After-tax Cost:	$99,608
Down Payment:	$9,700
+Initial Principal:	$6,500
+Starting Loan:	$90,900
Mortgage Rate:	7.750%
Loan Length (in Yrs):	30
+Monthly Payment:	$651
Real Estate Tax:	2.640%
Add Repair/Utility Cost:	0.10%
Closing Commission Rate:	6.0%

GENERAL:

Tax Bracket:	31.0%
Savings Rate:	4.0%

RENT:

Starting Rental Amount:	$538
Monthly Rental Incr./Yr (in %):	2.5%
+Initial Monthly Savings Amt:	$177

COMPARISON (3 YRS):

+Principal Paid:	$2,591
+Interest Paid:	$20,853
+Amount Renter Can Save:	$7,162
+Amount Difference Rent/Own:	$4,571
+Appr. Required to Break Even:	$13,429
+Required Home Sales Price:	$110,829
+Yearly % Appr. to Break Even:	4.4%
+Total % Appr. to Break Even:	13.8%

COMPARISON (5 YRS):

+Principal Paid:	$4,683
+Interest Paid:	$34,390
+Amount Renter Can Save:	$11,865
+Amount Difference Rent/Own:	$7,182
+Appr. Required to Break Even:	$16,206
+Required Home Sales Price:	$113,606
+Yearly % Appr. to Break Even:	3.1%
+Total % Appr. to Break Even:	16.6%

COMPARISON (10 YRS):

+Principal Paid:	$11,575
+Interest Paid:	$66,571
+Amount Renter Can Save:	$23,239
+Amount Difference Rent/Own:	$11,664
+Appr. Required to Break Even:	$20,975
+Required Home Sales Price:	$118,375
+Yearly % Appr. to Break Even:	2.0%
+Total % Appr. to Break Even:	21.5%

Figure 57

Myth Breakers®

Summary Information / Home Ownership / Rental Difference

Yr	Current Loan	Mortgage Payment	After Tax Layout	Cumulative Principal Paid	Cumulative Interest Paid	Amount Diff Rent/Own	Amount Renter Can Save	Annual Principal Paid	Annual Interest Paid	Real Estate Tax	Income Tax Break	Repairs + Add Utils	Mthly Rent	Ave Mnthly Savings Amount	Before Int Diff Rent/Own	Int on Diff & **ATDP	
0	$90,900																
1	$90,102	$7,815	$8,582	$798	$7,017	$1,601	$2,399	$798	$7,017	$2,571	$2,972	$1,169	$538	$177	$2,126	$272	$272
2	$89,240	$7,815	$8,676	$1,660	$13,970	$3,127	$4,787	$862	$6,953	$2,636	$2,972	$1,198	$551	$172	$4,185	$330	$602
3	$88,309	$7,815	$8,773	$2,591	$20,853	$4,571	$7,162	$931	$6,884	$2,702	$2,971	$1,228	$565	$166	$6,175	$386	$987
4	$87,303	$7,815	$8,873	$3,597	$27,662	$5,926	$9,523	$1,006	$6,809	$2,769	$2,969	$1,259	$579	$160	$8,096	$439	$1,427
5	$86,217	$7,815	$8,978	$4,683	$34,390	$7,182	$11,865	$1,087	$6,728	$2,838	$2,966	$1,290	$594	$154	$9,947	$491	$1,918
6	$85,043	$7,815	$9,086	$5,857	$41,030	$8,331	$14,188	$1,174	$6,641	$2,909	$2,960	$1,322	$609	$148	$11,728	$541	$2,460
7	$83,774	$7,815	$9,198	$7,126	$47,577	$9,363	$16,489	$1,268	$6,546	$2,982	$2,954	$1,355	$624	$143	$13,440	$590	$3,049
8	$82,404	$7,815	$9,315	$8,496	$54,021	$10,270	$18,766	$1,370	$6,445	$3,057	$2,945	$1,389	$640	$137	$15,081	$636	$3,685
9	$80,924	$7,815	$9,437	$9,976	$60,356	$11,041	$21,016	$1,480	$6,334	$3,133	$2,935	$1,424	$656	$131	$16,651	$680	$4,365
10	$79,325	$7,815	$9,563	$11,575	$66,571	$11,664	$23,239	$1,599	$6,216	$3,211	$2,922	$1,460	$672	$125	$18,152	$722	$5,087
11	$77,598	$7,815	$9,695	$13,302	$72,659	$12,130	$25,433	$1,727	$6,087	$3,292	$2,907	$1,496	$689	$119	$19,583	$763	$5,850
12	$75,732	$7,815	$9,832	$15,168	$78,607	$12,427	$27,595	$1,866	$5,948	$3,374	$2,890	$1,534	$706	$113	$20,944	$801	$6,651
13	$73,716	$7,815	$9,975	$17,184	$84,406	$12,541	$29,725	$2,016	$5,799	$3,458	$2,870	$1,572	$724	$108	$22,237	$838	$7,489
14	$71,538	$7,815	$10,124	$19,362	$90,042	$12,460	$31,822	$2,178	$5,637	$3,545	$2,846	$1,611	$742	$102	$23,461	$872	$8,361
15	$69,185	$7,815	$10,280	$21,715	$95,504	$12,169	$33,885	$2,353	$5,462	$3,633	$2,819	$1,651	$760	$96	$24,619	$905	$9,266
16	$66,643	$7,815	$10,442	$24,257	$100,777	$11,656	$35,913	$2,542	$5,273	$3,724	$2,789	$1,693	$779	$91	$25,711	$936	$10,202
17	$63,897	$7,815	$10,612	$27,003	$105,845	$10,903	$37,907	$2,746	$5,069	$3,817	$2,755	$1,735	$799	$86	$26,740	$965	$11,167
18	$60,930	$7,815	$10,790	$29,970	$110,694	$9,896	$39,866	$2,967	$4,848	$3,913	$2,716	$1,778	$819	$81	$27,706	$993	$12,160
19	$57,726	$7,815	$10,976	$33,174	$115,303	$8,616	$41,790	$3,205	$4,610	$4,010	$2,672	$1,823	$839	$76	$28,612	$1,018	$13,178
20	$54,263	$7,815	$11,170	$36,637	$119,856	$7,046	$43,682	$3,462	$4,352	$4,111	$2,624	$1,869	$860	$71	$29,462	$1,043	$14,221
21	$50,523	$7,815	$11,374	$40,377	$123,730	$5,166	$45,543	$3,740	$4,074	$4,213	$2,569	$1,915	$882	$66	$30,257	$1,065	$15,286
22	$46,483	$7,815	$11,588	$44,417	$127,504	$2,956	$47,373	$4,041	$3,774	$4,319	$2,509	$1,963	$904	$62	$31,001	$1,086	$16,372
23	$42,117	$7,815	$11,812	$48,783	$130,954	$395	$49,177	$4,365	$3,450	$4,427	$2,442	$2,012	$926	$58	$31,699	$1,106	$17,478
24	$37,402	$7,815	$12,047	$53,498	$134,053	($2,541)	$50,957	$4,716	$3,099	$4,537	$2,367	$2,062	$949	$55	$32,354	$1,125	$18,603
25	$32,307	$7,815	$12,295	$58,593	$136,773	($5,876)	$52,716	$5,094	$2,720	$4,651	$2,285	$2,114	$973	$51	$32,971	$1,142	$19,745
26	$26,804	$7,815	$12,554	$64,096	$139,084	($9,636)	$54,461	$5,504	$2,311	$4,767	$2,194	$2,167	$997	$49	$33,556	$1,159	$20,904
27	$20,858	$7,815	$12,828	$70,042	$140,953	($13,847)	$56,195	$5,946	$1,869	$4,886	$2,094	$2,221	$1,022	$47	$34,116	$1,175	$22,079
28	$14,435	$7,815	$13,116	$76,465	$142,345	($18,540)	$57,925	$6,423	$1,388	$5,008	$1,984	$2,277	$1,048	$45	$34,657	$1,190	$23,268
29	$7,496	$7,815	$13,419	$83,404	$143,220	($23,745)	$59,659	$6,939	$876	$5,134	$1,863	$2,334	$1,074	$44	$35,186	$1,204	$24,473
30	$0	$7,815	$13,739	$90,900	$143,539	($29,495)	$61,405	$7,496	$318	$5,262	$1,730	$2,392	$1,101	$44	$35,713	$1,219	$25,692

* Represents the approximate amount of money which should be saved monthly
** After Tax Down Payment is the initial principal plus the after-tax value of the closing cost

Figure 58 - Page 147

Rent vs Buy Analysis for Various Metropolitan Cities

St. Louis, MO

Using the Median Home Price and the Average Monthly Rent

HOME:

Purchase Price:	$81,700
Closing Cost:	$2,700
+Total Home Cost:	$84,400
+After-tax Cost:	$83,563
Down Payment:	$8,200
+Initial Principal:	$5,500
+Starting Loan:	$76,200
Mortgage Rate:	7.750%
Loan Length (in Yrs):	30
+Monthly Payment:	$546
Real Estate Tax:	1.150%
Add Repair/Utility Cost:	0.10%
Closing Commission Rate:	6.0%

GENERAL:

Tax Bracket:	31.0%
Savings Rate:	4.0%

RENT:

Starting Rental Amount:	$529
Monthly Rental Incr./Yr (in %):	2.5%
+Initial Monthly Savings Amt:	$1

COMPARISON (3 YRS):

+Principal Paid:	$2,172
+Interest Paid:	$17,481
+Amount Renter Can Save:	$322
+Amount Difference Rent/Own:	($1,850)
+Appr. Required to Break Even:	$5,229
+Required Home Sales Price:	$86,929
+Yearly % Appr. to Break Even:	2.1%
+Total % Appr. to Break Even:	6.4%

COMPARISON (5 YRS):

+Principal Paid:	$3,926
+Interest Paid:	$28,828
+Amount Renter Can Save:	($14)
+Amount Difference Rent/Own:	($3,940)
+Appr. Required to Break Even:	$3,006
+Required Home Sales Price:	$84,706
+Yearly % Appr. to Break Even:	0.7%
+Total % Appr. to Break Even:	3.7%

COMPARISON (10 YRS):

+Principal Paid:	$9,703
+Interest Paid:	$55,806
+Amount Renter Can Save:	($3,036)
+Amount Difference Rent/Own:	($12,739)
+Appr. Required to Break Even:	($6,355)
+Required Home Sales Price:	$75,345
+Yearly % Appr. to Break Even:	-0.8%
+Total % Appr. to Break Even:	-7.8%

Figure 59

Myth Breakers

Year	Current Loan	Mortgage Payment	After Tax Layout	Cumulative Principal Paid	Interest Paid	Amount Renter Can Save	Amount Diff Rent/Own	Annual Principal Paid	Annual Interest Paid	Real Estate Tax	Income Tax Break	Repairs + Add Utils	Mthly Rent	Ave Mthly Savings Amount	Before Int Diff Rent/Own	Int on Diff	**ATDP
		Summary Information						Home Ownership						Rental Difference			
Yr 0	$76,200																
Yr 1	$75,531	$6,551	$6,356	$669	$5,882	$211	($457)	$669	$5,882	$940	$2,115	$980	$529	$1	$8	$203	$203
Yr 2	$74,809	$6,551	$6,413	$1,391	$11,710	$320	($1,071)	$723	$5,828	$963	$2,105	$1,005	$542	($8)	($85)	$202	$405
Yr 3	$74,028	$6,551	$6,473	$2,172	$17,481	$322	($1,850)	$781	$5,770	$987	$2,095	$1,030	$556	($16)	($281)	$198	$603
Yr 4	$73,185	$6,551	$6,535	$3,015	$23,188	$212	($2,803)	$843	$5,708	$1,012	$2,083	$1,056	$570	($25)	($582)	$191	$794
Yr 5	$72,274	$6,551	$6,600	$3,926	$28,828	($14)	($3,940)	$911	$5,640	$1,037	$2,070	$1,082	$584	($34)	($989)	$181	$975
Yr 6	$71,290	$6,551	$6,668	$4,910	$34,395	($360)	($5,270)	$984	$5,567	$1,063	$2,055	$1,109	$599	($43)	($1,503)	$168	$1,143
Yr 7	$70,227	$6,551	$6,738	$5,973	$39,883	($831)	($6,804)	$1,063	$5,488	$1,090	$2,039	$1,137	$613	($52)	($2,126)	$152	$1,296
Yr 8	$69,078	$6,551	$6,812	$7,122	$45,285	($1,431)	($8,552)	$1,149	$5,402	$1,117	$2,021	$1,165	$629	($61)	($2,860)	$134	$1,429
Yr 9	$67,837	$6,551	$6,889	$8,363	$50,595	($2,164)	($10,527)	$1,241	$5,310	$1,145	$2,001	$1,195	$645	($70)	($3,705)	$112	$1,541
Yr 10	$66,497	$6,551	$6,970	$9,703	$55,806	($3,036)	($12,739)	$1,340	$5,210	$1,173	$1,979	$1,224	$661	($80)	($4,663)	$87	$1,627
Yr 11	$65,049	$6,551	$7,054	$11,151	$60,909	($4,050)	($15,201)	$1,448	$5,103	$1,203	$1,955	$1,255	$677	($89)	($5,735)	$58	$1,686
Yr 12	$63,485	$6,551	$7,142	$12,715	$65,895	($5,210)	($17,925)	$1,564	$4,986	$1,233	$1,928	$1,286	$694	($99)	($6,922)	$27	$1,713
Yr 13	$61,795	$6,551	$7,234	$14,405	$70,756	($6,520)	($20,925)	$1,690	$4,861	$1,264	$1,899	$1,319	$711	($109)	($8,225)	($7)	$1,705
Yr 14	$59,969	$6,551	$7,331	$16,231	$75,481	($7,985)	($24,216)	$1,826	$4,725	$1,295	$1,866	$1,351	$729	($118)	($9,645)	($45)	$1,660
Yr 15	$57,996	$6,551	$7,433	$18,204	$80,060	($9,607)	($27,811)	$1,972	$4,578	$1,328	$1,831	$1,385	$747	($128)	($11,182)	($86)	$1,574
Yr 16	$55,866	$6,551	$7,539	$20,334	$84,480	($11,392)	($31,726)	$2,131	$4,420	$1,361	$1,792	$1,420	$766	($138)	($12,836)	($130)	$1,444
Yr 17	$53,564	$6,551	$7,651	$22,636	$88,729	($13,342)	($35,978)	$2,302	$4,249	$1,395	$1,750	$1,455	$785	($148)	($14,608)	($178)	$1,266
Yr 18	$51,077	$6,551	$7,769	$25,123	$92,793	($15,460)	($40,583)	$2,487	$4,064	$1,430	$1,703	$1,492	$805	($157)	($16,498)	($228)	$1,038
Yr 19	$48,390	$6,551	$7,893	$27,810	$96,657	($17,750)	($45,560)	$2,687	$3,864	$1,465	$1,652	$1,529	$825	($167)	($18,506)	($282)	$756
Yr 20	$45,488	$6,551	$8,024	$30,712	$100,306	($20,214)	($50,926)	$2,902	$3,649	$1,502	$1,597	$1,567	$846	($177)	($20,630)	($339)	$416
Yr 21	$42,353	$6,551	$8,161	$33,847	$103,721	($22,855)	($56,702)	$3,135	$3,416	$1,540	$1,536	$1,606	$867	($187)	($22,872)	($400)	$16
Yr 22	$38,966	$6,551	$8,306	$37,234	$106,885	($25,675)	($62,909)	$3,387	$3,164	$1,578	$1,470	$1,647	$888	($196)	($25,228)	($463)	($447)
Yr 23	$35,306	$6,551	$8,458	$40,894	$109,777	($28,675)	($69,569)	$3,659	$2,892	$1,618	$1,398	$1,688	$911	($206)	($27,698)	($530)	($977)
Yr 24	$31,353	$6,551	$8,620	$44,847	$112,374	($31,858)	($76,704)	$3,953	$2,598	$1,658	$1,319	$1,730	$933	($215)	($30,280)	($600)	($1,577)
Yr 25	$27,083	$6,551	$8,790	$49,117	$114,655	($35,223)	($84,340)	$4,271	$2,280	$1,699	$1,234	$1,773	$957	($224)	($32,972)	($673)	($2,250)
Yr 26	$22,469	$6,551	$8,970	$53,731	$116,592	($38,770)	($92,501)	$4,614	$1,937	$1,742	$1,141	$1,818	$981	($233)	($35,771)	($749)	($2,999)
Yr 27	$17,485	$6,551	$9,160	$58,715	$118,159	($42,501)	($101,216)	$4,984	$1,567	$1,785	$1,039	$1,863	$1,005	($242)	($38,674)	($828)	($3,827)
Yr 28	$12,101	$6,551	$9,362	$64,099	$119,325	($46,414)	($110,513)	$5,384	$1,167	$1,830	$929	$1,910	$1,030	($250)	($41,677)	($909)	($4,736)
Yr 29	$6,284	$6,551	$9,575	$69,916	$120,059	($50,506)	($120,422)	$5,817	$734	$1,876	$809	$1,957	$1,056	($258)	($44,776)	($994)	($5,730)
Yr 30	$0	$6,551	$9,801	$76,200	$120,326	($54,776)	($130,976)	$6,284	$267	$1,923	$679	$2,006	$1,083	($266)	($47,965)	($1,081)	($6,811)

* Represents the approximate amount of money which should be saved monthly

** After Tax Down Payment is the initial principal plus the after-tax value of the closing cost

Copyright © Myth Breakers - 1993

Figure 60 - Page 149

Rent vs Buy Analysis for Various Metropolitan Cities

San Francisco (Bay Area), CA

Using the Median Home Price and the Average Monthly Rent

HOME:

Purchase Price:	$262,000
Closing Cost:	$8,000
+Total Home Cost:	$270,000

+After-tax Cost:	$267,520
Down Payment:	$26,200
+Initial Principal:	$18,200
+Starting Loan:	$243,800

Mortgage Rate:	8.250%
Loan Length (in Yrs):	30
+Monthly Payment:	$1,832

Real Estate Tax:	1.250%
Add Repair/Utility Cost:	0.10%
Closing Commission Rate:	6.0%

GENERAL:

Tax Bracket:	31.0%
Savings Rate:	4.0%

RENT:

Starting Rental Amount:	$785
Monthly Rental Incr./Yr (in %):	2.5%
+Initial Monthly Savings Amt:	$979

COMPARISON (3 YRS):

+Principal Paid:	$6,326
+Interest Paid:	$59,612
+Amount Renter Can Save:	$38,565
+Amount Difference Rent/Own:	$32,240
+Appr. Required to Break Even:	$56,893
+Required Home Sales Price:	$318,893
+Yearly % Appr. to Break Even:	6.8%
+Total % Appr. to Break Even:	21.7%

COMPARISON (5 YRS):

+Principal Paid:	$11,498
+Interest Paid:	$98,398
+Amount Renter Can Save:	$65,655
+Amount Difference Rent/Own:	$54,157
+Appr. Required to Break Even:	$80,210
+Required Home Sales Price:	$342,210
+Yearly % Appr. to Break Even:	5.5%
+Total % Appr. to Break Even:	30.6%

COMPARISON (10 YRS):

+Principal Paid:	$28,841
+Interest Paid:	$190,949
+Amount Renter Can Save:	$138,319
+Amount Difference Rent/Own:	$109,477
+Appr. Required to Break Even:	$139,061
+Required Home Sales Price:	$401,061
+Yearly % Appr. to Break Even:	4.3%
+Total % Appr. to Break Even:	53.1%

Figure 61

Myth Breakers®

			Summary Information					Home Ownership						Rental Difference			
Yr	Current Loan	Mortgage Payment	After Tax Layout	Cumulative Principal Paid	Cumulative Interest Paid	Amount Renter Can Save	Amount Diff Rent/Own	Annual Principal Paid	Annual Interest Paid	Real Estate Tax	Income Tax Break	Repairs + Add Utils	Mthly Rent	Ave Mthly Savings Amount	Before Int Diff Rent/Own	Int on Diff & **ATDP	Int on Diff & **ATDP (cum)
0	$243,800																
1	$241,862	$21,979	$21,170	$1,938	$20,041	$12,580	$10,642	$1,938	$20,041	$3,275	$7,228	$3,144	$785	$979	$11,750	$830	$830
2	$239,758	$21,979	$21,357	$4,042	$39,917	$25,435	$21,394	$2,104	$19,875	$3,357	$7,202	$3,223	$805	$975	$23,451	$1,154	$1,984
3	$237,474	$21,979	$21,551	$6,326	$59,612	$38,565	$32,240	$2,284	$19,695	$3,441	$7,172	$3,303	$825	$971	$35,105	$1,476	$3,460
4	$234,995	$21,979	$21,754	$8,805	$79,111	$51,971	$43,166	$2,480	$19,499	$3,527	$7,138	$3,386	$845	$967	$46,714	$1,797	$5,257
5	$232,302	$21,979	$21,965	$11,498	$98,398	$65,655	$54,157	$2,692	$19,287	$3,615	$7,100	$3,470	$866	$964	$58,281	$2,117	$7,374
6	$229,379	$21,979	$22,186	$14,421	$117,454	$79,618	$65,197	$2,923	$19,056	$3,705	$7,056	$3,557	$888	$961	$69,809	$2,435	$9,809
7	$226,206	$21,979	$22,416	$17,594	$136,259	$93,863	$76,269	$3,173	$18,806	$3,798	$7,007	$3,646	$910	$958	$81,301	$2,753	$12,562
8	$222,760	$21,979	$22,657	$21,040	$154,793	$108,392	$87,353	$3,445	$18,534	$3,893	$6,952	$3,737	$933	$955	$92,760	$3,070	$15,632
9	$219,020	$21,979	$22,909	$24,780	$173,031	$123,209	$98,429	$3,741	$18,238	$3,990	$6,891	$3,831	$956	$953	$104,192	$3,386	$19,017
10	$214,959	$21,979	$23,173	$28,841	$190,949	$138,319	$109,477	$4,061	$17,918	$4,090	$6,822	$3,926	$980	$951	$115,601	$3,701	$22,718
11	$210,549	$21,979	$23,450	$33,251	$208,519	$153,725	$120,475	$4,409	$17,570	$4,192	$6,746	$4,025	$1,005	$949	$126,992	$4,015	$26,733
12	$205,762	$21,979	$23,740	$38,038	$225,711	$169,435	$131,397	$4,787	$17,192	$4,297	$6,662	$4,125	$1,030	$948	$138,372	$4,330	$31,063
13	$200,565	$21,979	$24,044	$43,235	$242,493	$185,454	$142,219	$5,197	$16,782	$4,405	$6,568	$4,228	$1,056	$948	$149,747	$4,643	$35,706
14	$194,922	$21,979	$24,364	$48,878	$258,829	$201,789	$152,912	$5,643	$16,336	$4,515	$6,464	$4,334	$1,082	$948	$161,126	$4,957	$40,664
15	$188,796	$21,979	$24,700	$55,004	$274,682	$218,451	$163,447	$6,126	$15,853	$4,627	$6,349	$4,442	$1,109	$949	$172,515	$5,272	$45,936
16	$182,145	$21,979	$25,054	$61,655	$290,010	$235,448	$173,793	$6,651	$15,328	$4,743	$6,222	$4,553	$1,137	$951	$183,926	$5,586	$51,522
17	$174,924	$21,979	$25,426	$68,876	$304,768	$252,791	$183,915	$7,221	$14,758	$4,862	$6,082	$4,667	$1,165	$953	$195,368	$5,902	$57,423
18	$167,084	$21,979	$25,818	$76,716	$318,907	$270,494	$193,778	$7,840	$14,139	$4,983	$5,928	$4,784	$1,194	$957	$206,853	$6,218	$63,642
19	$158,572	$21,979	$26,232	$85,228	$332,374	$288,570	$203,343	$8,512	$13,467	$5,108	$5,758	$4,904	$1,224	$962	$218,003	$6,536	$70,177
20	$149,331	$21,979	$26,669	$94,469	$345,112	$307,035	$212,567	$9,241	$12,738	$5,236	$5,572	$5,026	$1,255	$967	$230,003	$6,855	$77,033
21	$139,298	$21,979	$27,130	$104,502	$357,059	$325,907	$221,405	$10,033	$11,946	$5,366	$5,367	$5,152	$1,286	$975	$241,697	$7,177	$84,210
22	$128,406	$21,979	$27,618	$115,394	$368,145	$345,205	$229,810	$10,893	$11,086	$5,501	$5,142	$5,281	$1,318	$983	$253,494	$7,501	$91,711
23	$116,580	$21,979	$28,135	$127,220	$378,298	$364,951	$237,730	$11,826	$10,153	$5,638	$4,895	$5,413	$1,351	$993	$265,411	$7,829	$99,540
24	$103,740	$21,979	$28,681	$140,060	$387,437	$385,169	$245,109	$12,840	$9,140	$5,779	$4,625	$5,548	$1,385	$1,005	$277,470	$8,160	$107,699
25	$89,800	$21,979	$29,261	$154,000	$395,477	$405,886	$251,887	$13,940	$8,039	$5,924	$4,328	$5,687	$1,420	$1,019	$289,693	$8,495	$116,194
26	$74,666	$21,979	$29,875	$169,134	$402,321	$427,133	$257,998	$15,134	$6,845	$6,072	$4,004	$5,829	$1,455	$1,034	$302,104	$8,835	$125,029
27	$58,235	$21,979	$30,528	$185,565	$407,869	$448,940	$263,375	$16,431	$5,548	$6,223	$3,649	$5,975	$1,492	$1,052	$314,731	$9,181	$134,209
28	$40,395	$21,979	$31,221	$203,405	$412,009	$471,346	$267,941	$17,839	$4,140	$6,379	$3,261	$6,124	$1,529	$1,073	$327,604	$9,533	$143,742
29	$21,028	$21,979	$31,958	$222,772	$414,620	$494,389	$271,617	$19,368	$2,611	$6,539	$2,836	$6,277	$1,567	$1,096	$340,755	$9,892	$153,634
30	$0	$21,979	$32,742	$243,800	$415,572	$518,114	$274,314	$21,028	$951	$6,702	$2,373	$6,434	$1,606	$1,122	$354,220	$10,260	$163,894

* Represents the approximate amount of money which should be saved monthly

** After Tax Down Payment is the initial principal plus the after-tax value of the closing cost

Copyright © Myth Breakers - 1993

Figure 62 - Page 151

Rent vs Buy Analysis for Various Metropolitan Cities

Seattle, WA

Using the Median Home Price and the Average Monthly Rent

HOME:

Purchase Price:	$145,900
Closing Cost:	$4,900
+Total Home Cost:	$150,800
+After-tax Cost:	$149,281
Down Payment:	$14,600
+Initial Principal:	$9,700
+Starting Loan:	$136,200
Mortgage Rate:	7.750%
Loan Length (in Yrs):	30
+Monthly Payment:	$976
Real Estate Tax:	1.050%
Add Repair/Utility Cost:	0.10%
Closing Commission Rate:	6.0%

GENERAL:

Tax Bracket:	31.0%
Savings Rate:	4.0%

RENT:

Starting Rental Amount:	$517
Monthly Rental Incr./Yr (in %):	2.5%
+Initial Monthly Savings Amt:	$421

COMPARISON (3 YRS):

+Principal Paid:	$3,882
+Interest Paid:	$31,245
+Amount Renter Can Save:	$16,720
+Amount Difference Rent/Own:	$12,838
+Appr. Required to Break Even:	$26,567
+Required Home Sales Price:	$172,467
+Yearly % Appr. to Break Even:	5.7%
+Total % Appr. to Break Even:	18.2%

COMPARISON (5 YRS):

+Principal Paid:	$7,017
+Interest Paid:	$51,528
+Amount Renter Can Save:	$28,274
+Amount Difference Rent/Own:	$21,257
+Appr. Required to Break Even:	$35,523
+Required Home Sales Price:	$181,423
+Yearly % Appr. to Break Even:	4.5%
+Total % Appr. to Break Even:	24.3%

COMPARISON (10 YRS):

+Principal Paid:	$17,343
+Interest Paid:	$99,747
+Amount Renter Can Save:	$58,546
+Amount Difference Rent/Own:	$41,203
+Appr. Required to Break Even:	$56,742
+Required Home Sales Price:	$202,642
+Yearly % Appr. to Break Even:	3.3%
+Total % Appr. to Break Even:	38.9%

Figure 63

Myth Breakers

	Current Loan	Mortgage Payment	After Tax Layout	Cumulative Principal Paid	Cumulative Interest Paid	Amount Renter Can Save	Amount Diff Rent/Own	Annual Principal Paid	Annual Interest Paid	Real Estate Tax	Income Tax Break	Repairs + Add Utils	Mthly Rent	Ave Mthly Savings Amount	Before Int Diff Rent/Own	Int on Diff & **ATDP	
			Summary Information							**Home Ownership**					**Rental Difference**		
Yr 0	$136,200																
Yr 1	$135,005	$11,709	$11,258	$1,195	$10,514	$5,490	$4,295	$1,195	$10,514	$1,532	$3,734	$1,751	$517	$421	$5,054	$437	$437
Yr 2	$133,713	$11,709	$11,358	$2,487	$20,931	$11,064	$8,577	$1,291	$10,314	$1,570	$3,716	$1,795	$530	$417	$10,052	$575	$1,012
Yr 3	$132,318	$11,709	$11,462	$3,882	$31,245	$16,720	$12,838	$1,395	$10,314	$1,610	$3,696	$1,839	$543	$412	$14,996	$712	$1,724
Yr 4	$130,811	$11,709	$11,570	$5,389	$41,447	$22,457	$17,068	$1,507	$10,202	$1,650	$3,674	$1,885	$557	$407	$19,885	$848	$2,572
Yr 5	$129,183	$11,709	$11,683	$7,017	$51,528	$28,274	$21,257	$1,628	$10,081	$1,691	$3,649	$1,933	$571	$403	$24,720	$982	$3,554
Yr 6	$127,424	$11,709	$11,801	$8,776	$61,478	$34,171	$25,395	$1,759	$9,950	$1,733	$3,622	$1,981	$585	$399	$29,502	$1,115	$4,669
Yr 7	$125,523	$11,709	$11,925	$10,677	$71,287	$40,147	$29,470	$1,900	$9,809	$1,777	$3,591	$2,030	$600	$394	$34,232	$1,246	$5,915
Yr 8	$123,470	$11,709	$12,053	$12,730	$80,943	$46,201	$33,472	$2,053	$9,656	$1,821	$3,558	$2,081	$615	$390	$38,911	$1,376	$7,290
Yr 9	$121,253	$11,709	$12,188	$14,947	$90,434	$52,334	$37,387	$2,218	$9,491	$1,867	$3,521	$2,133	$630	$386	$43,540	$1,504	$8,794
Yr 10	$118,857	$11,709	$12,329	$17,343	$99,747	$58,546	$41,203	$2,396	$9,313	$1,913	$3,480	$2,187	$646	$382	$48,120	$1,631	$10,425
Yr 11	$116,269	$11,709	$12,476	$19,931	$108,868	$64,837	$44,905	$2,588	$9,121	$1,961	$3,435	$2,241	$662	$378	$52,655	$1,757	$12,182
Yr 12	$113,472	$11,709	$12,630	$22,728	$117,781	$71,208	$48,480	$2,796	$8,913	$2,010	$3,386	$2,297	$678	$374	$57,145	$1,881	$14,064
Yr 13	$110,452	$11,709	$12,792	$25,748	$126,469	$77,661	$51,913	$3,021	$8,688	$2,060	$3,332	$2,355	$695	$371	$61,593	$2,005	$16,068
Yr 14	$107,188	$11,709	$12,962	$29,012	$134,915	$84,197	$55,185	$3,263	$8,446	$2,112	$3,273	$2,413	$713	$367	$66,002	$2,127	$18,195
Yr 15	$103,663	$11,709	$13,140	$32,537	$143,098	$90,818	$58,281	$3,525	$8,184	$2,165	$3,208	$2,474	$731	$364	$70,375	$2,248	$20,443
Yr 16	$99,854	$11,709	$13,326	$36,346	$150,999	$97,528	$61,182	$3,809	$7,900	$2,219	$3,137	$2,536	$749	$362	$74,717	$2,368	$22,811
Yr 17	$95,740	$11,709	$13,523	$40,460	$158,594	$104,328	$63,868	$4,114	$7,595	$2,274	$3,059	$2,599	$767	$359	$79,030	$2,487	$25,298
Yr 18	$91,295	$11,709	$13,730	$44,905	$165,858	$111,224	$66,319	$4,445	$7,264	$2,331	$2,975	$2,664	$787	$357	$83,319	$2,606	$27,904
Yr 19	$86,493	$11,709	$13,947	$49,707	$172,765	$118,219	$68,512	$4,802	$6,907	$2,389	$2,882	$2,731	$806	$356	$87,590	$2,724	$30,629
Yr 20	$81,306	$11,709	$14,176	$54,894	$179,286	$125,319	$70,425	$5,188	$6,522	$2,449	$2,781	$2,799	$827	$355	$91,848	$2,842	$33,471
Yr 21	$75,701	$11,709	$14,418	$60,499	$185,391	$132,530	$72,031	$5,604	$6,105	$2,510	$2,671	$2,869	$847	$354	$96,100	$2,959	$36,430
Yr 22	$69,647	$11,709	$14,672	$66,553	$191,046	$139,858	$73,306	$6,054	$5,655	$2,573	$2,551	$2,941	$868	$354	$100,352	$3,077	$39,506
Yr 23	$63,107	$11,709	$14,941	$73,093	$196,215	$147,313	$74,219	$6,540	$5,169	$2,637	$2,420	$3,014	$890	$355	$104,612	$3,194	$42,701
Yr 24	$56,041	$11,709	$15,224	$80,159	$200,858	$154,901	$74,742	$7,066	$4,643	$2,703	$2,277	$3,089	$912	$356	$108,889	$3,312	$46,012
Yr 25	$48,408	$11,709	$15,524	$87,792	$204,934	$162,634	$74,842	$7,633	$4,076	$2,771	$2,122	$3,167	$935	$359	$113,192	$3,430	$49,443
Yr 26	$40,162	$11,709	$15,841	$96,038	$208,397	$170,523	$74,485	$8,246	$3,463	$2,840	$1,954	$3,246	$958	$362	$117,531	$3,550	$52,992
Yr 27	$31,253	$11,709	$16,177	$104,947	$211,197	$178,580	$73,633	$8,909	$2,800	$2,911	$1,771	$3,327	$982	$366	$121,918	$3,670	$56,662
Yr 28	$21,629	$11,709	$16,532	$114,571	$213,282	$186,820	$72,249	$9,624	$2,085	$2,984	$1,571	$3,410	$1,007	$371	$126,366	$3,792	$60,454
Yr 29	$11,232	$11,709	$16,908	$124,968	$214,594	$195,258	$70,289	$10,397	$1,312	$3,059	$1,355	$3,495	$1,032	$377	$130,888	$3,916	$64,370
Yr 30	$0	$11,709	$17,307	$136,200	$215,071	$203,911	$67,711	$11,232	$477	$3,135	$1,120	$3,583	$1,058	$384	$135,499	$4,042	$68,412

* Represents the approximate amount of money which should be saved monthly
** After Tax Down Payment is the initial principal plus the after-tax value of the closing cost

Figure 64 - Page 153

Rent vs Buy Analysis for Various Metropolitan Cities

Washington, DC

Using the Median Home Price and the Average Monthly Rent

HOME:

Purchase Price:	$159,900
Closing Cost:	$5,300
+Total Home Cost:	$165,200
+After-tax Cost:	$163,557
Down Payment:	$16,000
+Initial Principal:	$10,700
+Starting Loan:	$149,200
Mortgage Rate:	7.750%
Loan Length (in Yrs):	30
+Monthly Payment:	$1,069
Real Estate Tax:	0.910%
Add Repair/Utility Cost:	0.10%
Closing Commission Rate:	6.0%

GENERAL:

Tax Bracket:	31.0%
Savings Rate:	4.0%

RENT:

Starting Rental Amount:	$707
Monthly Rental Incr./Yr (in %):	2.5%
+Initial Monthly Savings Amt:	$308

COMPARISON (3 YRS):

+Principal Paid:	$4,252
+Interest Paid:	$34,227
+Amount Renter Can Save:	$12,418
+Amount Difference Rent/Own:	$8,165
+Appr. Required to Break Even:	$22,783
+Required Home Sales Price:	$182,683
+Yearly % Appr. to Break Even:	4.5%
+Total % Appr. to Break Even:	14.2%

COMPARISON (5 YRS):

+Principal Paid:	$7,687
+Interest Paid:	$56,446
+Amount Renter Can Save:	$20,635
+Amount Difference Rent/Own:	$12,948
+Appr. Required to Break Even:	$27,871
+Required Home Sales Price:	$187,771
+Yearly % Appr. to Break Even:	3.3%
+Total % Appr. to Break Even:	17.4%

COMPARISON (10 YRS):

+Principal Paid:	$18,999
+Interest Paid:	$109,268
+Amount Renter Can Save:	$40,763
+Amount Difference Rent/Own:	$21,765
+Appr. Required to Break Even:	$37,251
+Required Home Sales Price:	$197,151
+Yearly % Appr. to Break Even:	2.1%
+Total % Appr. to Break Even:	23.3%

Figure 65

Myth Breakers

	Summary Information							Home Ownership						Rental Difference			
Yr	Current Loan	Mortgage Payment	After Tax Layout	Cumulative Principal Paid	Cumulative Interest Paid	Amount Renter Can Save	Amount Diff Rent/Own	Annual Principal Paid	Annual Interest Paid	Real Estate Tax	Income Tax Break	Repairs + Add Utils	* Mthly Rent	Ave Mthly Savings Amount	Before Int Diff Rent/Own	Int on Diff & **ATDP	
0	$149,200																
1	$147,890	$12,827	$12,179	$1,310	$11,517	$4,147	$2,837	$1,310	$11,517	$1,455	$4,021	$1,919	$707	$308	$3,695	$451	$451
2	$146,476	$12,827	$12,285	$2,724	$22,929	$8,287	$5,563	$1,415	$11,412	$1,491	$4,000	$1,967	$725	$299	$7,284	$552	$1,003
3	$144,948	$12,827	$12,395	$4,252	$34,227	$12,418	$8,165	$1,528	$11,298	$1,529	$3,976	$2,016	$743	$290	$10,765	$649	$1,652
4	$143,296	$12,827	$12,510	$5,904	$45,403	$16,535	$10,631	$1,651	$11,176	$1,567	$3,950	$2,066	$761	$281	$14,139	$744	$2,396
5	$141,513	$12,827	$12,630	$7,687	$56,446	$20,635	$12,948	$1,784	$11,043	$1,606	$3,921	$2,118	$780	$272	$17,404	$835	$3,231
6	$139,586	$12,827	$12,755	$9,614	$67,346	$24,714	$15,100	$1,927	$10,900	$1,646	$3,889	$2,171	$800	$263	$20,559	$924	$4,155
7	$137,504	$12,827	$12,885	$11,696	$78,091	$28,770	$17,074	$2,082	$10,745	$1,687	$3,854	$2,225	$820	$254	$23,606	$1,009	$5,164
8	$135,255	$12,827	$13,022	$13,945	$88,669	$32,798	$18,854	$2,249	$10,578	$1,730	$3,815	$2,281	$840	$245	$26,543	$1,092	$6,256
9	$132,826	$12,827	$13,165	$16,374	$99,066	$36,797	$20,423	$2,429	$10,397	$1,773	$3,773	$2,338	$861	$236	$29,370	$1,171	$7,427
10	$130,201	$12,827	$13,314	$18,999	$109,268	$40,763	$21,765	$2,625	$10,202	$1,817	$3,726	$2,396	$883	$227	$32,089	$1,247	$8,674
11	$127,366	$12,827	$13,471	$21,834	$119,259	$44,695	$22,861	$2,835	$9,991	$1,863	$3,675	$2,456	$905	$218	$34,700	$1,321	$9,995
12	$124,303	$12,827	$13,635	$24,897	$129,023	$48,589	$23,692	$3,063	$9,764	$1,909	$3,619	$2,518	$928	$209	$37,203	$1,391	$11,386
13	$120,994	$12,827	$13,807	$28,206	$138,540	$52,445	$24,239	$3,309	$9,518	$1,957	$3,557	$2,581	$951	$200	$39,600	$1,459	$12,845
14	$117,419	$12,827	$13,988	$31,781	$147,792	$56,261	$24,480	$3,575	$9,252	$2,006	$3,490	$2,645	$975	$191	$41,892	$1,523	$14,368
15	$113,557	$12,827	$14,177	$35,643	$156,757	$60,035	$24,393	$3,862	$8,965	$2,056	$3,416	$2,711	$999	$182	$44,082	$1,585	$15,953
16	$109,385	$12,827	$14,377	$39,815	$165,412	$63,769	$23,954	$4,172	$8,655	$2,107	$3,336	$2,779	$1,024	$174	$46,172	$1,644	$17,597
17	$104,878	$12,827	$14,587	$44,322	$173,731	$67,461	$23,139	$4,507	$8,319	$2,160	$3,249	$2,848	$1,050	$166	$48,164	$1,700	$19,297
18	$100,009	$12,827	$14,807	$49,191	$181,688	$71,112	$21,921	$4,869	$7,958	$2,214	$3,153	$2,920	$1,076	$158	$50,061	$1,754	$21,051
19	$94,749	$12,827	$15,040	$54,451	$189,255	$74,725	$20,273	$5,260	$7,566	$2,269	$3,049	$2,993	$1,103	$151	$51,869	$1,805	$22,856
20	$89,066	$12,827	$15,285	$60,134	$196,399	$78,299	$18,165	$5,683	$7,144	$2,326	$2,936	$3,067	$1,130	$143	$53,591	$1,853	$24,709
21	$82,927	$12,827	$15,543	$66,273	$203,087	$81,840	$15,567	$6,139	$6,688	$2,384	$2,812	$3,144	$1,159	$137	$55,231	$1,900	$26,608
22	$76,295	$12,827	$15,815	$72,905	$209,281	$85,349	$12,444	$6,632	$6,195	$2,444	$2,678	$3,223	$1,187	$130	$56,797	$1,944	$28,552
23	$69,130	$12,827	$16,103	$80,070	$214,943	$88,833	$8,485	$7,165	$5,662	$2,505	$2,532	$3,303	$1,217	$125	$58,295	$1,986	$30,538
24	$61,390	$12,827	$16,407	$87,810	$220,029	$92,295	$4,485	$7,740	$5,086	$2,568	$2,373	$3,386	$1,248	$120	$59,731	$2,026	$32,564
25	$53,028	$12,827	$16,729	$96,172	$224,494	$95,744	($427)	$8,362	$4,465	$2,632	$2,200	$3,471	$1,279	$115	$61,115	$2,065	$34,629
26	$43,995	$12,827	$17,069	$105,205	$228,288	$99,188	($6,018)	$9,033	$3,793	$2,698	$2,012	$3,557	$1,311	$112	$62,456	$2,103	$36,732
27	$34,236	$12,827	$17,430	$114,964	$231,355	$102,634	($12,330)	$9,759	$3,068	$2,765	$1,808	$3,646	$1,344	$109	$63,763	$2,139	$38,871
28	$23,693	$12,827	$17,812	$125,507	$233,639	$106,096	($19,411)	$10,543	$2,284	$2,834	$1,587	$3,737	$1,377	$107	$65,050	$2,175	$41,046
29	$12,304	$12,827	$18,216	$136,896	$235,077	$109,584	($27,312)	$11,389	$1,437	$2,905	$1,346	$3,831	$1,412	$107	$66,328	$2,210	$43,256
30	$0	$12,827	$18,646	$149,200	$235,599	$113,114	($36,086)	$12,304	$523	$2,978	$1,085	$3,927	$1,447	$107	$67,612	$2,245	$45,501

* Represents the approximate amount of money which should be saved monthly

** After Tax Down Payment is the initial principal plus the after-tax value of the closing cost

Copyright © Myth Breakers - 1993

Figure 66 - Page 155

Rent vs Buy Analysis for Various Metropolitan Cities

Your City, USA

Using Your Home Price and Your Monthly Rent

These results could be for your city.

For $17.50, you can have the results

shown on the previous pages run with

your personal information.

To order, just fill out the order form on the next page for the "Scen 1"
column.

If you want to run the numbers

For two scenarios, you pay only $32.50.

For three scenarios, you pay only $45.00

NOTE: All prices include tax and freight.

Please use the form on the next page to order.

Have Myth Breakers Run the Numbers* through the Spreadsheet

HOME:	Example	Scen 1	Scen 2	Scen 3
Purchase Price:	$250,000			
Closing Cost:	$5,000			
+Total Home Cost:	$255,000	calculated	calculated	calculated
+After-tax Cost:	$253,600	calculated	calculated	calculated
Down Payment:	$25,000			
+Initial Principal:	$20,000	calculated	calculated	calculated
+Starting Loan:	$230,000	calculated	calculated	calculated
-	-	-	-	-
Mortgage Rate:	9.000%			
Loan Length (in Yrs):	30			
+Monthly Payment:	$1,851	calculated	calculated	calculate
-	-	-	-	-
Real Estate Tax:	1.125%			
Add Repair/Utility Cost:	0.10%			
Closing Commission Rate:	6.0%			
-	-	-	-	-

GENERAL:	Example	Scen 1	Scen 2	Scen 3
Tax Bracket:	28.0%			
Savings Rate:	6.0%			
RENT:				
Starting Rental Amount:	$910	-	-	-
Monthly Rental Increase/Yr (in %):	2.5%			
+Initial Monthly Savings Amount:	$878	calculated	calculated	calculated
COMPARISON (in Yrs):				
Holding Period:	30	-	-	-
+Principal Paid:	$230,000	calculated	calculated	calculated
+Interest Paid:	$436,228	calculated	calculated	calculated
+Amount Renter Can Save:	$467,793	calculated	calculated	calculated
+Amount Difference Rent/Own:	$237,793	calculated	calculated	calculated
+Appr. Required to Break Even:	$272,758	calculated	calculated	calculated
+Required Home Sales Price:	$522,758	calculated	calculated	calculated
+Yearly % Appr. to Break Even:	2.5%	calculated	calculated	calculated
+Total % Appr. to Break Even:	109.1%	calculated	calculated	calculated

To have Myth Breakers run the numbers*, please fill out the appropriate columns and send a check for the amount on the previous page to Myth Breakers. Visa and Mastercard are welcome.

Card # (Visa or Mastercard): _____
Cardholder Name: _____
Cardholder Signature: _____
Phone Number: _____

*You need to interpret the numbers yourself. Myth Breakers does not give financial or legal advice. Please see a professional before making a decision to buy or sell a home.

Name: _____
Address: _____

Order Now or Share with a Friend!

Name: _____

Address: _____

_____

City/State/Zip: _____

MAILING LIST REGISTRATION and ORDER FORM
Please put me on the Myth Breakers' mailing list   ☐ yes ☐ no

Send a "Home Ownership: The American Myth" disk in the following format:

		QTY	Price	Amount
IBM: ☐ 3.5" ☐ 5.25" Mac: ☐ 3.5"				
Book		_____	$11.95	_____
Spreadsheets (Lotus & Excel formats)		_____	$32.50	_____
Tax (California residents add local tax)				_____
Postage & Handling ($3.50 1st piece, $1.00 each add. piece)				_____
Total				_____

Method of Payment

☐ Check Enclosed. Make checks payable to: Myth Breakers

☐ VISA   ☐ MasterCard

Card # _____   Exp. Date _____

Cardholder Name _____

Authorized Signature _____

Here is my phone number in case you need to call: _____

Mail to: yth Breakers®

19672 Stevens Creek Blvd, Suite 200
Cupertino, CA 95014

Myth Breakers
is customer driven

Please write us with a myth you would
like explored

If we write about your myth, you will receive 5 copies
of the new book and we'll publish
a quote of yours

Don't wait
Please send us your Myth Breaking ideas today!

Your Myth